Paul Dickson Knows How America Speaks—Today!

Critical Acclaim for Paul Dickson's

WORDS

"Like dictionarist Samuel Johnson, Dickson is good at words, great at definitions."

—Boston Herald American

"There's something for every sort of word collector in these pages."

—The New York Times

". . . Enough wonderfully weird and outlandish chapters on the language to leave you speechless for hours."

—The Los Angeles Times

THE DICKSON BASEBALL DICTIONARY

"A valuable reference work that provides absorbing and enlightening reading."

—Sports Illustrated

NAMES

"The best and most varied book of its kind that I've ever come across."

—The New York Times

FAMILY WORDS

"Paul Dickson is a national treasure."

—Communications Quarterly

SLANG!

The TOPIC-BY-TOPIC DICTIONARY of CONTEMPORARY AMERICAN LINGOES

PAUL DICKSON

POCKET BOOKS

New York   London   Toronto   Sydney   Tokyo   Singapore

An *Original* publication of POCKET BOOKS

POCKET BOOKS, a division of Simon & Schuster Inc.
1230 Avenue of the Americas, New York, NY 10020

Dickson, Paul.
  Slang! : the topic-by-topic dictionary of contemporary American
lingoes / Paul Dickson.
    p. cm.
  Includes bibliographical references.
  ISBN 0-671-67251-7 : $9.95
    1. English language—United States—Slang—Dictionaries.
2. English language—Provincialisms—United States—Dictionaries.
3. English language—Slang—Dictionaries. 4. Americanisms—
Dictionaries. I. Title.
PE2846.D44   1990
427'.973—dc20   89-49628
                                                      CIP

First Pocket Books trade paperback printing April 1990

10 9 8 7 6 5 4 3 2 1

POCKET and colophon are registered trademarks of
Simon & Schuster Inc.

Printed in the U.S.A.

A people who are prosperous and happy, optimistic and progressive, produce much slang; it is a case of play; they amuse themselves with the language.

—W. Sumner, A. Keller,
M. Davie (sociologists), 1927

CONTENTS

PREFACE xi

INTRODUCTION xiii
It Ain't No Big Thing

❏ 1
ADVERTISING AND PUBLIC RELATIONS 1
Let's Try a Few and See If They Repeat 'Em

❏ 2
AUCTIONESE 8
What's Your Pleasure?

❏ 3
AUTOMOTIVE SLANG 22
How to Speak Car Talk

❏ 4
AVIATION AND SPACE 37
Words from the Wild Blue Yonder

❏ 5
BUREAUCRATESE 44
The Talk of the White Collar Bailiwick

❏ 6
BUSINESS AND FINANCE 55
Buzzwords for Big Shots

❏ 7
COMPUTERESE 69
What Do You Say to a Chiphead?

❏ **8**

COUNTERCULTURAL SLANG   85
The Slang of Yesterday Sounds a Lot Like Today

❏ **9**

CRIME, PUNISHMENT, AND THE LAW   101
Words You Didn't Hear on Hill Street Blues

❏ **10**

THE DRUG TRADE   112
The Spacey Talk of the Junkie, Cokie, Druggie, and Pothead

❏ **11**

FANTASY, THE FUTURE, AND SCIENCE FICTION   120
Coming to Terms with Parallel Worlds

❏ **12**

FOOD AND DRINK   131
Words and Phrases to Fill a Doggie Bag

❏ **13**

MEDICAL SLANG   142
Words You Don't Want to Hear from Your Hospital Bed

❏ **14**

MENTAL STATES   148
Cutting with a Dull Tool

❏ **15**

NAUTICAL SLANG   152
At Sea with the Language

❏ **16**

PENTAGONESE   161
Fort Fumble Speaks

❏ **17**

PERFORMING SLANG   170
Terms from Out of the Green Room

❏ **18**

POLITICAL SLANG—CONGRESSIONAL
VERSION   179
The Lingo of the Hill People

❏ **19**

REAL ESTATE   188
Vocabulary to Go with a 3br./CAC/WBFP

❏ **20**

SEX, THE BODY, AND BODILY FUNCTIONS   194
R-Rated Terms You Probably Won't Find in
Your Collegiate Dictionary

❏ **21**

SPORTS SLANG   201
Introductory Jockese

❏ **22**

TEEN AND HIGH SCHOOL SLANG   211
Along with a Smattering of the Collegiate and
Skateboard Jargon

❏ **23**

WAR SLANG   231
Out of the Jungles of Southeast Asia

❏ **24**

YUPPIES, DINKS, AND OTHER MODERNS
A Field Guide to the Last Quarter of the
Twentieth Century   251

BIBLIOGRAPHY—SORT OF   261

INDEX   265

PREFACE

A few years ago I got in a cab and found that the elderly driver was a former carnival man. I told him I was fascinated with slang and hoped to put together a collection someday. Rising to the bait, he gave me a fast tutorial in carnival lingo, and I stepped out of the cab with the feeling that a stamp collector must have when he buys a sheet of stamps and finds they contain some spectacular rarity. Most of the terms were traditional circus and carnival terms, but one was new to me and I liked it more than any of the others. The term was *hard flash,* and is used to describe a carnival prize that is so appealing that a person will spend vast sums trying to win it. As the man put it, hard flash could be anything from an immense stuffed animal to a lamp in the form of a large bronze palomino horse with a clock implanted in its side.

At that moment I became convinced that I should stop talking about writing a book on slang and actually do it. Actually doing it and getting such a book published became my own version of hard flash. About that same time I became convinced there was a potentially popular and useful reference book begging to be created. It would be a topic-by-topic slang dictionary which would stand in contrast to the fine A-through-Z slang dictionaries then on the market.

The idea is not new, but it is one that has not been done in more than fifty years. The last—and as far as I can tell, only—American topical slang book was Maurice H. Weseen's long out of print *Dictionary of American Slang,* which is a marvelous book but primarily of historic interest today because it was published in 1934. It went into many printings but was never updated and went out of print when the immense amount of new World War II slang made it obsolete. It is a good companion for reading James T. Farrell or John Dos Passos. Weseen's book has twenty topical slang categories (Aviation, Theatre, Food, etc.) which are followed by a general slang section. The topical sections are still fun to browse because they give a good overall flavor for the topic at hand as it sounded during the Great Depression.

Despite and because of the fact that the idea has not been tried in such a long time, it was an attractive one. One major reason for a topical slang book is, I think, that most of us tend to approach slang topically rather than as a huge alphabetical body of words from many realms. If we are trying to decipher teenage slang, we don't want to have to wade through scores of terms used by the police, computer specialists, and GI's.

So here goes, with a tip of the hat to the carnival guy in the cab and Maurice H. Weseen and his original *Dictionary of American Slang.* After a short introduction on the subject of slang, there follow two dozen separate chapters, each covering a separate area of slang by topic.

The book is also meant to be contemporary, so the latest examples have been sought. This was particularly true in a chapter like that on teenage slang, where the list is dominated by terms that will be unfamiliar to older ears. No doubt a few that are passé have slipped through and in one chapter on the slang of the counterculture (1965–75), a sizable handful may have drifted out of popular use and live on mostly through the music of the period, which, as anyone who owns a radio knows, is still very much with us. As to the question of including acronyms and initialisms, it was decided to cite them, but only if they were used as slang.

A number of people will be acknowledged for their help throughout the book, but three people were of such great assistance to this effort, I would be remiss in not thanking and acknowledging their contributions here and now. They are researcher Charles D. Poe, writer Joseph C. Goulden, and archivist Randy Roberts of the Tamony Collection at the University of Missouri, Columbia.

—Paul Dickson,
Garrett Park, Md.

INTRODUCTION

It Ain't No Big Thing

> "Correct English is the slang of prigs who
> write histories and essays. And the strongest
> slang of all is the slang of poets."
>
> —George Eliot, 1872

1. THE QUICK & DIRTY

People seem fascinated by slang, and it is widely beloved, especially in the abstract by people who cringe when it is actually spoken. If you can accept it, you can't get all bent out of shape—and start yelling "double negative"—when someone says that something "ain't no big thing."

Slang is. Period. Whether it is in favor or out of favor does not matter. It is renegade language that thumbs its nose at the very people who study and write about it. It is unruly, unrefined, irreverent, and illogical. It can be brutally frank and direct, or deceptively kind and euphemistic. Euphemism is the verbal trick that has been termed the deodorant of language, and slang has given us dozens of terms for drunkenness and insanity that are remarkably gentle.

What else is it? This is what amounts to the current conventional wisdom on the subject, or at least this slang watcher's beliefs about the beast.

—That slang is as old as language itself, and that American slang started on the *Mayflower*. Mario Pei, in *The Story of Language*, points out that the slang use of a piece of pottery for the head found in "crackpot" has counterparts in ancient language, including Latin and Sanskrit. He also points out that Shakespeare used the slang of his time, and by doing so gave us such words as *hubbub, fretful, fireworks,* and *dwindle.*

—That it binds and identifies and thrives in groups with a strong sense of novelty and group activity. Farmers produce little slang, but boxers, science fiction fans, surfers, high school students, and actors produce a lot.

—That slang is produced by living languages, and the moment it stops being produced, the language in question is dead. It is also true that slang replenishes standard language. English words as diverse as *snide, hold up, nice* (as in "nice work"), *bogus, strenuous, clumsy,* and *spurious* were regarded as slang not that long ago. Contemporary slang terms such as *sleazy, hassle,* and *gridlock* look like locks on acceptance—as does *lock on* for that matter. Much slang has become so common that when we use it we forget that it is slang: "Pick up the *phone* and find out what time the *movie* starts."

—That it is all but impossible to destroy slang, especially with the argument that it is improper or impolite. For most of the twentieth century there has been a battle waged against the word *ain't*. The anti-ain't-ers never had a chance. When, for example, they criticized the late Dizzy Dean for using the a-word on his radio broadcasts, he all but liquidated their argument by pointing out, "Lots of people who don't say 'ain't' ain't eatin'."

—That America is particularly hospitable to slang, and it tends to be embraced rather than spurned. American slang has been called one of the "successful stories" of English, and one estimate, made in the *Reader's Digest Success with Words,* claims that there are some 35,000 expressions which are, or once were, American slang. There are those, including the author of this book, who suspect that

that immense estimate of 35,000 may be on the low side. In terms of the overall language, the number skyrockets when one considers the British, Irish, Scotch, Australian, and Canadian contributions to the pool.

—That it is not that hard to create slang, but it is hard to sustain a "new slang" without a group that continues to speak it. This is exactly what happened to the short-lived Valley Girl (1982–83) and the Citizen's Band radio slang (1975–77). Each of these received tremendous media attention, but a few months after each had peaked, they seemed to live on mostly in yellowing paperback quickies like *The Official CB Slanguage Language Dictionary* and *How to Be a Valley Girl.* If there is a high mortality rate with new slang, it is also true that terms making it through infancy tend to be absorbed as part of the standard language.

—That it often has as much to do with who says something as what they are saying. A simple word like *hot* has many conventional and slang meanings, depending on whether you are talking to a musician, police officer, electrician, florist, radiologist, cook, or basketball player. If a television talk-show guest talks about the Green Room, he's referring to the room in which guests wait to go on camera, regardless of its actual color. On the other hand, to a surfer on a California beach, the Green Room is the sought-for-realm inside the curl of a wave. By extension, at some West Coast colleges, to be doing exceptionally well is to be in the Green Room.

—That slang is often as much defined by context and position (in the sense that cowgirl and girl cow, OK and KO, and breaking ball and ball breaker, all differ) as by the expression itself. The word *say* is not slang unless it is used at the beginning of a sentence, in the sense of "tell me." This is as much true of the contemporary teenager who says, "Say, how much did that cost?" as it is in the line, "Oh, say, can you see, by the dawn's early light."

Despite all of this, people still have a tough time defining slang.

2. DEFINITIONS

Consider these questions:
- "Hey! No bullshit, but what the hell is slang anyhow?"
- "Could you please define slang?"
- "Can a suitable set of parameters be developed through which slang can be, first, identified and defined, and second, distinguished from conventional English, jargon, dialect, lingo, and argot?"

These three questions are, of course, the same question posed three separate ways. But their impact is quite different because of how they are stated. The first version of the question is stated in simple street slang. It is both direct and rude. The second version is phrased in standard, or conventional, English. It is at once forthright and polite. The third question approximates what has been called *bureaucratese* but which is spoken beyond the bureaucracy. It is bloated, indirect, and sleep-inducing. For lack of a better term, it is the jargon of a sizable slice of white-collar America.

The three questions only answer themselves to a point. Slang, conventional English, and jargon sound different, and if we speak English we pretty much know which is which. But exactly how does slang distinguish itself from argot, cant, and jargon?

The answer is not an easy one. In his monumental *American Language (Supplement Two)*, H. L. Mencken grappled with it and, without even mentioning jargon, wrote, "The boundaries separating true slang from cant and argot are not easily defined," adding later, "There is a constant movement of words and phrases from one category to another." Mencken's conclusion was that cant and argot belonged to the speech of small and cohesive groups, with cant having the extra characteristic of deceiving and mystifying outsiders. At another point (*The American Language*, 4th edition), he says, "The essence of slang is that it is of general dispersion, but still stands outside the accepted canon of the language."

Mencken believed that slang was driven by exuberance and word-making energy. He compared slang's relationship to language to that between dancing and music.

What about jargon? The rough distinction that seems to work is that jargon is technical, professional talk which as often as not, like cant, acts as a barrier to keep outsiders from understanding what is going on. But not always. For instance, medical doctors have a polysyllabic, latinate jargon as well as a blunt and sometimes cruel slang. It is one thing to say that one has a *bilateral probital hematoma* (jargon), but quite another to say that you have a shiner, black eye, or mouse (slang).

But, by the same token, some slang and some jargon are one and the same; for example, the slang and jargon of truck drivers overlap considerably. Perhaps the simplest definition of jargon was the one made by Mario Pei many years ago in the *Story of Language,* in which he termed it ". . . the special terminology in use in any given walk of life."

Finally there is dialect, which appears to be a different manner of speaking the same language with a different but consistent grammar and set of distinct expressions. By this definition the black English that was so widely discussed and debated in the 1970s would qualify as a dialect. By the same token, many of the words used in predominantly black rap music are slang. Rap slang is much more likely to be understood by a nonblack teenager than by a middle-aged black person. One can, in fact, make the case that rap slang and general teenage slang have so much in common, there are only a handful of words and phrases they do not share.

So if we can give slang a place, it occupies a perch between conventional English on one hand and the private, in-group cants, jargons, and dialects.

3. I HEARD IT ON TV

One final point that should be covered here has to do with the state of slang today. How is it faring in this the last decade of the twentieth century?

The simple answer is that it appears as dynamic a force in language as it has ever been during a period of peace and stability. Conflict is a catalyst for the creation of new slang, and English is still digesting terms created during World War II.

But there is another factor now in place that over time will rival anything else in history as a dispenser of language.

Television has become this great dispenser, soaking up words and phrases from one part of the population and repeating it for all of us to hear. Kids who have never been on a sled know what a luge is, and people who have never sat in a Catskills hotel and listened to a Brooklyn-born comic speak of *shtick* and *schlock*. For a moment we all knew enough CB talk (Ten-four, Good Buddy) and Valley Girl talk (gag me with a spoon) to fake those slangs. This was not because we all drove eighteen-wheelers or hung out in the shopping malls and video parlors of the San Fernando Valley, but because we *heard* it on television.

This fact has not been missed by the professional linguists and students of television. Frederick Mish, editorial director at Merriam-Webster Inc. in Springfield, Massachusetts, points out the electronic media has become a major influence on American English, especially when it comes to new words. "It overarches all the other influences and promulgates them. Whether you're talking about a new word or phrase from technology or cookery, it is likely to come to us through television," says Mish. Tom Shales, the *Washington Post* TV critic, has termed television "America's dictionary as well as its mirror."

Perhaps the most dramatic case of electronically transmitted slang occurred in the spring of 1989 after a gang of Harlem teenagers entered Central Park and brutally beat and raped a jogger. Within hours of the arrest of the teenagers, the New York police announced that their interrogation had yielded a name for vile rampage and other acts of senseless violence: *wilding.*

Although the police pointed out that they had never heard the term before that night, the word *wilding* had spread into every nook and cranny of the English-speaking world within hours. Television, with assists from radio and the wire services, had put the term and its grotesque connotations into the minds of tens of millions.

Hearing is the key to all of this. So much is said and written about the visual impact of television, we sometimes forget that it is equally auditory. This was particularly true of both Watergate and Iran-contra—what was spoken and "misspoken"—and America's manned ventures into outer space. The launches, the splashdowns and costly animation were memorable, but so were the voices of the

astronauts, the reporters, and even the official NASA spokesmen.
For a while we were all saying A-okay and counting backwards 10–
9–8–7 . . . Television is a linguistic paradise. You can flip to *Don-
ahue* and hear the latest in sensitive psychological talk, dial up the
news and hear the latest in boardroom or diplomatic jargon, screen
the new sitcoms for the next catch phrase, and catch a few innings of
the ball game to listen for the latest nickname for spit balls (referred
to of late as "wet ones"). Most Americans know what they know of
police slang from cop shows ranging from *Dragnet* to *Hill Street
Blues*. TV westerns of the 1950s invented a slang for the Old West
with new terms like *gunslinger* and *bounty hunter*.

If this sounds a bit too passive, go to the other extreme and think
of the quirky little ways TV talk affects us. Kids who dream of being
asked to spell "relief" by their teacher so they can reply, "R-O-
L-A-I-D-S," or how they will someday try to tell their kids how they
sat back and waited for Hans and Franz, the Teutonic body builders
on *Saturday Night Live,* to say "Ve're going to pump *you* up." If half
the teenagers in America are at this moment imitating Hans and
Franz, the other half are imitating the Church Lady saying "Isn't
that special." Their kids probably won't understand what was so
special about it, just like my kids draw a blank when I try to tell
them how I loved the Burns and Allen signature—"Say goodnight,
Gracie." "Goodnight, Gracie."

Television, in fact, creates its own indigenous slang in the form of
rallying cries and catch phrases. A case in point is "Where's the
beef?" which is gone now but marked the winter of 1984 linguistically as it was repeated over and over by the late Clara Peller
in a series of ads for the Wendy's hamburger chain and then became
a rejoinder in the presidential debates on television.

This kind of thing is nothing new, but the Wendy's commercials
are an especially dramatic example of how we mark time with catch
words and phrases in the television age. It goes on all the time, and
the odds favor a major, new national pet phrase every few years and
numbers of minor ones. It will be fresh one moment and a cliché
emblazoned across a million tee-shirts the next.

Such was the case with the late Gilda Radner's chirpy "Never
mind," from *Saturday Night Live* and Steven Martin's "Well, ex-

cuuuuuse me." Then John Belushi took the word *no,* extruded it
into something that took three seconds to say, and it became his
signature.

The most obvious impact has come with signature lines uttered
by characters, comedians, and advertisers. If there were a Hall of
Fame for such phrases, it would be hard to know where to begin.
Just for starters, you'd have to consider: "Would you believe?" from
Don Adams as Maxwell Smart; McGarrett's "Book 'em," from
Hawaii Five-O; Flo's endearing "Well, kiss my grits," from *Alice;*
Jack Paar's "I kid you not," Mork's "Nano-nano," and the Fonz's
"Aaaaaaaay!" There was a bunch from *Laugh-In,* including Artie
Johnson's "Verrrrrrry interesting!" And the ubiquitous "Sock it to
me!" Then there is "Heeerrrre's Johnny," Tommy Smotherss's
"Mom always loved you best," and Charlie Brown's "Good grief,"
which appeared first in the comic strips but needed television to
make it a household term.

It can be argued that *yucky* was in use before *Sesame Street,* but
that show did for that article of slang what *The A-Team* did for
sucker. And speaking of *Sesame Street,* it can be argued that this
was the instrument by which the term *you guys,* as slang for males
and females as opposed to males alone (as in *Guys and Dolls*)
became popular. Shows like *Star Trek* created their own vocabulary
and left a noun in its wake, *Trekkies,* for those who follow the show.

This ability to change the way we speak by electronically transmitted buzzwords and catch phrases is not new. Radio had its
impact: "the $64 question" is a permanent part of the language, and
people over forty shudder nostalgically with a line like "Gotta
straighten out that closet one of these days, Molly." But it is
television that has really moved the process into high gear and given
it "may-jor mo-tion."

If we like them because of the way they are said, we remember
them because they are our mental souvenirs, and we hang on to
them for the same reason the Smithsonian hangs on to Archie
Bunker's chair, the Fonz's jacket, and J.R.'s cowboy hat. Our souvenirs can, in fact, be the least funny element in a show. For all the
great, funny lines from M*A*S*H, what we will all recall, even after
the reruns have stopped, is the chilling phrase "Incoming

wounded." And scores of funny lines from *All in the Family* have been forgotten by people, like me, who can only remember that Archie called his son-in-law "meathead" and his wife "dingbat."

The big question is, Where's the magic? Why do so many of these phrases work? It clearly defies full analysis, but it would appear that timing is terribly important. It is doubtful we all would have been running around saying "Where's the beef?" during the Iranian hostage crisis or during last days of the Vietnam War. It wouldn't have been an appropriate catch phrase at the time or a verbal souvenir to recall a time of crisis.

If you listen carefully, you'll be among the first to catch someone who will have the touch and give us not one hot, new line or phrase, but a whole bunch of them. Looking back, it can be argued that the last great television phrase maker was Jackie Gleason, a man with as many signatures as a second mortgage. "To the moon, Alice," "How sweet it is," "One of these days," "And away we go," were all his. He even had words for the times, in the person of *The Honeymooners'* Ralph Kramden, when he got too nervous to talk: "Hommina, hommina."

Television itself is never at a loss for words.

SLANG!

1

ADVERTISING AND PUBLIC RELATIONS

"Let's Try a Few and See If They Repeat 'Em"

> "Advertising, for its part, has so prostrated itself on the altar of word worship that it has succeeded in creating a whole language of its own. And while Americans are bilingual in this respect, none can confuse the language of advertising with their own."
>
> —William H. Whyte, Jr. and the editors of *Fortune*, in *Is Anybody Listening?* Simon & Schuster, 1952

There was a period in the late 1950s when the nation went gaga over the slangy metaphoric hyperbole of Mad Ave. They were dubbed "gray flannelisms" (from the novel *The Man in the Gray Flannel Suit*) by syndicated columnist Walter Winchell, while fellow columnist Dorothy Kilgallen called them "ad agencyisms." They were all convoluted and most were based on whether or not something—an ad, a campaign, a slogan, etc.—would work. The most famous flannelism was "Let's send it up the flagpole and see if they salute it," but there were hundreds more which columnists and TV personalities repeated with relish. A few of many:

- Let's pull up the periscope and see where we're at.
- I see feathers on it but it's still not flying.
- Let's toss it around and see if it makes salad.

1

- Let's guinea pig that one.
- Let's roll some rocks and see what crawls out.
- Well, the oars are in the water and we're headed upstream.
- Let's drop this down the well and see what kind of splash it makes.

Were these real or were they created to get a line in a column and then forgotten? No less an observer than John Crosby of the old New York *Herald Tribune* deemed them "the curiously inventive (and, in some cases, remarkably expressive) language of the advertising industry." This is not to say a few were not created for outside consumption. In late 1957, when the Soviet Union put a dog in orbit, the metaphoric handstand that attracted attention was: "Let's shoot a satellite into the client's orbit and see if he barks."

That fad has passed—at least the public side of it has—and things are a little less colorful advertising- and public relations–wise, but plenty remains.

A

account side. That half of an ad agency that attracts and keeps clients. The other half is the *creative side*.

ad. Print advertisement as opposed to a *commercial,* which appears on radio or television.

advertorial. An advertisement that sells an editorial point of view as opposed to a product or service.

advid. Advertising video.

agency copy. Material printed or broadcast just as it was when it came from an advertising or public relations firm.

art. Anything graphic—photography, typography, illustration—in advertising. It is used to distinguish everything else in an ad or commercial from *copy.*

B

beauty shot. A well-staged and -lit view of a product in a commercial.

bleed. An ad, photo, or illustration that extends to the very edge of a page.

book. A magazine or other periodical. The *front of the book* is the portion of the magazine before the main editorial section, and the *back of the book* follows it.

boutique. Small ad agency, often noted for its creativity.

brandstanding. Supporting a race car, sponsoring a rock tour or some other "special event" to promote one's product.

C

clutter. The collective name for the many advertising spots on television.

commish. A commission paid to an agency.

comp. Short for (1) comprehensive, and (2) complimentary.

co-op. A cooperative advertisement, jointly paid for by the manufacturer and the retailer.

copy. Written or typewritten text in an ad or commercial.

creative side. That part of an advertising agency that actually creates ads. The other side is the *account side.*

customer golf. Term for recognizing the fact that an agency has to go along with and not "beat" the client. It is based on the notion that you don't go out with your best customer and whomp him at golf.

D

DINFO. Defense Information; public relations office and function of the Pentagon.

double truck. A two-page ad.

E

equity. A theme that has worked over time and increases in value.

F

face. A particular alphabet or typeface.

flack/flak. (1) a public relations person. (2) To push a product, service, or story.

G

greek. Garbled letters used to indicate text in a dummy ad.

H

hand-holding. Reassuring an advertising or PR client.

hotdogger. Publicity seeker.

hymns. Hidden messages.

I

ink. Press coverage; a goal of public relations.

J

jingle. Short musical refrain

used on radio or television commercials.

K

kickapoo. The customer's product.

kotex. A free newspaper "shopper," which is seldom read but scanned for ads. It is a derogatory allusion to the brand name of a popular sanitary napkin.

L

live tag. Voice at the end of a commercial that gives current or local information, such as the words "Opens Wednesday at the Cineplex 6" at the end of a movie commercial.

M

magalog. Blend of "magazine" and "catalog" for a catalog that acts like a magazine in that it carries ads—among its own ads—for other companies and products.

media. Ad space or time one buys. Not to be confused with the media that is the press.

mention. A short item in the press. Publicists like to be able to say, "Did you see this morning's mention in the *Wall Street Journal?*"

O

overexposure. What happens to a celebrity who endorses too many products and thereby becomes ineffective.

P

P.A. Short for Public Affairs. This is what some companies and almost all government agencies call their public relations operations—usually P.A.O.'s for Public Affairs Offices—to avoid the label, which is seen as manipulative.

peg. That which is newsworthy or notable in a press release or campaign. Also a *slant* or a *handle*.

pick-up. The use of a press release, photo, etc., by the media; public relations placement.

place. To use public relations techniques to get a favorable mention or story in the media.

plug. A favorable positioning for a product or service in public relations.

pluggery. A PR firm.

PR. Public relations, both as a noun and a verb. To "PR the public" is to put a message across.

praisery. A PR firm.

product PR. Publicity gained for an item rather than a person or a company. Product publicists work to get their products shown on TV or in the movies.

puffery. Exaggerated claim or promise given to a product or service. Calling something the best that money can buy is often regarded as pure puffery.

puff piece. A flattering article in the press about a client or product. Publicists try to place such articles.

pull. (1) The ability to create sales which is said of the most effective ads. (2) To remove an ad or kill an advertising campaign.

put on the map. Successfully promote and advertise a relatively unknown product or service.

R

release. (1) In public relations, a press release. (2) In advertising, a written okay to use a person's face, voice, or name commercially.

remnant space. Odd page spots sold at a discount.

S

sandwich man. A human billboard; a person wearing a huge sign fore and aft, making a human sandwich. Though less common today than they once were, they are used as an image of disparagement; "We'd be better off with a sandwich man."

shop. An ad agency.

shot. A publicist's attempt at placement.

sizzle. Image. From the advertising maxim that holds that you should sell the sizzle, not the steak.

slant. The attitude or opinion that a publicist is trying to sell. For instance, a PR slant on nuclear power might be that it is essential to America's future.

space. Paper or air time that has been purchased for a client. Space can also be obtained through public relations.

spin/spin control. In public relations, the ability to present a client in a certain light and with a certain *slant*. It implies control, and probably derived from the word "top-spin."

spin doctor/spin master. PR person with the proven ability to put a certain *slant* or story across.

stunt. An event staged as news for the purpose of public relations.

sweeps. Periods during which television shows are rated and ranked by audience size. The outcome determines the advertising rates for the show in question.

T

teaser. Ad or announcement that arouses interest without naming the product, as in, "Coming soon, the movie of the year."

thirty. A thirty-second commercial.

throwaway. Handbill or other printed ad that the advertiser assumes will be looked at for a few seconds before being thrown away.

trade out. Goods or services given for ad space or broadcast time; for instance, meals given in exchange for a restaurant ad in a directory.

tub-thump. To make an obvious appeal or pitch for a client or product.

U

up-cut. To edit a television show, usually a rerun, to fit in one or more extra commercials.

USP. Unique Selling Proposition, that which separates a product or service from its competitors.

V

Videocart. Recently introduced type of grocery shopping cart with a video screen that plays commercials for the customer while shopping.

VO or voice-over. Narration in a commercial by person not seen.

W

white coat rule. Nickname for the Federal Trade Commission prohibition against commercials that claim or imply that the person on the screen is a doctor.

——— Z ———

ZOO. Acronym for Zero On Originality. To work for a zoo agency is to work for one lacking innovation.

SOURCES

A good source of "flannelisms" is two articles by John Crosby on Madison Avenuese which appear in B. A. Botkin's *Sidewalks of America* (Bobbs-Merrill, 1954). Material in the Tamony Collection at the University of Missouri was of great help in preparing this glossary.

2 | AUCTIONESE

What's Your Pleasure?

"In New York dealers call the items 'cultural antiques,' in Northern California the favorite word is 'collectibles,' in Dallas 'new antiques.' In Memphis and Madison, Wisconsin, they simply call the stuff junk—but they spell it, with verbal pinkie extended, J-U-N-Q-U-E."

—Wayne King, *The New York Times*, August 22, 1970

How does one get a handle on the world of antiques, collectibles, and flea markets? Simple. At the auctions where the slang of the auctioneer is the most interesting and colorful slang of the trade.

Auctioneers are under a lot of pressure to be clever. Not only do they have to keep their audience entertained, but they have to keep potential bidders interested in what they are selling. This is especially true of country auctioneers, who may have to move an occasional box lot of rusted chains or a 1974 Dodge Dart without an engine. After all, you don't have to be that clever if you are able to offer a Monet or a Bentley.

In order to get a handle on the stuff of that cleverness—the rich slang and pat phrasing of country auctioneers—I began collecting terms from auctioneers at auctions in Maine over the course of more than a half-dozen summers (1982 through 1989). I was helped by other auction buffs who tape recorded or took notes on auctions that I was not able to attend. To be sure, these are regional, but they are authentic country and give a sense of the flavor of the larger whole.

A

aggravation. Flaw. "This bottle is perfect except for a little aggravation in the neck." Also *agitation, distortion*.

agitation. Same as *aggravation*. The extent to which this term and "aggravation" can be applied was shown at a 1988 Rangeley, Maine, auction where the glass covering a framed print was held together by several yards of masking tape. The auctioneer noted playfully that the glass had "some agitation." Later in the same auction a really decrepit child's chair was described as agitated with the explanation, "You'd have a lot of agitation if you were that old." See also *distortion*.

all for one money. The whole lot is sold as one: "Here are five chairs all for one money." One of three ways of selling a lot, the other two are listed under *so much for one*.

all in and all done. Final bid; last call.

all over the house. Too many bids at one price; need a higher bid to sort them out. "I've got fifty dollars all over the house. Somebody give me sixty quick."

ancestral. Seldom invoked term in auction ads which is only used when *early* and *old* do not convey the proper sense of antiquity. One of its rare appearances was in an ad for a 1985 Robert W. Skinner auction which contained the line, "Ancestral property from central and eastern Massachusetts families."

Arizona Windsor. Style designation for an odd or funny-looking chair; not a classic.

as is, where is. No claim is being made for the condition of an item, and it must be removed from the premises by the buyer. A more colorful admonition: "Don't buy it if you haven't helt it, smelt it, and felt it."

auction fever. The belief on the part of the buyer that everything on the block is a bargain. Auctioneers encourage this malady.

_____ **B** _____

backfield. The back of the hall. "I've got fifty dollars in the backfield."

believe he stole it. Auctioneer's pat response to a desirable item selling for a seemingly low price.

bidder's paddle. Object on which the bidder's assigned number is written. The number must be recorded after every successful bid. Bidder's paddles can range from rather nice wooden affairs (which must be returned) to paper plates on which the numbers are written in crayon.

boat anchor. A heavy item with less than universal buyer appeal. Applied, for instance, to a monstrous old calculating machine at a Northport, Maine, auction. "Come on, folks, what am I bid? You can always use it for a boat anchor."

buyer's premium. Fee charged to the buyer by the auctioneer for the privilege of spending money, usually ten percent of the gavel price. Some make no small point about *not* charging this fee: OF COURSE, NO BUYER'S PREMIUM IS EVER CHARGED, trumpets an ad from a Rhode Island auctioneer in *Maine Antique Digest*. An ad from Mike True in the *Maine Sunday Telegram* avoids the word "premium" for this practice and says NO BUYERS PENALTY.

buy-in. When a *reserve* has been set by the seller and no bidder reaches that reserve, the auctioneer "buys-in" for the seller. Often the other buyers do not know that a buy-in has taken place until the final list of prices realized is printed and the space next to the buy-in is blank.

_____ **C** _____

can't cut it any closer. Point at which the auctioneer will take no more half or fractional bids. If the bid is for $160 and the auctioneer is asking for $170, he may accept $165 but "can't cut it any closer," so will not take $162.50.

catered. Food will be served.

change your tune. Something

fine is coming up. "Change your tune for this one." Auctioneer Dan Andrews, who believes he was the first to use this phrase in this manner, often prefaces it with a loud "Whoa." Also *time to open your eyes.*

choice and privilege. Auctioneer's shorthand used when offering a multiple lot, such as six chairs, and then giving the buyer his "choice" of taking just one at the winning price, or having the "privilege" of having several or all of them at a multiple of the winning price.

clean. (1) Unadulterated. It can be embellished, as when, at a Northport, Maine, auction, C. W. "Chas" Hare pointed to a Sheraton washstand and declared that it was "clean as a smelt."

country auction. "A true country sale," says a man who runs them, "is when the buyer and seller are allowed to make a fast deal without hidden reserves or other forms of protection. It will contain everything from period chests and fine jewelry to pots and pans and the outhouse door."

D

did you want to buy it or rent it? Auctioneer's response to a low opening. Variations: "He's here to rent it," and, "That's not a bid, that's the rental fee."

distortion. Flaw or damage. A large L-shaped rip in an oil painting was termed "a little distortion" in a 1987 auction. Also *aggravation, agitation.*

don't dwell, sell. Motto used by an auctioneer trying to get the action going. Alternative line: "Scream, holler, shout: do something."

don't shoot, I'll marry your daughter. Auctioneer's pat response to a loud noise made when a runner drops a large object.

dusty. Untouched and not picked over, something still covered with the dust of an attic or barn loft. An ad for a George Morrill auction which appeared in *The Maine Sunday Telegram* (August 2, 1987) was headlined DUSTY COUNTRY AUCTION and promised "Many wonderful dusty primitives and country items in old paint from the barns and attics . . ."

E

early. Auctionese for old. Presputnik. See also *old*.

ended out. Added to. A chair leg that has been ended out is one has been given fresh wood. Also *pieced out*.

F

fair warning. Name for the auctioneer's warning that bidding is nearing a close, but you still have a moment in which to spend your money.

feed. Auctioneer's term for the flow of goods being brought to the front for sale. A good auctioneer will control the feed so that the items are diverse and the best come up when the buyers are most eager to pay top dollar.

feeder. One who feeds goods to the auctioneer. See *runner*.

finding story. Tale about how the item came to be in the auction. An account of a 1978 James Julia auction in *Maine Antique Digest* tells of a rare political banner that brought $1,150. Samuel Pennington wrote, "There even was a 'finding' story to go with this one, too. According to auctioneer Julia, the banner had been found by a man hired to clean out a Belfast hall. Part of his payment was that he could keep whatever he found in the hall—not a bad keep, this one."

An occasional finding story involves a treasure discovered at the town dump.

flake. Small chip, as in "a perfect Depression glass decanter with a small flake."

flea-market kit. Kind name for a large pile of stuff that could never sell individually, say, a nonworking clock, five unwashed canning jars, four unrelated saucers, a padlock without a key, and a long run of clean *Poultryman* magazines. If this lot did not sell, a few other items would be added to make it "an intermediate-level flea-market kit."

flow blue. Desirable form of china decorated in blue.

It has also been known to flow from one place to another. At a 1987 Franklin County estate auction a lot of flow-blue china that had attracted a lot of interest during the inspection period suddenly disappeared as the auction was about to start. A runner found the plates at the bottom of a box of farming magazines just as he was putting it on the block. The magazines brought five dollars. The runaway china was offered separately and fetched $190.

folky. Describing an item with folk-art qualities, such as "a great folky rug." Not to be confused with the noun "folkie" for a devotee of folk music.

G

gallery. Building used for auctions and where sale goods are displayed prior to sale. Galleries are often also used to store recycled newsprint and snowplows.

gimmie what? Words of an auctioneer begging for an opening bid.

give 'em away for Christmas. Consumer tip given by auctioneer Clyde Allen when he was unable to move bidders up from $35 on a lot of augers.

gone. Missing, as in a mug with a "gone handle."

good. One of the most overused words in auctionese. It seems to be a filler word used when the auctioneer is not sure

what else can be said. At a July 1988 auction in the western Maine mountains, a totally undistinguished painting was described as "a good early painting, quite good." It sold for $35 with its good frame.

good, early ware. Generic description of a whatsit that appears to have come out of the kitchen.

good trade. Words used when a noteworthy sale has been made that favors the buyer.

gowser. Generic term for an unconventional object or lot. In an article in the April 1981 issue of *Maine Antique Digest* there was a report on a Plainfield, New Hampshire, auction conducted by William A. Smith during which an odd-shaped box came on the block. Smith called it a "gowser" and it sold for $45.

H

hairlines. Network of small cracks.

he ain't too drunk, let him bid against himself. Comment leveled at a bidder who has made two bids in a row. Heard at the Fryeburg (Me.) Fair on October 6, 1989, by the legendary R. I. "Razor" Crossman.

he/she came early. Common comment when a bidder with number 1, 2, or 3 gets a winning bid.

he'll be back. Said of someone who has just gotten a very good deal on something.

hernia special. Said of any item that is so heavy that it causes the runners holding it up to turn blue in the face.

honest. Not adulterated; pure.

I

I can't buy 'em for that. Cry of despair that goes up when an auctioneer has put an item in the auction that he has bought for more than it is about to be sold for.

If you was that old you'd have a lot more than chips. Said of a flawed item that is not moving.

important. Expensive.

I never would have thought of it. Commonly said when a half bid is made, especially when the bidding is low. "I've got five dollars, give me ten, give me ten. Okay, seven-fifty—I never would have thought of it."

infraction. A high-toned name for a chip or flaw. "There's been a small infraction here."

It's got some age on it. Old. Said for emphasis. (JT.)

It's no ___ (fill in the blank) ___ but it's a good ___ (fill in the blank) ___ anyhow. Phrase used to link an item being offered with a hot property, as in, "It's no $50,000 decoy, but it's a good bird anyhow."

K

kippers. In some parts of the country, members of an auction pool are referred to as kippers. See *pool*.

knockdown auction. Informal auction among members of a pool. See *pool*.

L

left bid. Bid left by a prospective buyer who has the auctioneer bid for him up to a certain limit.

let's show a little respect for this one. Something excellent is coming along.

lookers. Auctioneer's derisive term for people who do not bid. "What's the matter, you all just lookers?"

looks like somebody missed the road to the dump. Candid admission of a low-quality lot. Quoted in a *Maine Sunday Telegram* account of a 1971 auction. Variation on this was, "Throw it in the swamp," said auction items attracting no bids or interest at a Earl Hare auction in Northport, Maine, July 1986.

lot. Any and all auction items are called lots whether they be a single item or box full of kitchen utensils. The term has been used by auctioneers for so long that it is the source of such long-established idioms as "a lot of them," "a lot of time went into this," and "a bad lot."

lots per hour. Measure by which the speed of auction or auctioneer is judged. A fast auction is one at which items are knocked down at a hundred per hour.

M

majolica. Gaudy pottery style. Overheard at a Northport, Maine, auction as piece was being offered:
First Woman: What's majolica?

Second Woman: It's Italian for ugly.

married. Said of two incomplete pieces joined to form one bizarre whole.

N

new blood. A new bidder(s). Also, *new fire*.

New Jersey. State on the East Coast beloved of Yankee auctioneers. It is a special place where the ugly looks good ("This would look great back home in New Jersey") and values climb meteorically ("Just think what you'd have to pay for it in New Jersey," or, in reference to an item stuck at $25, "Come on, folks, you know you could get $350 for this back in Jersey"). It is believed that most people who buy New Jersey items at auction are from Massachusetts or Connecticut.

New Jersey tourist birds. Lesser decoys in the $15 to $25 range.

no excuses to be made on this one. A good lot. Pet phrase of auctioneer James E. Talbot of Turner, Maine. "Here's a Lincoln rocker. No excuses to be made for it. Let's start the bidding at fifty dollars."

no more partying, let's get with it. Said when an important bid was missed by a man who was talking.

No refund. No return. This isn't J. C. Penney. Caveat line uttered at the beginning of a no-nonsense Maine country auction.

no's. Auction notices commonly contain one or more of these (no children, no pets, no out-of-state checks, etc.). It has been suggested that the greater the number of no's, the tonier the auction.

nothing to hide. Without a problem or flaw.

nothing wrong with it, it just needs a new home. Invitation to bid.

"Not that well-known in these parts." Said of an unknown painter or artisan who presumably is known elsewhere. Heard at a Turner, Maine, auction of an Arizona dessert scene painted by one Sterling Mock.

O

of the period. Short for "of the colonial period" and describing seventeenth century goods. It is also used as an inspired bit of vagueness for a piece of indeterminate age. "Here's a sturdy ladderback chair—could be of the period. What's your pleasure?" Or, "I don't know if this is period, but it sure looks it."

old. Term of emphasis for that which is *really old*.

one hundred percent. Flawless; perfect.

P

pass. To move on to the next item without selling the lot on the block. Items are usually passed when there is no bid or the bid is too low. One coastal Maine auctioneer announced at an August 1987 auction that he would pass on any item that was not bid up to twenty percent of its value.

phantoms. Nonexistent bids.

picker. One who finds selected items which he will resell for auction consignment; a middle person.

pickin' bids. Accepting a nonexistent bid to help jimmy up the price of a lot. The term seems to derive from the idea of "pickin' bids out of thin air," "pickin' bids off the wall," etc.

pool. Illegal, informal agreement among dealers not to bid on an item, in order that one or more dealers in the pool can get the item at a low price. Those who sit on their hands are paid not to bid *(kippers)*. For instance, auctioneer Dan Andrews tells of selling a fine china closet for $950 and later learning that the bidder was a dealer who had paid $200 to the pool to get it at that price. Sometimes one dealer will bid for the whole pool, with one item going to one dealer and the next going to another. Dividing up a pile of pooled goods is often done at a *knockdown auction* near the location of the legitimate auction.

As more collectors and independent dealers enter an auction, effectiveness of the pool diminishes. Auctioneer Elsie Andrews adds that "really good stuff tends to break up the pool; greed takes over. This is when you see a member of the pool trying to sneak in a bid from the door of the coatroom."

pop it right out of here. Let's move this quickly.

POS. Piece of shit, pronounced as if it were "paas." Said of a lot that is not good and will be passed on. This is an inside joke between some auctioneers and their best customers, who know that when the word "pos" is heard it does not mean the same thing as *pass* (although a pos is usually passed).

posteds. Specific printed or written ground rules for the sale which are displayed at the auction site. For example, here is one of the rules attached to a tentpole for a Clyde Allen auction in Carthage, Maine, on July 25, 1987: "In the event that two or more persons believe they have the purchasing bid, the item must be resold with only those persons participating."

prime time. The best time for selling, generally the hour to ninety minutes after the first half hour. This is the time for the best stuff.

probably. Adverb used to link an item to a possible source. For instance, almost any old sled that comes to the block in Maine is "probably from South Paris" (a former hotbed of sled manufacturing).

puffer. Bidder in league with the auctioneer, bidding up prices; a *shill*.

pulling teeth time. One auctioneer's term for the first half hour of the auction, which comes before *prime time*. During this time, says the auctioneer who used the term, "people gawk, sit on their hands, and generally forget that they have wallets." He stopped short of saying that this was a time when junk was offered, but said that he kept his really good stuff away from the first half hour.

Q

quick knockdown. Method by which an auctioneer will mumble a few numbers and then award a plum to a friend or a partner.

R

reserve. The lowest amount the seller will allow an item to be sold for at auction.

right. Pure and unadulterated; a piece that you don't have to worry about. Also *right as rain*.

"right where we should've started." Said sometimes when the bidding reaches the point from which the auctioneer tried to start the bidding.

S

sameway. To the same person as the bid before. Instead of saying "sold to number 42," the auctioneer may say "sold sameway."

sell ya' one in a minute. Auctioneer's possible response to: "You wouldn't have an extra chair for me?" (Bidders at auctions are often required to bring their own chairs.)

set it in at. Injunction to start the bidding. "Do I have a hundred, do I have a hundred? Okay, let's set it in at fifty." Alternatively, "kick it in at," or "fifty and go."

shill. Bidder who is working for the auctioneer and working to inflate bids. Also *puffer*.

sick. Term applied to glass that is cloudy, usually because it was used as a vessel for chemicals, or china that is stained or so weak that it lacks the characteristic ring you should get when you flick it with your fingernail.

signed. Said of anything with the maker's name on it, ranging from an oil painting to a soup strainer. An item that was not moving at an August 1986 auction at the Blue Goose Dance Hall in Northport, Maine, had the auctioneer making the plaintive cry, "But, folks, it's a signed Archibald."

smalls. Little items that are presumably appealing to out-of-state dealers and collectors without trucks. Smalls are good for the summer trade, and the best of all are listed in the ads as "Shaker Smalls." Also *tabletops.*

so much for one, take 'em all. One way of selling a group of items. In this case you bid on one but are obliged to pay the same for the others. If one of a set of six chairs is sold this way for $20, the buyer has bought $120 worth of chairs.

so much for one; take one, take all. The buyer of the first item can just take that item—$20 in the case of the aforementioned chair—or take the whole lot for $120. Also known as *choice and privilege,* as in you can take your choice or have the privilege of taking them all.

steal of the evening. Good trade. At a good country auction the auctioneer will usually deem something the steal of the evening about every half hour.

T

tabletops. Same as *smalls.*

ten-and-ten. The scheme by which both the buyer and the seller pay the auctioneer a ten-percent commission on a lot. In other words, if an item sells for $100, the buyer pays $110 at settle-up time, and the consignor gets $90. It is legal but not always popular.

thanks for your help. Said when a bidder drops out after helping to get the bidding up to a level that pleases the auctioneer. Alternatively, "Appreciate the help."

the old (insert name of color) paint. Old or original paint. For reasons unclear, the word "the" is almost always attached to the word "old" when talking about paint.

there's still plenty of money to be made on this one. There's still money in this one. Applied to a lot that is still cheap and about to be sold. The auctioneer says this to wake dealers up to the fact that he thinks there is still a lot of room left for profit.

throw it in the swamp. Reaction

to a lot attracting no interest and no bids.

thunder jug / thunder mug. Chamber pot, from the noises created when they were used. There are auctioneers who will present the most decrepit example or the lid of one just to be able to say "thunder jug" in public.

time to open your eyes. Same as *change your tune*.

treewood. Unknown wood. "What's it made of?" is the question from the floor. The auctioneer's answer, "Looks like treewood to me."

turnpike cruiser. A bedpan. Also referred to as a "New York tureen."

twenty-percenter. Auctioneer who does not charge a buyer's premium but rather takes all of the traditional twenty-percent commission from the seller. Besides the traditional twenty percent and the new *ten-and-ten* scheme, there are other variations. A sign noted in Clyde Allen's auction house in New Sharon, Maine, a few years back said, "Twenty percent commission—thirty percent on junk and leftover lawn sale items."

U

unfortunately, he isn't here. The last line of a story used by an auctioneer to get a piece of antique furniture over the hundred-dollar bid then on the floor. "A man was in here the other day and offered me $260 for it. Pleaded with me to let him have it, but I told him that it was advertised as part of the auction. Unfortunately, he isn't here tonight."

use it for packing. Suggestion made by an auctioneer having a hard time selling a homely brown quilt.

W

we're goin' the other way. One way of telling a bidder that he is bidding lower than the amount now on the floor.

what's wrong with it? Challenge to the crowd to start bidding.

where's the pleasure? Who will make an opening bid?

whimsy. Something made to occupy one's time, such as a carving made by a sailor on a long voyage. Often an odd or fanciful object, for instance, an intricate carving of a chain made from one piece of wood. The word is currently popular among auctioneers, museum curators, and antique dealers to describe objects of uncertain utility but clear charm.

white goods. Refrigerators, washing machines, and other large appliances. Some auctioneers will not handle them. "Good antiques and household items; no white goods."

Y

you battin' a fly or are you bidding? Query used to determine if a party is actually bidding. Also, "Is that a bid or are you waving at someone?"

you folks on this side are allowed to bid. Line used when only one side of the hall seems to be bidding.

you just can't seem to win. Said to a bidder who keeps dropping out before the next highest bid takes the item. Sometimes embellished by a line like, "One more time you might get it."

you'll never see another one like this. Said of a particularly ugly painting.

you're the expert. All-purpose disclaimer, usually followed by something on the order of, "You can tell if it's Louis XIV or Louis XV, I can't."

you wanna stand up so everyone can see you? Used by a disgusted auctioneer after a bidder had asked to have a lot of good china put up early and then bid $26 when the auctioneer was trying to get an opening bid at a hundred.

SOURCES

The following have helped me in the collection of auction terms. Auctioneers appear with their license numbers: Daniel W. Andrews (Me. 0385), Elsie M. Andrews (Me. 0389), Bill and Virginia Cressey, Frank Dingley, Barbara Hardenbrook, Susan Kenney, Patricia McIlvaine, M.D., and Joe Reilly. Additional material came from the "auction" files in the Tamony Collection. The compiler was helped considerably by reading *Maine Antique Digest,* the excellent tabloid from Waldoboro, Maine.

3 | AUTOMOTIVE SLANG

How to Speak Car Talk

"Ever since the first car wheel put rubber to the road, cars have evolved a language of their own. Today, although just about everybody owns and drives a car, few know how to talk car-talk."

—From a booklet on Detroitese, published by Chrysler in 1959, found in the Tamony Collection

If the automotive world is one that always seems to be in a constant state of flux and change, the informal language associated with the internal combustion engine is not. To be sure, new terms are always being coined, but the old terms endure. *Four on the floor* is still the accepted way of describing a four-gear car with stick shift on the floor, and a *ragtop* is a convertible, just as it was when Ike was in the White House. In fact, some of the slang from the late 1940s found in the Tamony Collection remains remarkably current. A 1949 San Francisco *Examiner* article on hot rodders talks about *skins*, *jugs*, and *bent eight*'s.

It is also slang with its own subsets and dialects. Depending on whether you talk to a used-car salesman, race-car driver, hot rodder, or mechanic, you will hear a different version of automotive slang.

Even within auto racing there are distinct differences depending on whether you are talking to a NASCAR or Indy competitor.

Here is a heavy sampling from all of those realms within a realm.

A

A-bone. Model A Ford, especially one that has been converted into a 1950s-style street rod.

alki / alky. Methanol or alcohol as a fuel.

anchors. Brakes.

apron. The portion of a racetrack that separates the racing areas from the infield.

arching / arcing. Racing; going all out.

ark. One of many terms for a hulking, older American car; also a canoe, bomb, sled, boat, etc.

B

back light / backlite. Industry term. Rear window.

back off. To throttle down in racing.

bagel. A poorly maintained car, to a person looking at it for trade in.

baldies. Drag-racing tires that are supposed to lack tread, as well as badly worn tires.

banzai. All-out.

barefoot. Describing a car with worn-out tires.

barefoot pilgrim. Trusting car buyer who questions nothing.

barrel. (1) Engine cylinder. (2) Carburetor throat, alluded to in the term "four-barrel carburetor." (3) To speed.

base. Dealer's price.

B-back / beback / be-back. Sales term. Derogatory name for a potential customer who says he or she will return but clearly has no intention of doing so. From the time-honored departure line, "I'll be back."

beauty bolts. Exposed, brightly finished bolt heads displayed for looks.

beefer. A complaining consumer, in the lingo of the sales room.

bent eight. V-8.

big arm. Piston with a long stroke.

big banger. Big engine; one with large displacement.

Bimmer. A BMW. In his "Dream Machines" column in the *Washington Post,*

Brock Yates points out that "Beemer" is proper when referring to one of the company's motorcycles.

binders. Brakes.

bite. The adhesion of a tire to a road or track; traction.

black box. Device housing electronic components. Many traditional mechanics do not go inside black boxes.

black-flagged. Describing a race car that has been waved off the track (with a black flag) because of a mechanical problem that endangers other drivers.

blower. Supercharger. Sometimes a turbocharger.

blow lunch. Blow an engine.

blown engine. (1) Engine with a supercharger, in racing circles. (2) All-inclusive term for a serious engine breakdown.

blown gasser. Supercharged car that is fueled by gasoline.

blow off / blow off his doors. In racing, to pass a challenger.

blue book. The stated value of a car, such as "I'll give you a hundred dollars over blue book for your Ford wagon." From the name and color of the guidebook listing standard prices for used cars.

boneyard. Junkyard.

boondocks. Off the course, in racing.

booth. Where the papers are signed in closing a sale on a new or used car. It can be an office, cubicle, or desk.

boots. (1) Tires. (2) Tire inserts to reinforce the casing at weak points.

boss. Perfection.

Botts' dots. Raised, reflective pavement markers which rumble when run over to alert drivers to tollbooths and other hazards. They are called Botts' dots because they were invented by Dr. Elbert Botts, working for the state of California, in the 1950s. They are also known as *idiot buttons*.

box. Transmission.

brain bucket. Racing helmet.

brains blown out. Describing a car with a sunroof.

brass hat. Sales term. A slightly used car; a demo.

Brickyard. The Indianapolis racetrack.

bucket. Contour seat for one person.

buff. A great-looking car. "That thing is totally buff."

bull ring. A short—less than half a mile long—dirt racing track. Bull rings are common to the South.

bumble bee. Small foreign car.

bumper tag. (1) To drive close to another car, as one were to play at; (2) touching other cars' bumpers in a game of tag in which one car is "it." This game is from the same era and state of mind as *chicken*.

buried. Describing a car owner who owes more on the car than its trade-in value.

burn rubber. To accelerate with smoke and tire squeal.

bushing. Jacking up the price of a car after the buyer has signed an agreement to buy it. The classic bushing occurs when a salesman uses a high trade-in figure to estimate the final cost to the buyer, only to have the sales manager disallow the figure after the contract to buy has been signed.

busted lung. Sparkplug that is not firing.

C

cam. Camshaft.

cancer. Rust or corrosion.

carcass. An old tire.

cement mixer. Car that makes loud noises.

channel. To lower the floor by lowering the chassis.

charger. Aggressive car racer; one who gets to the front and stays there.

cherry. Older car in excellent condition.

Chevrolet BB. A tiny, four-cylinder foreign car.

chicken. Hot-rod game in which two cars drive toward each other on a head-on collision course, with the first driver to turn away being the chicken. This game, more talked about than actually played, was part of the outlaw image of the fifties hot-rod culture, but it is still used as a metaphor for unreasonable automotive risk.

chizzler. A Chrysler engine, to a hot rodder.

chop. To cut the top of a car down; to edit. Custom cars are sometimes chopped and channeled (cut down and lowered).

chop shop. Place where stolen cars are cut up for their parts, which are sold separately.

Christmas tree. (1) Electronic device using lights to ready and start drag races. (2) An array of flashing lights atop a police car, tow truck, fire engine, and ambulance. (3) Car loaded with gadgets and gizmos.

chute. A racetrack straightaway.

clamshell. Large hinged rooftop luggage carrier that is easily installed and removed and accepts luggage like it was being ingested by a giant clam.

clean deal. Car sale that does not involve a trade-in.

cold car / cold one. In the used-car business a make, model, or year of car that is not popular and hard to sell. A car can be cold for no apparent reason.

corner. A curve in auto racing.

crank. (1) The crankshaft. (2) To start a car; to crank her up.

crash cage. The confines of a stock car used in racing. It consists of tubular steel formed into a cage which protects the driver when the car crashes.

cream puff. A used car in fine, clean condition that has customer appeal.

creeper. Board on wheels, on which mechanic lies to slide under a car.

cruising. (1) Driving slowly up and down a particular stretch of town or city street, or through a particular area of town. (2) Moving along at a good clip—such as "cruising down the highway."

crunch. A crash in racing.

curbstoner. Used-car dealer who operates with a few cars, a telephone, and splashy ads.

D

dagoed. Dropped front axle on a custom street car, giving it the classic high-in-the-back and low-in-the-front look. It is pronounced "day-goed" and derives from the ethnic slur for Italian.

Darlington stripe. The distinctive right-side scrape on the side of a stock car; every NASCAR driver eventually acquires this on turn three at Darlington International Speedway in South Carolina.

dash. Dashboard.

dead sled. Nonworking or abandoned car.

death trap. A car that is rusted through, banged up, and probably has bad brakes and/or faulty steering.

deck lid. Lid of a trunk.

demo. Sales term for a demonstrator.

detailing. Sales term. The art of touching up a car to hide minor damage and imperfections. It is commonly performed in getting a used car ready for resale.

Detroit. American, as in, car air conditioning was a Detroit idea.

deuce. As always, a 1932 Ford coupé. Both the car and term have been given a long lease on life through the Beach Boys' hit "Little Deuce Coupe." The deuce alludes to the two in 1932.

dimple. Dent.

dirt tracking. A controlled slide in auto racing.

dog. Lousy car; one that nobody wants, usually because it needs a lot of work; a junker.

donuts. (1) Tires. (2) Intentionally spinning around in snow-filled parking lots, known as "Doin' donuts."

doping. Any method used to hide the flaws in a car being prepared for resale. Some of these are legal, some are not.

down / downstroke. Down payment.

downsizing. Reducing the size and weight of a vehicle to achieve better fuel economy. The term came into prominence in 1977, when Detroit began talking like this: "I think when the downsizing gets going we're going to push them right out to the shores." (Henry Ford II, on foreign competition.)

D.P. Down payment, deposit.

drafting. Driving or racing close to the tail of another car to take advantage of the vacuum created, to literally be "pulled" by the lead car. It gives the drafted car extra power without using extra fuel.

drift. To make a controlled slide in racing.

drop the hammer. To pop the clutch in drag racing.

E

edgy car. Car that needs body work, interior work, etc. Automotive equivalent of the "handyman's special" in real estate.

E.T. Elapsed time in car racing.

executive. Sales term. A car that has been used by the dealership; a fancy name for a *demo.* On occasion it has been implied that an executive car was driven by a Detroit executive of the company.

exotics. Unusual—usually foreign—cars; for example,

when a rental-car company offers a Porsche or Rolls, they are said to be offering "exotics."

F

factory. Manufacturer, or as manufactured. In racing, a factory team is one sponsored and supported by a manufacturer.

fender-bender. Accident.

flat-out. As fast as possible.

flea. Car buyer out to get a tremendous bargain.

forked-eight. V-8 engine.

four-banger. Four-cylinder engine.

455 air-conditioning. Cooling obtained while driving with four windows open at 55 mph.

front-end bra. Nylon wire or plastic mesh cover fitted to the front of a car to protect it from flying gravel and other minor road hazards.

frozen. Locked up or jammed.

fueler. Short for *top fueler.*

full house. Car or engine loaded with all the accessories and performance gimmicks.

G

gas guzzler. Car that drinks fuel. Also simply known as a *guzzler.*

Georgia credit card. Siphon for stealing gas from other people's tanks. Texan Joseph C. Goulden notes, "In Texas we call them Okie credit cards; in southern California, they are Tijuana credit cards."

glass. Fiberglas.

gobble. To drive fast; to "gobble" up the road.

gourd guard. Crash helmet.

grenade. To blow an engine.

grid. The alignment of cars for the start of a race.

gridlock. Initially a name for a mythical moment at which all the cars and trucks in Manhattan would stop, thereby turning the city into a mammoth used-car lot. The term is on its way to becoming a conventional term for any severe traffic jam.

grind. (1) Car buyer who is able to negotiate a low price on a new car. (2) To work a price down, "to grind the salesman." (3) Also to "grind" gears.

groove. The best route around a track.

gut. To remove upholstery and other items.

guts. The interior of a car.

guzzler. Car that consumes a lot of gasoline.

H

hairy. Describing racetrack traffic that is thick and fast.

hang. Turn. Once considered a teenage or hot rodder term, "hanging a left" has become general slang.

happy man. Traditional term for finance companies or loan officers among car dealers.

hat. Crash helmet.

hauler. Car that is really fast; one that "hauls ass."

header. An exhaust manifold that is designed for the free flow of exhaust gases.

hides. Tires.

high ball. (1) In sales, an estimate that is too high. For instance, a salesman may suggest a higher price for a trade-in than the customer will get after it has been "re-appraised." See also *bushing*. (2) To haul ass.

honking. At top speed in racing: "Boy, was I honking."

hot car. (1) Stolen car. (2) Used car in great demand because of such factors as condition (a *cream puff*), mileage, make, model, and/or year.

house. A car dealership.

HOV. High-occupancy vehicle, usually one with three or more people inside. The term is used on interstate highways to indicate preferential lanes for rush-hour cars with more than one or two riders. Since it is really a reference to car pools, HOV has been said to stand for "highly obtuse verbiage."

huffers and puffers. Turbochargers and superchargers.

I

idiot buttons. Same as *Botts' dots*.

idiot lights. Red lights on the instrument panel that flash on to warn the driver of an engine, brake, or electrical problem. They are stand-ins for formerly standard gauges with needles, and presumably take less intelligence to understand. The term also alludes to the fact that these lights have been known to go on when nothing is wrong.

igniter. Ignition distributor.

Indy. Of or relating to the Indianapolis 500 and the cars that race in it, which are Indy cars.

iron. Dog of a car; a clunker.

J

jack. Showroom nickname for a looker with no intention of buying.

jackknife. To fold like a blade closing in a pocket knife or jackknife. Usually used to describe a tractor-trailer truck gone out of control, with its trailer folded around or broken loose from the cab.

jug. Carburetor.

June bug. Derisive term used by stock-car racers for the Indianapolis racing car. Sometimes called a *water bug.*

junker. Car that is in bad shape; one that is almost ready for the junk heap.

K

kissed by the Santa Fe. A car that was wrecked and then repaired, according to an article on auto showroom slang in *Newsweek* (August 7, 1989). The reference is not to the city of Santa Fe but to the Santa Fe railroad.

knock-off. Quickly removable wheel lug.

L

LAHA. Acronym for Life, Accident, and HeAlth insurance.

lay. Leave, as in "lay rubber," meaning to accelerate so fast as to leave black rubber tire marks on the pavement.

leadfoot. Person who drives fast; one who keeps a heavy foot on the accelerator.

Le Mans start. A racing start in which drivers run across the track, jump in their cars, and start up. It is named for the famous French race where this start originated.

lemon. A bad car, specifically, a new one with mechanical problems although it can be used to describe a used car.

light the rug / light the tires. To make the tires smoke.

lipstick. Cosmetic changes made to a new model car to give the illusion of a new version of it.

loaded. Describing a car with many extras and options.

loop. To spin out in auto racing.

low ball. (1) To offer a car at a low price to make a buyer interested. When the deal is about to be consummated, the seller will jack the price up. (2) To offer a car at an outrageously low price for a trade-in or sale to a used-car dealer.

low-rider. A car with springs and suspensions adjusted so that it rides only a few inches above the pavement.

lump. The engine.

lunch. To blow an engine, especially in drag racing. "He just lunched his second engine this month."

M

mag. (1) Short for magneto. (2) Wheel cast from magnesium; a mag wheel.

main. Street where cars cruise; not necessarily Main Street.

make. Manufacturer.

marbles. Racer's term for track debris—pebbles, tire fragments, etc.

mashed potato drive. Automatic transmission.

Mexican overdrive. Coasting downhill.

mill. An engine.

moth-eaten. Describing a car from a harsh-weather state where snow, ice, and road salt have caused corrosion.

mouse house. Dealership in which customers (mice) are fed through an assembly-line sales operation—from salespeople to contract writers or closers.

mud doggin'. Driving a four-wheel-drive vehicle off the road for pleasure.

muscle. Power in a car, as opposed to the illusion of power given by styling, names, racing stripes, etc.

N

nerf. To nudge another vehicle with your vehicle.

nerf bars. Special bumpers used for pushing other vehicles.

O

ocean fenders. Rippled or dented fenders—that is, those with waves in them.

on the floor. Describing a gearshift mechanism on the floor at the driver's right hand, as opposed to the mechanism on the steering post. Depending on the number of forward gears, a car may be said to have three, four, or five on the floor. An automatic floor post can said to be "automatic on the floor."

on the hook. In tow; at the rear of a tow truck.

open the tap. Open the throttle.

outlaw. Race-car driver who runs in a nonsanctioned event.

out of the chute / gate / hole. The start of a drag race.

_____ **P** _____

pacer. (1) Driver who drives a racetrack at a predetermined speed before the green flag is dropped. (2) Car which sets the pace for a race.

packing. Adding extra charges to the base price of a car—dealer prep, document prep, finance fees, etc.

piece. Car that is a piece of junk; piece of shit.

pipes. Dual exhaust system.

pit. Service area; place where one makes a "pit stop."

pop the clutch. To engage the clutch suddenly.

post. The steering column.

pot. Carburetor.

power. Sales term for electrically operated windows, breaks, and seats.

preacher's car. Car without expensive options.

puke. Blow an engine.

pull. To remove, especially in auto repairs where components are always pulled—never lifted—from under the hood.

_____ **R** _____

ragged edge. Racing term for the limit; to run on the ragged edge is to push oneself to the point where it is difficult to maintain control.

ragtop. Convertible.

rail job. Dragster built on bare frame rails, or one that has been created by stripping a car down to its frame.

rails. Frame for a dragster.

raked. Describing a car with a lowered front end—a classic hot-rod look.

R and R. In auto mechanics, to Remove and Repair or Remove and Replace.

rap. Motor knock.

rat. Car that performs poorly.

rest cure. Practice of sending a car to the repair shop and having it returned to the customer without anything being done to it.

rice burner. Japanese motorcyle or car.

ride. Car.

ride the rails. Racing technique that calls for taking the outside course on the flats and the high part of the banked curves.

roach. Car buyer without credit or with bad credit.

road tar. Truckstop coffee.

roller. (1) Rolls-Royce. (2) A car in stock; one that a buyer can come into a dealership and see, buy, and drive home in.

roller skate. Subcompact.

rubber. Tires.

rubberneck. To slow down and turn one's head around, as if attached to one's body with a rubber neck, to look at an accident or other roadside event, usually into the lane of oncoming traffic.

rust bucket. A car that is rusted through.

S

say hello. To give a competing race car a tap on the rear bumper to let the driver know that you intend to drive through his space—a means of telling him to move over.

scuff. Racing term for a tire that has been used.

shaved. A car stripped of ornaments.

shillelagh. Chevy engine, especially an old V-8.

six-banger / six-holer. Six-cylinder engine.

skeeching. Holding onto the bumper of a slow-moving car on a snowy street and getting pulled along.

skins. Tires.

sled. Big car; also a *tank,* boat, etc.

slicks. Wide, smooth-tread racing tires.

slingshot. (1) A racing maneuver in which a car following in the draft of another breaks out of the vacuum and gets a sudden burst of speed. See *drafting.* (2) Dragster in which the driver sits behind the rear wheels, like a rock in a slingshot.

slippery. Streamlined.

slipstreaming. Driving or racing close to the tail of another car to take advantage of the reduced air resistance. Also *drafting.*

slow motion. Prospective car buyer who tends to think things over.

slug. Piston.

slush / slush box. Automatic transmission.

sneakers. Tires.

snowballs. Traditional big, showy whitewall tires; the kind you'd put on a restored Packard.

souped up. Customized for greater power and speed.

spaghetti. Excess chrome or trim on a car.

special. One of several terms used in car sales for a vehicle that has been advertised or promoted but not necessarily reduced in price—such as cars offered in "Sellathons."

spoiler. Metal strip used to control drag, downforce, and airflow. Primarily found on race cars, they appear under the front end and atop the back end (where the trunk would be on a sedan.)

squint. Tinted windshield glass.

squirrelly. Racing term describing a car that is given to sliding. It is said to come out of turns "loose in the rear."

squirt. Windshield spray-cleaning solution.

stick. Describing a manual, as opposed to automatic, transmission.

sticker. (1) A new tire; from the fact that the manufacturer's paper label has to be pulled off a new tire. (2) Short for sticker (undiscounted) price, so called because an itemized price list is stuck to one of the car's windows with glue.

sticks. Furniture, in the context of collateral for a car loan.

stock. From the factory; to take from the normal stock.

stove bolt. Chevrolet six-cylinder engine.

straw hat. Convertible.

stroked. Souped or hopped up; specifically, an engine in which the piston stroke length has been increased.

stroker. (1) The opposite of a *charger;* a driver who never tries to set the pace and is simply content to win. (2) A racer who cannot afford to replace a blown engine; but gets money and a chance to race the following week if he finishes. To finish he "strokes along."

submarine. Car that has been damaged by flooding. The term came into prominence in late 1965 when, according to the March 1968 *Esquire,* some 30,000 cars were waterlogged by Hurricane Betsy and "many were reconditioned to hide water damage, [and then] shipped out of state."

sugar scoop. An indented surface leading to an air scoop.

T

tank. Big car.

T-bone. (1) Model T Ford. (2) To take an accidental right-angle shot at the doorside of another car.

Texas rat. Used car originally owned by a long-distance driver.

tired iron / tired rat. A beat-up car.

tool. To drive.

top eliminator. Overall winner at a drag race, so called because he has eliminated all other drivers.

top fueler. State-of-the-art dragster.

tossing a rod. Blowing an engine.

trannys. Transmission.

turbo lag. The split second between slamming the accelerator to the floor and experiencing the takeoff of a turbocharged car.

turn. To generate or achieve a speed; "to turn eighty in the curve," for example.

turtle shell. Trunk or trunk lid of a car.

tweak. Small engine modification made to improve performance.

U

unblown. Without a blower or supercharger.

unglued. Blown, as in a *blown engine*.

unhorsing. Getting a customer to give up his/her car for a long appraisal period so that the time can be used to sell the customer.

unloading. Losing part of a car, such as a dragster unloading a tire.

upside down. Same as *buried*.

V

vanity plate. License plate customized for the owner of the car. Usually initials, nickname, spouse's name, etc.

ventilate the block. To throw a rod through the engine; to wreck the engine.

vette. Corvette.

W

wagon. Station wagon.

wail. To run fast and free.

water bug. Same as *June bug*.

wayback. The area behind the backseat in a station wagon or van.

wheels. A car.

windmill. Radiator fan.

wiped. To be beaten or overtaken in a race.

wires. Wire wheels.

wrecker. A tow truck.

Y

yellowtail. A rookie driver who may be required to race with a yellow back bumper to alert others to his inexperience.

Z

z. To reinforce and lower the frame of your car, as in "that car's been z'd."

SOURCES
Important help for this chapter has come from Joseph C. (Stroker) Goulden, James W. Darling, the Tamony Collection, and Gary B. Van Voorhis of the Daytona International Speedway. Matthew Fass, Stephanie Flathman, and Cathy Sanders also contributed.

4 | Aviation and Space

Words from the Wild Blue Yonder

"Can You Talk the Language of the Age of Space?"

—Title of Air Force recruiting
brochure, late 1950s, found in the
Tamony Collection

During World War II there was so much aviation slang that the newspapers had to run occasional articles to point out that bombs were *eggs*, antiaircraft balloons were *pigs*, planes were *kites* or *crates*, student pilots were *kiwis*, a routine flight was a *milk run*, and the cockpit was a *pulpit*.

It was a basic slang that obtained until the 1950s, when jets, missiles, and satellites came into the picture and to a large degree slang gave way to technical terminology. But this is not to say that there aren't ripe, colorful terms flying about. Here are examples from commercial aviation, the Air Force, and space exploration.

37

A

A-Okay. (Space) Fine; the best.

auntie. (Air Force) Anti-, as in "antimissile missile."

B

backout. (Space) Reversing a countdown because of a component failure or bad weather.

barbecue mode. (Space) An orbiter taking a slow roll in space for thermal conditioning.

bazuco. Cheap coca paste.

bird. (1) (Space and Air Force) Pilotless objects that fly—satellites, probes, and the like. (2) Helicopter.

birdman. (Air Force) Pilot.

blowoff. (Space) The separation of an instrument section or other package from a rocket vehicle by explosive force.

blue letter. (Commercial aviation) Letter of complaint about a stewardess.

blue room. (Commercial aviation) Lavatory on an airplane.

bug smashers. (Commercial aviation) Small private planes, especially when they are in congested areas.

burnout. (Air Force and Space) The moment of final oxidization or combustion of fuel. Burnout velocity is the speed of a rocket or airborne vehicle at the moment it runs out of fuel.

This term, which at least dates back to the early 1950s, was adopted for work in the form of "teacher burnout," "job burnout," etc.

C

carryon. (Commercial aviation) Luggage carried aboard an airplane by the passenger.

chicken switch. (Space) An abort switch or any other control that stops the mission.

cod. (Naval aviation) Plane that delivers mail and other supplies to an aircraft carrier. It stands for Carrier Onboard Delivery.

crawlerway. (Space) Heavily reinforced road built for transporting space vehicles and rockets.

D

dayside. (Space) The portion of a planet or moon in daylight.

deadheading. (Commercial aviation) For a crew member to

fly as a passenger, either to return home or to catch a flight to which they are assigned. One is only considered to be deadheading when in uniform, so going on vacation in civvies does not count.

decay. (Space) Loss of energy.

deep space. (Space) Beyond Pluto.

dogs. (Commercial aviation) Passengers.

doolie. (Air Force) Air Force academy cadet.

drone. (Air Force) Unmanned aircraft.

dry run. (Air Force and Space) A practice or rehearsal.

E

empty kitchen. (Commercial aviation) Name given to female pilots by males—presumably from the fact that the woman is in the cockpit of a plane rather than in her house.

equipment. (Commercial aviation) The plane. If you are told that there has been a slight delay in the arrival of the equipment, it means your plane is late.

exotic. Fuel that delivers a great deal of power for its weight and volume.

F

fat Albert. (Air Force) Jumbo jet that is wide-bodied.

fly by wire. (Air Force and Space) To fly by autopilot.

footprint. (Space) The space taken up by a spacecraft after it has landed.

G

go-no-go. (Space) The decision to launch or not launch; the point of no return.

grav field. (Space) Gravitational field.

H

hawk. (Commercial aviation) Passenger who causes trouble. Sometimes called a *vulture*.

I

icing. (All) The phenomenon of ice accumulating on aircraft.

Indians. (Commercial aviation) Same as *bug smashers*.

J

jump-seat sniffer. (Commercial aviation) Derogatory "stew talk" for a passenger who chases stewardesses. Stewardesses sit in the plane's jump seats. This term was first given wide circulation in Jay David's *Sex and the Single Stewardess* (Playboy Press, 1976). Also *lobby locust.*

K

KOPS. (Space) Short for 1000 (K) Operations per Second. The speed and quantities required for space exploration call for much use of the letter K, as in K-gal, which is short for a thousand gallons.

L

LAX. (Commercial aviation) Los Angeles and/or Los Angeles International Airport. LAX, suggestive of laid-back, is the three-letter baggage-ticket code for that destination. Others that have been adopted for conversation are ORD for O'Hare Airport in Chicago and MIA for Miami.

layover. (Commercial aviation) Time spent by a member of a flight crew in a city other than that person's home base.

leather or feather. (Commercial aviation) "The choice between filet mignon and chicken cordon bleu that pilots are offered on board," according to *Newsweek,* July 3, 1989.

lobby locust. (Commercial aviation) Term used by stewardesses for man who hangs around hotel lobbies trying to pick up stewardesses.

LOX. (Air Force and Space) Liquid OXygen.

loxing. (Air Force and Space) The job of loading liquid oxygen into the fuel tanks of a missile or space vehicle.

M

mark one eyeball. (All) Human sight. This term came into play during the moon landings, which were helped considerably by the mark one eyeball.

marsdoggle. (Space) Wasteful and highly expensive mission to Mars. It is a blend of "Mars" and "boondoggle."

metsat. (Space) Short for "meteorological satellite."

N

near space. Near the earth.

no-op. A plane that will not operate; one that has been canceled.

no-show. (Commercial aviation) A passenger who does not appear for a flight on which he or she holds reservations.

O

offline. (Commercial aviation) Travel on a carrier other than the one that sold the passenger the ticket.

P

PAX. (Commercial aviation) A passenger, from the ticket code for passenger.

penalty box. (Commercial aviation) An inactive runway where an incoming aircraft waits until a gate becomes available.

pit. (Commercial aviation) The belly of the plane where baggage is stored.

pod. Detachable compartment of a spacecraft.

Q

quiet sun. (All) Condition of the sun when it is relatively free of sun spots and other factors that interfere with radio transmission.

R

red-eye. (Commercial aviation) A late-night flight, commonly a midnight flight from the West to the East Coast, as in, "I came in on the red-eye from L.A."

retros. (Space) Breaking rockets or retro-rockets.

roach coach. (Commercial aviation) Flight to the tropics.

S

scramble. (Air Force) To take off in a hurry.

scrub. (All) To cancel or to back out of a countdown.

slam dunk. (Commercial aviation) Landing technique that allows the plane to stay above traffic until the last minute, at which point it quickly drops to land.

smoking materials. (Commercial aviation) Cigarettes, in the strange cant of the public address announcement. Smoking materials are never put out, they are extinguished.

soup. (All) Fog.

space junk. (Space) Debris in earth orbit.

spacetug. (Space) Utility vehicle for servicing orbiting space stations.

spaghetti suit. (Space) The long underwear worn by astronauts, which is composed in part of tubes that carry cool water.

splashdown. (Space) The landing of a space vehicle in the ocean.

starship. (Space) Interstellar vehicle.

stew. (Commercial aviation) Stewardess.

stew zoo. (Commercial aviation) An apartment where a lot of stewardesses live, or a hotel where they lay over.

stick shaker. (Aviation) An alerting device used to indicate that a stall condition may be in the offing.

T

three pointer. Aircraft landing in which the three sets of wheels all touch down at the same time; a good landing.

tinman. (Space) Aluminum space suit.

touchdown. Landing of a manned or unmanned spacecraft on the surface of the moon, a planet, or on its return to earth.

turn around / turn around flight. (Commercial aviation) Flight that returns a crew or crew member to their home base on the day of departure.

U

unobtanium. (Space) A substance or piece of hardware that is desired but not obtainable.

upgrade. (Commercial aviation) To move from tourist to first class.

V

vulture. (Commercial aviation) A troublesome passenger. Also known as a *hawk.*

W

window. (Space) Period during which a space mission is possible and/or most economical.

X

XTAL. (Space) NASA-ese for crystal. Over time the National Aeronautics and Space Administration has developed thousands of acronyms and abbreviations. For reasons unclear, there are a bunch that shorten words using the letter X. Others include XFER for "transfer," XFD for "cross feed," XPNDR for "transponder," and XMT for "transmit."

Z

zero-g. (Air Force and Space) The state of weightlessness when there is no—or zero—gravity.

zip fuel. (Air Force and Space) High-energy jet fuel.

SOURCES

A remarkable collection of NASA acronyms and terms appear in NASA Reference Publication 1059, *Space Transportation System and Associated Payloads: Glossary, Acronyms and Abbreviations.* A good source of commercial aviation slang shows up as a glossary to Jay David's *Sex and the Single Stewardess* (Playboy Press, 1976). A small but important collection of commercial aviation slang appears in the July 3, 1989, *Newsweek.* A large collection of aviation and aerospace glossaries in the Tamony Collection proved invaluable, as did suggestions from Ralph Hamil.

5 BUREAUCRATESE

The Talk of the White-Collar Bailiwick

> "The language used is bureaucratic gobbledygook, jargon, double talk, a form of officialese, federalese and insurancese, and double speak. It does not qualify as English."
>
> —Federal Judge Jack B. Weinstein, ordering the government to remove gobbledygook from Medicare forms, July 11, 1984

> "WASHINGTON—This is the only town in Christendom where corrupting the English language is a community project."
>
> —Lead to an unsigned Scripps-Howard dispatch, December 28, 1959

Most people think of it in terms of the federal government, but it is spoken and written, with variations, in many other places. It seems to be used anywhere that people are sorted into departments and divisions and communicate with each other through memos.

It is the linguistic fuel of state and local government, think tanks and consulting firms, educational administration, nonprofit organizations, and much of corporate America. It is, in short and increasingly, the lingo of white-collar America. There are subdivisions of this lingo which have been created to serve education *(educanto)*, planning *(plannish,* or *urbabble* in the case of urban planning), the government *(bureaucratese* or *governmentese* or *officialese* or, as the ever-provocative Herb Caen put it, *bureaucrapese)*, and specific agencies of government (*statese* for the State Department, for example).

Lest there be any question, it is proliferating, seeming to grow and reinforce itself with each new leap in communications technology. Its breeding grounds are telephone lines and computer screens, and it reproduces through copy and fax machines. Even television plays a role in the proliferation as it covers events like Watergate and the Iran-contra hearings, in which many of the key roles were played by people who spoke it fluently.

Some points should be made about it.

1. This slang does not always sound like a slang but, rather, a bloated version of standard English. It is, however, slang in the classic sense of a language particular to a certain group that is *not* used by others and is meant for widespread dispersal. It also fits the definition of jargon, so it can be called a hybrid.

2. It dotes on extra syllables (*utilize* over *use, orientate* over *orient*) and loves to turn nouns into verbs. It hates simple words like *money* and *cash* (preferring terms like *resources, funds, allocations, appropriations,* etc.), and dotes on what one critic termed "reductive prefaces" (on the order of *debrief, dicensus, disadvantaged, disequilibrium,* and *disincentive.*)

3. The slang is accompanied by extended metaphors and colorful clichés. If one tries to saved a doomed project, that person is accused of "trying to rearrange the deck chairs on the *Titanic,*" and if one tries to get hold of the elusive, you are said to be "trying to nail jelly to the wall."

4. It has a penchant for the passive voice, the collective *we/us,* and acronyms.

5. It is much maligned and criticized, and has been since it first began to grow during World War II. A number of people, including Jimmy Carter, have tried to control it. Despite this, it chugs along in true bureaucratic style and seems to get the job done—that is to say, "it has displayed and demonstrated an ongoing efficacy when confined to certain logical parameters."

A

acceptable. Possibly acceptable. When used in terms like "acceptable level of unemployment," it means acceptable to those using the term (that is, those who have a job).

activate. Start.

alarmist. Anyone who rocks the boat or questions an important decision.

apologist. One who takes a position on an issue or industry that you don't like.

apples and oranges. That which defies comparison.

at this point in time. Now. This phrase came into its own during the Watergate hearings, when one suspected that witnesses used it to give themselves extra time to think.

B

back burner. Metaphor of delay or dismissal. "Let's put that one on the back burner and get back to it later." The back burner amounts to bureaucratic limbo.

backdoor spending. Spending that is provided for outside the normal channels of appropriations.

backgrounder. Session in which a ranking official gives information on the proviso that it is not quoted directly or attributed to an individual.

bailiwick. Realm or area of responsibility, commonly phrased in terms of something that is "not my bailiwick."

ball of wax. The entire situation; the whole enchilada.

ballpark figure. Estimate.

basically. In short.

Beltway bandit. Consultant working out of the many think tanks and consulting firms in the Washington, D.C., area. The Beltway is the name for the circumferential interstate highway that rings the city of Washington as it runs through the inner suburbs of Virginia and Maryland. It refers to more than the actual road, taking in a state of mind—an idea may make perfect sense inside the Beltway but not outside the Beltway. In this case "outside the Beltway" refers to the rest of the nation.

big picture. Larger considerations.

bird dog. To put something aside; to make no decision. In other quarters, this means to sniff something out; but not here where one can bird dog a project that is going nowhere.

brainstorm. A collective attempt to be creative, and find new ideas or solutions. As a verb, brainstorm describes group rather than individual thought.

broadbrush. Crude; rough.

buy. To approve, in the sense of "I'll buy that." This term is never used with money—that kind of buying is *procuring*.

––––––––– **C** –––––––––

can of worms. A mess, problems.

causal factors. Reasons.

charged. Ordered to; told to.

clearance mechanisms. What it takes to get an okay.

coequal. Equal.

cognitive skills. Book learning.

community. Group of people *not* linked geographically; for example, handicapped community, gay community, etc.

copy. To send a copy; "Copy me on that memo." It replaces the prephotocopy era verb "to carbon."

counterfactual. Untrue, as in a counterfactual proposition, or a lie.

counterintuitive. Surprising; not what you'd expect (unless you thought about it).

CYA. Initialism for Cover Your Ass; bureaucratic self-protection.

––––––––– **D** –––––––––

data. Anything in writing (numbers, figures, facts, graphs, etc.). A precise term that has lost its precision through overuse.

day one. The beginning; the first day. "I could have told you from day one that this would not work."

debrief. To get information from. This term emerged from the Pentagon and spread into other monolithic buildings along with *prebrief.*

destabilize. Overthrow or destroy.

detention center. Jail.

developing nation. A nation that may be developing economically and technologically, standing still, or mired in decay. Formerly undeveloped or underdeveloped nations.

dialogue. Conversation.

dicensus. Lack of consensus.

disadvantaged. Poor. In 1965 a Jules Feiffer cartoon character tells how he went from being poor to being poor but needy. Then they told him that it was self-defeating to think of himself as needy, so he became deprived. Then they told that he was under-privileged, and finally he was disadvantaged. The character summed it up, "I still don't have a dime, but I have a great vocabulary."

discipline. Occupational specialty. To be asked "What is your discipline?" is the bureaucratic equivalent of the singles bar question "What's your sign?"

disequilibrium. Out of whack; not in balance.

disincentive. Anything that tends to reduce motivation.

do-able. Workable.

domicile. Home.

double dipper. Person who takes dual compensation from the government and another public institution.

dysfunctional. Not working.

E

end result. Result.

end-user. Recipient.

etched in sand. Flexible.

etched in stone. Cannot be changed, but often stated in the negative: "This plan is not exactly etched in stone."

ethically disoriented. Describing a cheater in educanto.

exercise. Take or make, such as exercising an option or exercising one's opinion.

expertise. Experience. This term has come to encompass all things and has become totally divorced from the idea of a true expert.

F

facilitate. To ease.

facility. Thing; place.

fallback position. Bureaucratese for a defeat.

feedback. Reaction to; as in reporting. "I'd like some feedback on Friday's meeting."

finalize. End.

fine tune. To work out the details.

freeze. To stop or hold in place—from a nuclear freeze to a COLA [Cost of Living Adjustment] freeze.

functional. Working.

functional utilization. Actually being used.

fund. Pay for.

funding. Money. Funding is almost always spoken of in

terms of increased or decreased funding.

fungible. Interchangable, as in "All shopping centers are fungible."

fuzz. To blur on purpose; to make less direct.

F.Y. Abbr. for *fiscal year.*

——— **G** ———

good. Fair to poor, as in "good try, but let's try to do it right this time."

——— **H** ———

hands off. Not involved; as in "President Reagan had a hands-off management style."

hands on. Involved; participating.

heretofore. Before.

human resources. People at work. This used to be known as the "work force."

——— **I** ———

I can live with. Said of something that is mediocre or arrived at through compromise; a lukewarm okay.

impact. Effect, such as a school impacted by dwindling population.

implement. Do.

implementation. Doing.

indicated. Said. "You indicated that you would empty the garbage."

information processing center. Typing pool.

infrastructure. Bridges, sewers, roads, etc.

inoperative. Broken; not working.

insufficiency. Shortage.

interconnect. Connect.

interdependent. Dependent.

interdisciplinary. Describing anything involving people with different backgrounds.

interpersonal. Between humans.

intervention. Interference.

in the loop. Part of what is going on; in the know.

in view of. Since.

irrespective. Regardless.

is of the opinion that. Believes.

——— **K** ———

K-12. Educanto for the period from kindergarten through the twelfth grade, the last year of high school. It is stated as "K through 12."

L

let's discuss. Memo notation from a superior which tells a junior to "come down to my office."

low profile. Describing that which is being kept out of the limelight.

M

maximize. Make the most of.

media center. Library.

methodology. Method.

mobile response unit. Police car, ambulance, or fire truck.

motivationally deficient. Lazy.

multidisciplinary. Diverse. A committee with people from various departments or interests is invariably described as a multidisciplinary task force.

N

needless to say. Needs to be said (if it were actually "needless to say," it would not be said).

neonatal unit. Nursery.

O

off-load. Unload.

one would think. I think.

OTE. Overtaken by events.

Said of a program, report, or concern that has been rendered obsolete by time.

outreach. Reaching the consumer, public, target audience, etc.

overcrowded. Crowded.

oversight. A mistake; a screw-up.

P

paper pusher. Self-deprecating term for one in a bureaucracy. The term is sometimes useful when things go wrong: "Don't ask me, I'm just a paper pusher."

paper trail. Evidence left by a bureaucrat to prove that he or she acted in a particular way in dealing with a situation.

past history. History.

pencil in. To tentatively schedule something. It is based on the fact that pencil can be erased. "Pencil in lunch for Wednesday."

phase in. Start; implement.

phase out. Stop; dismantle.

phase zero. The beginning of something.

plum. A political appointment; a job given out by the President.

policy. Predetermined response.

prebrief. Brief in advance of a meeting or event.

preplanning. Planning.

prioritize. To decide what is most important; to assign priorities to things.

private sector, the. Business; anything that is not part of the government, which is the *public sector.*

proactive. Advance planning.

procedural safeguards. Defined by Don Ethan Miller in his *Book of Jargon* as "red tape."

process. Work or activity, as in the "planning process" or the "information process."

procurement/procuring. Buying; getting hold of.

program. Almost anything. In 1962 Senator Stephen M. Young of Ohio defined it as "any assignment or task that cannot be completed in one phone call."

project. See *program.*

promulgate. Announce; issue an order; start something.

prune. A *plum* with experience; an appointee who has held the job for a while.

public sector. The government—federal, state, and local—itself.

Q

qualitative. Having to do with quality and things that cannot be measured.

quantification. Putting a number on something.

quantitative. Having to do with numbers.

quick fix. That which does not exist. In the context of the bureaucracy it is common to state that there is "no quick fix" when a problem cannot be solved by money.

R

R&D / R and D. Research and Development.

redundancy of human resources. Too many employees.

reinventing the wheel. To study something that has already been studied; usually stated negatively, by those opposed to reinventing the wheel.

reskilling. Retraining. This term may have been invented by Maine Governor John R. McKernan, who in 1967 said to a reporter, "That tells you right off the bat that we need serious reskilling of our work force."

revenue shortfall. One of several clever ways of saying that there is a deficit without saying the word. If the word deficit is used, it is never "our deficit," but rather "the deficit."

revise to reflect. Revise.

revolving door. Metaphoric term used to describe the movement between public service and private employment.

RFP. Initialism for Request for Proposals, which is a notice to bid for a government job or contract.

RIF / riff. Derived from the acronym for Reduction in Force, it stands for a cutback in staff, or a layoff. It applies to the federal work force, including the military, and comes up as agency budgets are trimmed and riffing becomes rife.

root cause. Cause.

S

scenario. Hypothetical case; a prediction.

seed money. Money used to start something.

selected out. Fired.

shortfall. Not enough. A bud- getary shortfall is a shortage of money.

signage. Signs.

significant contribution. Contribution.

sound of the city. An inside-Washington reference to paper shuffling, as in "Listen carefully and you'll hear the sound of the city."

state of the art. Not out of date; current.

subject matter. Subject.

substandard housing. Slum.

sunset law. Legislation that specifies the periodic review of, or stated date of demise for, a program or agency.

sunshine rule. Rule that opens a previously closed proceeding to public scrutiny.

surviving spouse. A widow or widower.

T

take a fix / take a reading. To try to figure out; to attempt an answer.

target. (1) To aim or earmark. (2) Goal.

task. (1) Job. (2) To assign work.

tasker. Memo or other device used to assign a task.

task force. A temporary committee.

thrust. Direction.

time frame. When; a period of time.

trickle-down. To benefit from a law or a program after it has benefited and been filtered through its prime target.

U

underutilized. Not used very often.

unsubstantiated rumor. Rumor.

up to speed. Current.

utilization. Use.

utilize. To use.

V

verbalize. Say.

viable. Workable. This term came into its own when bureaucratese was criticized for its dependency on the word "feasible."

visualize. See.

W

watchdog. Term used to describe the *oversight* function of commissions, committees, and certain agencies, notably the General Accounting Office, the investigatory arm of Congress.

when deemed appropriate. When okay.

whistleblower. One who reveals corruption or mismanagement in an organization.

wiggle room. Quality of a public statement that sounds authoritative but is really so vague that the speaker can later change positions and still use the same words. Writing about such statements in the *Washington Post,* Susan Trausch reported, "The phrase 'cautious optimism' has about a mile of wiggle room on either side. So does 'tentative acceptance' and 'he is leaning in that direction.'"

window. Opportunity.

wired. Describing a grant, contract, or job whose winner is predetermined: "They said it was open to new bidders, but we thought it was wired from the beginning."

within the framework of. Within.

Y

your court. Your problem now, from the tennis metaphor of "the ball is now in your court."

_____ **Z** _____

zero fund. To not pay for.

zero-sum game. Conflict in which there will be a winner and a loser, but usually initiated by one who will be able to say "my gain is your loss."

SOURCES

Beyond the fact that the author has spent the last twenty years of his life inside and just outside the Beltway and is by now fluent in this lingo, the sizable file on bureaucratese in the Tamony Collection was most helpful, as were the suggestions from Chris Keller.

6 | BUSINESS AND FINANCE

Buzzwords for Big Shots

"That guy is no lamb at this game, and right now he's a bull on a lot of cats and dogs I'd never suggest you own. He doesn't get hung up in many pups, though, and some of his hot issues in recent years have been real yo-yos."

—Sylvia Porter recalling the gist of a conversation she had with a broker a few days earlier, her "Your Money's Worth" column of September 17, 1964

It has been long argued that slang tends to thrive in informal environments. The point is well taken, but it does not explain the fact that the highly structured, formal realm of money management is as slangy as any baseball dugout or high school locker room. After all, this is a realm in which the gray institutions of fiscal responsibility are known as Fannie Mae, Ginnie Mae, Freddy Mac, and the Fed.

——— A ———

Acapulco spread. Transaction with multiple commissions that is so complicated that, in the words of *The Wall Street Journal,* it will ". . . send the broker winging off to a Mexican vacation."

air-pocket stock. A security whose value has dropped sharply, like an airplane does when it hits an air pocket.

alligator spread. A transaction in which the commissions eat up the profit.

arbs. Arbitrageurs, or those who speculate in the stock of companies with announced or rumored deals.

at the market. The current price of a security.

B

Baby Bells. The regional telephone companies created as a result of the breakup of *Ma Bell*—the American Telephone and Telegraph System.

baby bond. Bond sold in denominations of less than the amount of $1 million.

back off. Sudden sinking of stock price after a rise.

bag job. Describing a security bought on a rumor that turns out to be false.

bar. One million.

basis point. One hundredth of one percent.

beard. To act as a front for another.

bear hug. The embrace that a large company puts on another (not always smaller) company, one that it is taking over. The term is apt. *Forbes* magazine explained a bear hug this way: "Big companies buy little companies and usually end up destroying the very thing they coveted the small company for."

bear market. One that is going down; a market driven by uncertainty and/or pessimism.

bear raid. Heavy selling of a stock to force its price down so that large quantities can be purchased at the depressed price.

bed and breakfast. Selling a security and buying it back quickly to minimize capital gains taxes.

belly up. Out of business; bankrupt. Also, *went toes*.

Big Blue. IBM.

big board. The New York Stock Exchange.

black book. A preplanned defense against a takeover.

black hole. The discrepancy in the global balance of payments.

black knight. Predator who mounts a hostile takeover bid.

Black Monday. October 19,

1987, when the stock market crashed.

blow back. To sell a new issue quickly. This is usually not popular with the underwriter who brought it.

blue chip. Common stock in a major corporation with a longstanding ability to generate profits and dividends.

blue-sky laws. State laws created to protect the public from securities fraud. Supposedly the phrase was coined when a judge likened the value of a stock to the value of a piece of blue sky.

bo dereks. Bonds maturing in the year 2010, from Bo Derek's role as the perfect woman in the movie *10*.

boiler room. Room in which fast-talking sales people use the phone to sell securities or commodities for outrageous commissions or markups which are usually overpriced and have poor investment characteristics.

boot. Cash thrown in with stock in an acquisition; a cash sweetener.

box. One's own holdings. To sell short against one's own portfolio is known as "selling short against the box." See *selling short*.

brass ring. Wall Street partnership.

breakup value. The value of a company after a takeover, as it is broken up for the value of its component parts.

bucketing. Broker arranging a trade for a customer at a higher price than a market open to all bidders would produce.

bucket shop. Dishonest brokerage house which gambles with its clients' stocks, bonds, and other holdings without permission.

Buck Rogers. Securities that enjoy a sudden rise in a short period of time.

bullet. Fixed-interest security with a fixed date of maturity and no sinking fund.

bull market. One that is going up.

C

cafeteria plan. Benefit plan that allows an employee some alternative choices, as if that employee were selecting dishes in a cafeteria.

callable. Describing some bonds and preferred stocks

that can be redeemed—or called—by the issuer before maturity.

candy-store problem. Situation involving a great variety of good choices.

car. A futures contract. According to *Lamont's Glossary,* prepared by Lamont and Partners of London, this is "a throwback from the days when commodities were transported in railway cars."

cascade. To send information through a company.

cash cow. Enterprise that creates a lot of surplus cash flow, as opposed to paper profits.

CATS. Certificates of Accrual on Treasury Securities. One of several financial "felines," including *TIGR's* (Treasury Investment Growth Receipts) and *LYON's* (Liquid Yield Option Notes). These are house names for zero-coupon "stripped" Treasury bonds. They are said to be *stripped* because the interest is separated from the principal and sold separately.

cats and dogs. Stocks of unproven value which, among other things, cannot be used as collateral.

CBOE. Chicago Board of Exchange.

CEO. Chief Executive Officer; the boss. As William Safire has pointed out, in olden times the boss was called the president or chairman.

Chinese Wall. Term characterizing the procedural barriers that prevent information known to people in one part of the business from becoming known to those in another part.

churn. To cause a client to buy and sell securities imprudently in order to generate commissions for the broker.

cold call. A call made to a stranger, often at night, to get the stranger to buy a security or securities.

comfort letter. Letter used by an issuer's accounting firm specifying procedures used to determine interior periods and dates employed by the firm to determine the status of a client's financial position.

contrarian. Person who thinks that the market will move in the opposite direction, up or down, from where the majority believes it is moving.

corner. To take control of the price of a security or commodity by obtaining a major interest in it.

creeping takeover. Gradual accumulation of large amounts of the shares in a company through purchases on the open market.

cut a melon. For a company to declare a large stock dividend.

----------- **D** -----------

dawn raid. Quick buy of substantial amounts of a company's stock on the market before the market becomes aware that something is going on.

day order. An order given to a broker that is only good for one day.

dead cat bounce. Small increase in the market averages after a substantial drop.

dividend-capture. Investment strategy in which stocks are bought just before they declare dividends and sold immediately thereafter.

dog. Enterprise that costs more to operate than it produces in income. The opposite of a *cash cow.*

down size. Term used to euphemistically describe layoffs.

DRIP. Acronym for Dividend ReInvestment Plan, which automatically reinvests cash dividends from stock into the purchase of new shares of that same stock.

drop-dead fee. Money paid to those who have backed a raider if the raid fails; a kill fee.

dummy. A member of a board of directors who has no direct interest in the company but represents someone who does; a human proxy.

dump. To unload goods in a foreign country at a very low price to prevent a domestic oversupply.

----------- **E** -----------

ERISA. Employee Retirement Income Security Plan.

ESOP. Employee Stock Ownership Plan.

ex-dividend. Without dividend—a stock whose settlement date is between the record and payment date. Such stocks are said to sell ex-dividend. A stock can sell ex-dividend before the dividend is paid. It first goes ex-, as declared by the exchange where it trades, four business days before the record date— on the company's books—on which the payment will be made.

F

Fannie Mae. The Federal National Mortgage Association.

fast track. Describing the path of quick ascent to the top of the heap.

Fed, The. The Board of Governors of the Federal Reserve System, and the Federal Reserve Bank; constituting *The System.*

Fed time. The half hour between eleven-thirty and noon, Eastern Standard Time, when Federal Reserve Banks are, by tradition, most likely to buy and sell securities.

FIFO. Acronym for First In, First Out, an accounting term used in areas ranging from computing interest to computing inventory value. *LIFO* stands for Last In, First Out.

fill or kill. The stock-trading equivalent of "Speak or forever hold your peace."

floor. The huge trading area of the New York Stock Exchange.

friendly takeover. Purchase of a company that is welcomed or unopposed.

front run. For a broker to load up one's friends and favorite customers on a stock, hype it, and then sell it to later customers at a higher price. Illegal.

G

garbitrageur. Derogatory blend of "garbage" and "arbitrageurs," for those who manipulate rather than simply speculate in stock of companies with announced or rumored deals.

gilt edge. Term used to describe the highest-quality stocks and bonds. The term originated in the British government-securities market.

golden handcuffs. Packaged perks and forms of delayed compensation that keep executives locked in their jobs. To qualify for these benefits, which include annuities and stock purchase plans, the executive must stay in place for a defined period of time.

golden parachutes. Compensation packages, usually a combination of money and benefits, for executives, providing them with substantial benefits to allay their fears in the event that the company is to be taken over.

go naked. To sell an option without owning the security to which it is linked or a stock one does not own.

go public. To sell the shares of a private company to the public.

gray knight. See *white knight*.

gray market. Retail operation that falls into the "gray" area between the legitimate and the illegal (or black market).

grease. Extraordinary amount of commission on the sale of a stock, resulting from the fact that the stock the firm acquired for sale to customers was cheap. This is usually legal.

greenmail. Money paid by a takeover target to a raider to thwart a takeover; blackmail of a different sort and color. It is usually paid in terms of a highly inflated stock price.

greenmailer. One who stages a raid, to be paid to call it off.

GTC order. Order to buy or sell a stock that is Good Till Canceled.

H

haircut. The percentage by which specific categories of securities and assets must be reduced—cut back neatly—

for the purpose of computing a registered broker-dealer's net capital.

hickey. Broker's loss from a customer's failure to deliver a check on a purchase (usually because the price went down by the payment date) or to deliver stock on sale (for the opposite reason).

hokey. Nickname for bonds of the Home Owners Loan Corp.

home run. Large capital gain in a stock in a short period of time.

hoovering. Acquiring stocks as if one were sucking them up with a vacuum cleaner.

hot new issue. A new stock or bond that is met with heavy demand, driving up the market price when it is first offered publicly.

hung up. Describing a situation in which one cannot sell a security without taking a large loss.

hushmail. Situation in which stock is bought from the director of a company by a raider at a substantial premium in return for the silence of that director.

hype. Excessively exaggerated news on a stock.

I

insiders. Top executives, directors, and large stockholders associated with a given stock. The buying and selling of insiders is watched carefully as a judge of the health of a stock.

J

james bond. A security due in the year 2007, a nickname inspired by the code number of the famous fictional spy.

January effect. Uncanny tendency for stocks with low capitalization to take off during the first month of the year.

junk bonds. Bonds that offer higher yields at the cost of higher risks. They have gained added notoriety because they have fueled takeover bids by providing leverage to assist in financing transactions.

K

killer bees. Firms and outside individuals used to help fight off a takeover. Killer bees include law firms, PR firms, and proxy solicitors.

killer technology. An invention or new technology that renders another invention or technology obsolete.

knockout. Share or shares of Coca-Cola stock whose New York Stock Exchange symbol is KO.

L

lamb. Inexperienced investor; one given to buying and selling on rumor and questionable tips.

leads. A list of prospects from which a broker works, making *cold calls*. Brokers sometimes pay for leads, or obtain them from some business or industry related to the stocks they're selling.

lettered stock. Restricted stock that cannot be sold unless registered with the SEC.

LIBOR / LIBID. Acronyms for City of London Inter-Bank Offer Rate or London Inter-Bank Bid Rate.

LIFO. Last In, First Out. See *FIFO*.

London fix. Price given twice each business day by London bullion dealers to set the value of an ounce of gold.

long. A bullish position in which one holds securities in anticipation that they will go up in price. By extension, anything that one has possession of: "This company is long on goodwill and short on cash."

LYON's. Liquid Yield Option Note. See *CATS*.

M

Ma Bell. The American Telephone and Telegraph Company.

Manny Hanny. The Manufacturer's Hanover Trust Co.

melon. Large stock or cash dividend.

meltdown. The October 1987 market crash.

mentor. Senior executive who takes on a younger protégé.

mommy track. One who is a mother and a career woman, but is often seen as "Female career path that is interrupted and slowed by having children."

mortgage-backed. A security whose value is based on a pool of home mortgages.

motors. Shares of General Motors stock.

mouse-milking. Term for an effort that seems too great for the results it generates; for instance, a broker spending a

lot of time on a very small account.

mullets. Broker's derogatory term for customers.

N

new issue whore. See *whore*.

noise. Stock market movement caused by phenomena not reflective of general sentiment. Programmed trading is a prime source of noise.

no-load. Investment that carries no fee for investment but may penalize you with a declining charge over a five-year period, if you redeem. Usually applied to mutual funds.

O

odd lot. (1) A lot of less than a hundred stocks, or a bond with less than $100,000 in principal value. (2) Used to describe anything out of the ordinary.

Old Lady of Threadneedle Street. The Bank of England.

P

Pac-Man defense. Named after the popular video game, it describes a move in which a target company turns around and tries to swallow the company that is trying to acquire it. Sometimes it works simply because it is an audacious move that scares away the pursuer. It is so named because a key element in Pac-Man is the ability of the pursued to turn on its pursuer.

paper profit. An unrealized profit on a security that is still being held.

penny stock. An inexpensive security, usually under five dollars a share, but many in this class sell for under a dollar and are priced in terms of pennies.

pink sheets. Listing of over-the-counter stocks that are not always listed in the newspapers. They list all traded OTC stocks.

pip. The smallest unit of any given currency: cents, pfennig, etc.

pit. Where commodities are traded, as opposed to a floor where stocks and bonds exchange hands.

plastic. Credit card(s).

plunge. Reckless speculation.

point. In terms of stocks, equal to a dollar.

poison pill. Device to make a takeover less attractive and more difficult.

porcupine provisions. Legal provisos made to deter takeovers.

privatize. The opposite of going public—that is, converting a publicly owned company into a private one.

product. Goods. "Anyone can talk about computers, but can he move product?"

prudent man rule. Common-law standard of care by which a trustee or other fiduciary must act to the standard of a man of discretion and intelligence seeking preservation of capital and reasonable profits.

puddle. Item in a company's overall inventory (or pool).

puds. Nickname for bonds of public utility districts.

pups. Cheap, inactive stocks; dogs.

Q

quants. Computer technologists working in the financial industry, designing sophisticated investment strategies and computer models; the folks who made "program trading" possible.

R

raider. One who swoops down and buys other companies by acquiring large amounts of stock.

red herring. Prospectus that cannot be used to confirm the sale of a security because it still lacks clearance from the Securities and Exchange Commission to become the final prospectus, so-called because such documents have a legend so stating, along with two red lines running down the left side and the top of the cover only.

repo. An agreement to sell a government bond for cash together with an agreement to repurchase the bond on a special date later, at a higher price reflecting the loan of the cash for a specified period.

resistance level. Dollar level at which a stock or bond seems to stop rising in a rally. The opposite of *repo.*

rig. To manipulate a stock.

ring the register. Take a profit.

RIPP. Acronym. A Reduction-in-Personnel Plan; a layoff, as in a 500-person RIPP.

round lot. A hundred shares, or a multiple of a hundred shares in the case of stock, and a milion par value for a bond.

S

Sallie Mae. The National Student Loan Marketing Association.

scenery. A board of directors selected for their status and respectability.

scorched earth. Destructive antitakeover measure by which a company takes steps to make itself less attractive.

sea-gull model. Term used to describe a consultation in which the consultant flies off, makes a couple of passes over his client, drops a strategy on the client and returns home.

seat. Membership in a commodity or securities exchange.

securitization. To change any asset into a security, such as loans, credit card loans, and home mortgages.

shake out. A period of market activity or crisis that causes small investors to drop out of the market.

shallow river running fast. Describing a stock, stocks, or the whole market moving in response to rumors.

shark. One who attempts a hostile corporate takeover; an avaricious raider.

shark repellent. Any measures that a target company uses to fend off a *shark;* for instance, changing a company's rules to require stockholder approval before a takeover can be accomplished.

short. To sell stocks one does not own, borrowing to make delivery in anticipation of buying the stocks back after a drop in value. In contrast, to be *long* is to actually own stock.

showstopper. Legal move made to thwart a hostile takeover.

skunk works. Backroom corporate think tank convened to foster new ideas.

slam dunk. A stock, usually a new issue, that is supposed to have a quick rise when it opens, so that it can be rapidly sold. A "sure thing."

SLOB. What else but a Secured Lease Obligation Bond?

smidge. Small amount of price; 1/8 of a point, for instance.

squeeze. See *corner.*

Stalingrad. To snow under with paper work, or, as Michael M. Thomas explains in *Hard Money,* "Russian winter with subpoenas instead of snowflakes."

steenth. Short for 1/16th of a point in verbal stock-and-bond reports. Also known as a *teeny.*

street name. The name of a brokerage house or bank that is put on a stock for the benefit of the client who owns it. This makes it easier to buy and sell stock.

stripped. See *CATS.*

swooner. Stock that is particularly sensitive to good or bad news.

System, The. See the *Fed.*

T

tape watcher. Small investor who monitors his or her investments by watching the transaction tape, whether it be in brokerage office or on the cable Financial News Network, which runs the tapes continuously.

target. Object of a takeover bid.

teeny. 1/16th of a point.

Texas disease. Epidemic S&L failure.

TIGR's. Treasury Investment Growth Receipts. See *CATS.*

tin parachute. Plan guaranteeing employees severance pay—the poor cousin of the *golden parachute*.

top tick. To buy a stock at the highest price of the day.

triple witching hour. One of the four Fridays in each year on which the options and futures contracts expire.

twiggy bond. Thin coverage.

U

ultra. Consumer who demands the best of everything.; the upper end of upscale.

up tick. Securities transaction made at a price higher than the last one.

V

velvet. An easy or quick profit.

W

war babies. Defense stocks.

wash tub. Bond issued by the Washington Suburban Sanitary District.

went toes. Synonym for *belly up*.

whisper stock. Stock in a company that is believed or rumored to be ripe for a major play.

white knight. A friendly suitor who intervenes in a hostile takeover and saves the target company and its assets. An opportunistic second bidder is a *gray knight*.

white squire. *White knight* who buys less than a majority interest.

whore. Customer who wants the hottest new-issue stocks coming out so that it can be sold quickly at a profit. Also known as *new issue whore*.

widget. Any unspecified product, commonly used in hypothetical situations: "Say I've got two million widgets and not enough trucks hired to haul them."

window dressing. Anything done to make a mutual fund or stock look good just prior to the end of a period, to improve, or dress up, the quarter or year-end reports sent stockholders.

with ice. When issued.

wooden ticket. A fictitious trade in an issue that a broker promised to sell, but couldn't get anyone to buy. He will quietly try to cancel the transaction later on.

X

xd. Ex-dividend, pronounced x.d.

Y

yankee bond. Foreign bond issued in dollars and registered for sale in the United States.

yard. A billion (dollars, yen, units, etc.).

yo-yos / yo-yo stocks. Pricey, volatile issues that fluctuate wildly in price.

Z

zero. A zero-coupon bond.
zero out. To not pay taxes legally.

SOURCES

Irving Hale, Charles D. Poe, and Stephen Brent Wells provided much help in the preparation of this chapter. This glossary was also built from a mammoth pile of clippings from the financial pages, magazines including *Forbes,* and a large collection of financial and business glossaries found in the Tamony Collection. Help was also rendered by *Lamont's Glossary,* prepared by Lamont and Partners of London, a first-rate contemporary guide to the financial terminology used on both sides of the Atlantic, as was the Equity Trading Glossary created and used by Goldman Sachs. It was helped to some degree by the author's year in a brokerage firm back when "Bessie" was the nickname for Bethlehem Steel and there was only *one* phone company.

7 | COMPUTERESE

What Do You Say to a Chiphead?

"The Chipheads Are (Sigh) Winning."

—Headline in the San Francisco
Examiner, January 3, 1983

Computers created a revolution. They also created an odd means of
expression through which it seemed everything got renamed. The
TV screen became a monitor, writing became word processing, and
a list of options became a menu. It also embraced an odd proclivity
for misnomer: floppy disks which are hard, hard copy which is
floppy, peripherals which are central, and global searches which are
intensely localized. As if to tweak the noses of the language purists,
the computerists converted large numbers of nouns into transitive
verbs—to format, to access, to array, to input, to output, and to
interface, to name but a few.

Computer slang is, in a word, quirky. Traditionally, this country
has created great slang. Whether you were talking about lumber-
jacks, hoboes, GI's, or short-order cooks, you were talking about
people with a rich, colorful slang. But then came the computer

revolution, and with it a less than dynamic slang—at least at first. But as computers got smaller and cheaper, all sorts of people got into the act, and soon there was a burgeoning slang which even included terms created by outlaw hackers. Here is a heavy sampling, including some that no longer sound like slang to those who are at home in the world of bits, bytes, K's, and modems.

A

abend. An *ab*normal or *ab*ortive *end*. This is what can happen when a machine is fed bad input data or shut down before it completes a routine.

algy. Algorithm for "short."

antidote. Program or programs used to protect computers from a computer virus. These programs tend to have apt names like "Vaccine," "Flu Shot," and "Syringe."

architecture. The selection and interrelationship of components of different kinds of computer systems—*mini, micro, A.T.,* etc.

A.T. It originally stood for Advanced Technology, an IBM Corp. PC that uses an 80286 chip. Now any 80286 chip.

B

bagbiter. Something or someone that has created problems.

barf. To fail or malfunction.

baud. Measurement, in bits per second, of the speed by which computers move data from one place to another. Also called *BPS*.

bead. A small program module.

bells and whistles. Unessential, but often alluring, features.

beta test. The first tests of new software outside the company that developed it (where the company did the alpha testing).

bit. The smallest unit of information, represented by a "0" or a "1." It is a compression of the words *bi*nary digi*t*.

black-box approach. To accept computed results without questioning the method used to get those results.

blue. An IBM computer, from the Wall Street nickname "Big Blue" for IBM. A "true-blue shop" is a computer center where all the equipment comes from IBM.

blue collar. Computer working in a factory.

Bogon. A person who is bogus or says bogus things. A Bogon is also a mythical subatomic particle bearing the unit charge of *bogosity*. These related terms were brought to national prominence by *The Hacker's Dictionary*.

bogosity. The degree to which something is bogus. See *Bogon*.

bomb. To fail or malfunction. Bombing is less than crashing; that is, a program may bomb, but a system crashes.

boot. To start. To restart is to reboot.

bootstrap. A small program that gets the computer up and running.

box. A computer.

BPS. Bits Per Second; see *baud*.

bridgeware. Hardware or software that serves as a bridge between one kind of system to another.

bug. An error, defect, or problem; cleaning up such a program is called *debugging*. Navy computer pioneer Grace Hopper has claimed that the term was coined in 1945 by her team, working on the Mark II, the first large-scale American computer. It was created in response to a glitch that occurred when a two-inch moth got stuck in one of the Mark II's relays.

The term had been used before to describe an error or failure, but this was its first application to computers. Hopper taped the original bug to the page of her logbook for the day on which it was dislodged from the machine.

bulletproof. Said of a program that is safe from both hackers and the inept.

burn in. To run a computer for a certain amount of time, usually at least twenty-four hours, to ensure its electronic components are not faulty.

burst. To tear printer paper along its perforated line; as in "Print and burst that report please."

bus. The physical and electronic connections that allow data to move where it needs to be in a computer. Sometimes used interchangeably with *architecture*, as in "A.T. bus."

byte. Eight bits. It is the standard unit of computer information. See *character.*

C

chad. Specks of paper that drop out of a computer card or paper tape when it is punched.

character. A letter, number, symbol, or space. A character is equivalent to one byte. *The Hacker's Dictionary,* by Guy L. Steele and others, points out that there is an elaborate hacker vocabulary for the various keyboard symbols; for instance the # is called a "Hash mark, MESH, SPLAT, CRUNCH, [and] pig-pen," and the ! is variously verbalized as "EXCL, exclam, BANG, SHRIEK [and] WOW."

chip. An integrated circuit on a wafer slice, usually made of silicon.

chiphead. Computer enthusiast. Listen to Sandy Grady writing on this term in the San Francisco *Examiner* (January 3, 1983): "The human race, you see, is now divided into Chipheads and Squareheads. The Chipheads—and there are millions of them—think computers are changing the world. A Chiphead will rhapsodize endlessly about his Atari or Osborne or IBM. A Chiphead swears computers are the greatest things since food and sex."

chomp. To fail or lose, or, as stated in *The Hacker's Dictionary,* "to chew on something of which more was bitten off than one can."

clone. (1) n. Generally a cheaper computer copy that operates identically to a name brand (IBM or Apple) unit. There are also software clones. (2) v. To make a copy.

cold fault. Any malfunction or fault that is apparent as soon as the machine is turned on.

computer virus. See *virus.*

connectivity. The ability of computers to talk to each other; generally applied to communication among different computer architectures. (Interestingly, software people usually say "connec*TIV*ity"; hardware people usually say "*CON*nectivity.") In this regard, the "connector conspiracy" is the tendency of manufacturers to come up with new products that are not compatible with old ones.

core dump. To unload a computer's main memory or—by

extension—to get something off your chest.

CPU. Short for Central Processing Unit. It is the electronic brain of any computer system.

crack. To gain unauthorized access to a computer; a more correct term than *hack* in this situation.

cracker. One who is adept at breaking into computer systems.

crash. (1) To stop working; to freeze up. (2) A major malfunction resulting in the loss of information.

CRT. Short for "cathode ray tube," the computer screen.

crufty. Bad, poorly built, yucky.

crunch. To process or compute routinely.

cursor. Movable screen character—usually a dash or a small square—that indicates where the next character will be generated.

cuspy. Excellent.

cybercrud. Cybernetic bullshit; hype.

cyberphobe. One with a fear of the computer.

cyberpunk. High-technology enthusiast with, as a writer for the *Los Angeles Times* put it, "futuristic ideas and outlaw natures."

D

daisy wheel. A print wheel on which type is positioned like the petals on a flower. They are used on some printers that rely on the impact of type on paper.

daughterboard. A small circuit board directly attached to the *motherboard*.

DDT. A debugging program, from the name of the famous insecticide.

deadlock. Stoppage created when two computer processes wait for the other to do something. In some circles this is referred to as a "deadly embrace."

debugging. See *bug*.

default. A preset value for a variable. For instance, the default in a word processing program might be to double-space each line of text.

diddle. To work aimlessly; not seriously.

display. What you look at while working on a computer; the *CRT*.

docs. documentation; the instruction manual.

dot matrix. Printing system that uses tiny dots to form characters and images.

down. Said of a system that has crashed; out of order.

dump. See *core dump.*

E

electronics hobbyist. Term used facetiously and euphemistically for and by those who have gotten into cybernetic mischief, such as illegally breaking into a system.

elegant. Describing a solution that is uncluttered and smooth; not clumsy. See *kludge.*

end user. The person who buys and/or uses the computer.

execute. To run a program.

F

feep. The soft beeping sound that a computer terminal makes when it is booted.

firmware. Elements of a computer system that are neither hardware or software, usually a program burned into *ROM.*

flavor. Variety.

floppy disk. An encapsulated sheet of plastic that is used to store information. Because of the stiff plastic jacket in which it is locked, it is bend-able but not the slightest bit floppy.

flyback. The time it takes for the cursor to go from the end of one line on a monitor to the beginning of the next.

footer. That which consistently appears at the bottom of the page in word processing.

footprint. Floor or desk space taken up by a computer or printer.

freeware. Public domain software.

frobnitz. An unspecified physical object; a widget; a black box.

fry. To fail, to become inoperable. *The Hacker's Dictionary* adds, "Said especially of smoke-producing hardware failures."

FUD / FUD factor. Initialism for Fear, Uncertainty, and Doubt, which is applied to the idea of recommending or buying potentially unknown hardware or software; part of what keeps IBM so profitable.

G

garbage. Unwanted data. To amass this data in a separate file, disc, or buffer to make room for more is to make a "garbage collection."

gearhead. Programmer.

GIGO. Garbage In, Garbage Out—that is, solutions from bad data will also be bad.

glitch. A flaw. It differs from *bug* in that bugs tend to appear in software while glitches appear in hardware. A loose wire is a glitch. (This is an interesting distinction, given the fact that the first *bug*, see, was in hardware.) Also, a sudden interruption in electric service.

global. Describing a search that covers an entire file; for instance, looking for all instances of a given name.

graunch. A devastating error.

gray market. The not quite legal buying and selling of computers through nonauthorized dealers.

gritch. To complain.

grok. To understand. It is a verb that made its terrestrial debut in Robert A. Heinlein's *Stranger in a Strange Land.*

gronk. To clear a machine that has been jammed or *wedged.*

gronked. Inoperative. It can be applied to people when they are sick or exhausted.

gronk out. To stop working.

growzy. Describing a computer that is slow to respond to commands. Said to be a blend of "grumpy" and "drowsy."

gubbish. Junk; bad data—a blend of "garbage" and "rubbish."

GUI. Pronounced "gooey," the term is an acronym for Graphical User Interface.

gulp. Multiple bytes, a play on words.

gweep. User.

H

hack. A term at the heart of computing slang, with many shades of meaning, including the twelve meanings given in *The Hacker's Dictionary.* The most common verb-form meanings are to work quickly, to work cleverly, to use a computer for pranks or deception, and to work aimlessly (as in "hacking around").

hack attack. A period of frenzied programming.

hacker. (1) One who enjoys getting into the details and creative side of computing, as opposed to one who simply uses a computer. (2) A malefactor who can range from a fun-loving but irritating prankster to a bona fide cybernetic criminal. (3) A genius programmer.

For hackers, there are even greetings (like "How's hacking?") and farewells (such as "Back to hacking)."

hair. Difficulty.

handshake. An introductory exchange of electronic signals.

hang. To wait—sometimes interminably, as in a *deadlock*.

hard copy. Printed version of what appears on the computer screen; printout.

hard disk. Rigid platter used for storing computer data magnetically. The speed and storage capacity of a hard disc is much greater than that of a floppy disk. Unlike a floppy disk, a hard disk is seldom removable.

hardware. Equipment: the computer, disk drivers, monitor, etc.

hash. Unwanted or meaningless data.

header. That which consistently appears at the top of the page in word processing.

hedgehog. Person whose abilities are limited to one machine or program.

home. The starting position for the cursor on a screen; usually in the upper left-hand corner.

host. The controlling unit in some computer networks, usually refers to a *mainframe*.

housekeeping. Routine chores —cleaning up files, getting rid of unneeded material, backing up, etc.—that have nothing to do with problem solving per se.

hungus. Large, unmanageable, humungous (from which it appears to derive).

hygiene. Describing steps taken to prevent systems from being infected by a computer virus. A tenet of computer hygiene is not trusting foreign data or other people's machines.

I

icon. A command in pictorial form.

J

jitter. The brief instability of a signal.

joystick. An input device, used primarily in computer gaming, that allows one to give the computer directions by tilting a stick. Like its namesake, the aviator's joystick of World War II, it is a reference to the erect male member.

—————— **K** ——————

K or kilobyte. A thousand bytes. Often used as a unit to measure how much information a computer can store at one time. It is also used to measure the size of a file or program. One K equals 1024 letters or characters. K is always written in uppercase.

KISS. Short for Keep It Simple Stupid, a long-established bit of computer dogma and graffiti.

kludge / kluge. A clumsy solution to a problem; a jury-rigged piece of hardware. Pronounced "klooje," it is the opposite of *elegant*.

—————— **L** ——————

launch. To start an application program running; commonly used by Macintosh users.

letter-quality. Said of a printer that produces letters that are as good as those produced by

an old-fashioned portable typewriter.

liveware. People, especially technicians, users, etc., found around computer systems.

logic board. Apple-speak for *motherboard*.

logic bomb. Outlaw term. A computer virus whose effects are triggered and felt when a certain result is specified during routine computation.

—————— **M** ——————

magic. Too complicated to explain, as in "How does it do that?" Answer: "Magic."

mainframe. A large computer, in terms of the size and amount of data it can process and its size. They are at least the size of a full-sized refrigerator and require their own air-conditioned rooms.

meatware. The human body.

menu. Listing of options; a table of contents.

micro. *PC.* Generally speaking, a micro—or microcomputer —implies a single user, while a *mini* has many.

mindshare. To discuss an idea or issue. "Let's mindshare on that one."

mini. A minicomputer; A mid-range machine between a *PC* and a *mainframe*.

MIPS. A Million Instructions Per Second; a measure of a computer's processing capability.

moby. Immense, as in Herman Melville's *Moby Dick*.

mode. State of. For instance, the HDX says that "night mode" is "The state a person is in when he is working at night and sleeping during the day."

modem. Short for *modulator/dem*odulator, it is a piece of hardware that allows two computers to "talk" to each other over a phone line.

motherboard. Circuit board to which the main processor chip, memory, and slots for additional cards are attached to form the guts of a computer.

mouse. A small electromechanical box with a button or buttons on it which is attached to a computer by a taillike cable. As it is moved across a desk, the *cursor* moves across the computer screen. A button on the mouse is pushed to give commands.

mung. To change irrevocably or to destroy, such as, "I really munged that program." In *The Book of Jargon,* Don Ethan Miller points out that this term began as an acronym of Mushed Until No Good.

N

n. A number, usually a large one.

nerdling. Immature hacker.

nerd pack. Plastic shirt-pocket protector pack in which one keeps pens and pencils.

nibble. Half a byte; a four-bit word. Sometimes written "nybble," presumably to match *byte*.

number crunching. Repetitive, routine numerical calculating. A computer or person employed to do this kind of work is sometimes called a number cruncher.

O

off-the-shelf. Standard program or piece of equipment that has not been customized or tailored for a specific group of users, nor needs to be. The military refers to it with the acronym COTS for Common Off-The-Shelf.

open architecture. Describing an expandable system that allows for the easy replacement and upgrading of circuit boards. It also implies that you can use boards made by third parties.

orphan. Computer system that gets no software support from its parent company. Orphans are usually created because the manufacturer has gone out of business or because the company has abandoned a line of computers.

P

PC. Personal computer; generally taken to mean one compatible with an IBM PC.

peripherals. Anything that connects to the computer, including disk drives, screens, and printers, or, as defined by John Held in the *Washington Post,* "what you discover you also need if you go to buy a personal computer."

pessimal. Terrible; the opposite of optimal.

phreaking. Gaining illegal access to phone lines.

pixels. Tiny dots that comprise the characters on a computer screen. The greater the number of pixels, the better the quality of the image.

planar / planar board. IBM-speak for *motherboard.*

ports. Connectors through which the computer sends and receives data to and from other computers, printers, keyboards, etc.

prompt. Signal from the computer telling the user that it is ready to take a command. A prompt can take various forms from blinking cursor to a full question stated in plain English.

propeller-heads. Programmers.

Q

QBE. Initialism for Query By Example. A technique by which a user shows a program how to ask questions of a data base to get information.

R

RAM. Acronym. Random-Access Memory. Chips on

which data are stored temporarily as the computer is working. That information is wiped out when the machine is turned off.

resident. That which exists in memory, generally taken to mean in *RAM* and therefore not permanent.

ROM. Acronym. (1) Read-Only Memory. Computer chips on which permanent information is stored. Unlike data in *RAM,* ROM is data installed by the manufacturer and cannot be altered. (2) Describing a person who does not listen. "I ran that idea by him, but he's strictly ROM."

RYFM. Initialism for Read Your F---ing Manual.

S

salami attack / salami technique. Outlaw term. Computer crime in which the culprit instructs the computer to do his dirty work a small slice at a time (hence salami). Typically, such an attack is mounted when the malefactor instructs the computer to transfer a few cents from hundreds of accounts and de-

posit them in his account. For instance, a few seldom-noticed cents might be added from every monthly service charge.

scroll. To move up or down through text on a screen.

scrub. To clean or purge a file of unneeded data.

SCSI. Pronounced "scuzzy," it is an acronym for Small Computer System Interface; a method of connecting *peripherals* to a computer.

shareware. A program that is distributed freely under the assumption that anyone who uses it will pay for it (that is, it is not *freeware*).

Silicon Valley. Area outside San Francisco that has attracted many semiconductor and computer manufacturers. Similarly, there is Silicon Beach in southern California and Silicon Prairie in the Midwest. The nickname for the area between Detroit and Ann Arbor has been called Automation Alley because of the concentration of robotics firms in the area.

slave. Machine that is under control of another.

smoke test. Test in which one turns on a machine and gives it a passing grade if it does not smoke, spark, or burst into flames.

snarf. To take with or without permission.

software. Programs that tell the hardware to do useful work.

spazz. To behave erratically.

spike. A sudden surge of electricity that can create computer havoc.

splash. To shoot something down; to cancel, especially a new program.

SQL. Structured Query Language; a specialized way of getting information from a data base; generally, one stored in a larger computer. Sometimes pronounced "sequel."

steel collar. Industrial robot in the sense that blue collar stands for industrial worker.

T

techie. Technician.

tech-mech. Engineer or techie who "sold out" to the military or a large corporation.

technoslut / technotrash / technoweenie. Brilliant technician who is a social disaster.

tiled. On-screen windows that do not overlap.

time bomb. Outlaw term. Instructions built into a program that cause destruction of data at a particular time in the future.

transparent. A process not obvious to the user.

trap door. Outlaw term. A gap in a program, created by accident or deliberately, that allows access to that program, by bypassing its security system. It may be designed on purpose by somebody who has legal entry but plans to make an illegal foray later, or who doesn't want to take the time to jump through all the security loops with each entrance to the program.

Trojan horse. Outlaw term. Any secret set of illegal instructions built into an existing program. The affected program acts normally until the hidden commands are triggered or a certain date and time are reached (for example, Friday the 13th at noon).

TSR. Terminate and Stay Resident. Said of a program that stays in memory *(RAM)* after it has been executed. By remaining in memory, it is readily available for the user to run again.

tweak. To fine tune; to make a slight adjustment.

U

up. Working or up-and-running. A machine is often said to be up after it has been down (crashed).

user. One who works with the computer but does not get into the innards of programs. Not a hacker.

user-friendly. Industry jargon for easy to use. User-friendly computers usually have many menus.

V

vanilla. Ordinary; standard; the usual flavor, such as a piece of equipment with no special features.

vaporware. Software that does not exist yet but which is often announced by a software company and discussed and given coverage in the trade press. It has been termed a realm of hype and illusion where promises and deadlines are sometime things.

VAR. Value-Added Reseller. Generally, a person who puts together computer systems complete with software, hardware, and peripherals.

virtual. Behaving as if; such as, "virtual real time."

virus. Outlaw term. Program or instruction created to cause mischief. A virus may clog a system with useless information or erase or alter existing information. Like true biological viruses, they spread and cause the electronic equivalent of epidemics. There are a number of individually named viruses along the lines of the infamous "Christmas virus" of December 1987, which hid its germ and transmission instructions in a Christmas greeting, or the older "cookie monster," which could only be stopped when the word "cookie" was typed into the machine.

W

wallpaper. Lengthy printouts that give more information than will ever be used.

wedged. To get stuck.

wetware. The human brain and its DNA code.

window. The portion of a text that appears on the computer screen at any given moment; also, divided or superimposed screens.

wirehead. Fanatic addicted to computers to the extent that other things in life are neglected.

word wrap. The ability of a word processing program to drop a word to the next line rather than allow a word to be broken at the end of the line. The word is literally wrapped around to the next line and eliminates the need for the carriage return at the end of each line.

work station / workstation. Described by the *Wall Street Journal* as "a souped-up personal computer typically used by engineers and scientists." Increasingly, however, it has come to mean little more than a computer sitting on a desk.

worm. A rogue program that endlessly duplicates itself, thereby causing the infected system to bog down. It was a worm that caused some 6000 computers to malfunction on November 2, 1988.

WYSIWYG. Pronounced "wizzy-wig." Initialism for What You See Is What You Get. It refers to the alleged ability to view a display and see exactly what will be printed in terms of typography and graphics.

X

X.T. IBM's second-generation personal computer. Reputedly standing for Extended Technology, the X.T. offered more memory and slots for new circuit boards.

Y

yo-yo mode. Condition of a system that is alternately up and down.

Z

zap. To erase.
zorch. To move quickly.

SOURCES

Richard Danca, writer and computer journalist, provided invaluable help in the preparation of this collection. Although it is fast becoming dated, the key work on computer slang is the aforementioned book called *The Hacker's Dictionary,* which was produced by a team of six professional computer wizards led by Guy L. Steele, Jr., and published by Harper & Row in 1983. Charles D. Poe and Matthew Fass were also most helpful.

8 | COUNTERCULTURAL SLANG

The Slang of Yesterday Sounds a Lot Like Today

> Remember when hippie
> meant big in the hips,
> And a trip involved
> travel in cars, planes,
> and ships?

—First line of an anonymous poem that appeared in *Parade* magazine for November 14, 1971. Peter Tamony had a mimeographed copy as early as 1968. Tamony's copy was titled "Psychedelirium Tremens."

The slang of the 1960s and 1970s is still very much with us. To be sure, there are few flower children around, and not many people can say "groovy" with a straight face. But there is a body of words and expressions—especially having to do with state of mind—that are as clearly of the period as teach-ins, underground newspapers, and face-painting.

The approximate period in which this slang came into being and showed strength was between 1965 and 1975. Some was old and borrowed, such as calling a job a gig, which was an old jazz term, but most of it was new, daring, and well-publicized. It was also quickly adopted by the mainstream, a point that was made in *Newsweek* (February 3, 1969):

Groovy. Beautiful. Out of Sight. The jargon of the alienated, the oppressed, the discontented is becoming the idiom of Middle . . . America. Television writers babble like acidheads, newspaper columnists sound like black militants, and advertising copywriters echo the slogans of teenyboppers."

As the 1970s wore on, there were periodic declarations that the language of Haight-Ashbury and Woodstock was dying out to be replaced by the banter of post-Watergate teens who called good-looking guys *hunks* and *studs*, deemed *bad* to be good, and called those who were "out of it" *airheads*.

Oddly, this was not to be. Much of the old slang hung on tenaciously, as those who grew up with it grew older . . . as they got into middle age, if you wish. Today they work hard to keep it together: to be up front about their hang-ups, to avoid confrontations and rip-offs, and to maintain a hassle-free lifestyle. They strive to keep from getting uptight, strung out, or down on their kids, even if they've trashed their rooms. Heavy.

What follows is a collection of the slang of "then" which is in large part still in use "now." In order to give this slang a special sense of time and history, 86 of the terms are labeled "P.O.W.—Air Force." These were terms the U. S. Air Force compiled and defined in 1973 for the prisoners of war returning from Vietnam. The glossary of 160 terms was called "semi-official" and was based on a poll of P.O.W. families, to see which terms were actually in use in their homes. It was published by the Air Force with this comment: "We hesitate whether or not to call the language progress, but facts are facts. This is part of the slang being used by your sons and daughters. The main purpose is to get you and your offspring off to somewhat of an equal start."

The original definitions from the Air Force list are contained in quotation marks.

A

acid. (P.O.W.—Air Force) "Refers to the hallucinogenic drug. Lysergic Acid Diethylamide (LSD)."

acid freak. (P.O.W.—Air Force) "Frequent user of LSD."

acid head. One who uses LSD.

acid rock. (P.O.W.—Air Force) "Psychedelic music; emphasizes electronic sounds, has a prominent beat and repeated sounds, very loud."

Afro. (P.O.W.—Air Force) "Naturally black hairstyle; hair not straightened, but left in its natural curly state and styled. Also prefix denoting black (ex: Afro-American)."

alternative. Nonconforming, as in alternative schooling, alternative press, etc.

Amerika. A bad America; the one that was the stage for the Kent State shootings.

at. (1) Place; where things are happening; where it's "at." (2) One's position; for instance, "This is where I'm at."

B

babe. Woman, girl, one's *old lady*.

bad news. (P.O.W.—Air Force) "A depressing or undesirable person."

bad scene. (P.O.W.—Air Force) "Unpleasant experience, place, or event; a disappointment."

bag. (P.O.W.—Air Force) "Person's way of life, now generally replaced by the term 'trip.' Ex: 'He's into a jazz trip.'"

ball. To copulate.

banji. Marijuana. This is one of thirty-one terms for the substance which appear in Joel Makower's *Boom! Talkin' About Our Generation*. Most of the other terms for marijuana come from Makower's collection.

beautiful. (P.O.W.—Air Force) "Expression of approval; usually exclamatory."

be down on. (P.O.W.—Air Force) "Dislike or disapprove of something or someone, usually intensely. Ex: 'He's down on pollution.'"

be-in. (P.O.W.—Air Force) "Gathering of people for spontaneous and hopefully creative activities."

Black Panthers. (P.O.W.—Air Force) "Militant organization of blacks who are engaged in promoting the welfare of black people. The organization is now downplaying armed confrontation and encouraging community self-help and building popular support in the black community."

blow your cool. (P.O.W.—Air Force) "Loss of control of temper or emotions. The term is still used, though far less frequently."

blow your mind. (1) To overwhelm; to make a startling point. (2) To amaze or delight. (3) To lose touch with reality because of drugs.

bogart. To be selfish; to "bogart a joint" is to not share a marijuana cigarette.

boo. Marijuana.

bopper. (P.O.W.—Air Force) "Hip, aware young person in tune with the modern scene. Usually short for teenybopper."

bread. Money. (Often forgotten is that this term began as a play on the slang "dough" for money.)

brick. A kilogram of marijuana.

brother. (1) (P.O.W.—Air Force) "Term mostly used by a black man or woman to identify a black male, and as a term of address. Also being used by Chicanos and American Indians." (2) Term used by hippies to indicate that another individual is *cool*: "Don't worry about him, he's a brother."

bud. Marijuana bud. This meaning was probably not forgotten in the Budweiser beer motto, "This Bud's for you."

bummer. (P.O.W.—Air Force) "Unpleasant experience, especially with drugs. It is also an exclamation of disgust or sympathy for anyone's bad experience." This term was derived directly from "bum trip."

burn. (1) (P.O.W.—Air Force) "Hurt emotionally, being taken." (2) To cheat, especially in a drug deal.

burned out. (P.O.W.—Air Force) "Incapacitated, mentally and/or physically, temporarily or permanently from drugs."

bush. Marijuana.

bust / busted. (P.O.W.—Air Force) "Arrest, arrested."

C

cactus. Peyote.

cat. (P.O.W.—Air Force) "Any male, especially a sharp dresser (dude is more common now.)" The term predates the sixties, especially in jazz circles.

catnip. To sell something other than drugs in a drug deal— catnip for marijuana, etc. A line in William Burroughs's *Naked Lunch* is "I'll catnip the jerk."

check it out. To pay attention to; to have a look at.

chick. (P.O.W.—Air Force) "Young girl."

commune. (P.O.W.—Air Force) "Community where nothing is privately owned, usually associated with hippies. Social structures and values vary considerably."

confrontation. Hostile demonstration.

connection. Source, especially for drugs.

contact high. (1) Vicarious experience of being high with someone on a trip. (2) Also, a marijuana high derived from being in a marijuana-smoke-filled room, but without having actually smoked it.

cool. (1) (P.O.W.—Air Force) "Self-assured, knowledgeable. One who is aware of the times." (In some circles to be "cool" was to be a user of drugs.) (2) To be calm, not overly excited or easily rattled.

This term predates the period in question, and along with *cat* and *dig,* go back to the *Dharma Bums* and the beats, to Kookie of *77 Sunset Strip* and—most important— the bop school of jazz.

cop. To obtain; for instance, to cop a joint.

cop out. (P.O.W.—Air Force) "Refuse to face issue or responsibility, usually a social one."

cosmic. (1) Very important. (2) Relating to anything inexplicable.

counterculture. (P.O.W.—Air Force) "A style of living. Values are different from current society. Usually associated with hippies and communes."

crash. (1) To collapse, or sleep, usually when high. (2) To come down quickly from a drug-induced high.

crash pad. Place to sleep, or to come down from being high.

D

deal. To sell or deal in; "I don't deal drugs."

devil weed. Marijuana.

dew. Marijuana.

dig. (P.O.W.—Air Force) "enjoy, comprehend to the fullest extent possible."

digger. Hippie social worker; altruist of the counterculture.

dig it. (P.O.W.—Air Force) "Exclamatory meaning enjoy it or appreciate it, get into it."

do. Take or participate in, as in "I don't do acid anymore." This meaning of do comes into play in the Hollywood invitation, "Let's do lunch."

do a number. (1) To effect or try to influence; to pester. "She tried to do her support-payment number on me again last night." (2) To deliberately mislead. See also *mindfucking.*

doobie. Marijuana cigarette.

dope. (P.O.W.—Air Force) "Any drug; though most frequently in reference to marijuana."

down. (P.O.W.—Air Force) "(1) Unhappy, depressed. (2) No longer under the influence of a drug." Also, (3) a barbituate

that is an activity suppressant, and (4) to be upset with or feel negative about: "I'm down on school."

downer. (1) A depressant drug, especially a barbituate, which lessens activity. (2) An unpleasant person or activity.

do your own thing. (P.O.W.—Air Force) "Follow your own interest and activities. Usage has decreased in frequency."

drag. (P.O.W.—Air Force) "Boring. A tedious experience."

drop. To take LSD.

drop out. To turn away or withdraw from conventional society.

dude. (P.O.W.—Air Force) "Any male."

dynamite. Great.

E

earth. (1) The home planet. (2) Of the natural environment, the opposite of plastic; organic. Earth Day, "Spaceship Earth," *The Mother Earth News, The Whole Earth Catalog,* the earth mother, earth tones.

ego trip. (P.O.W.—Air Force) "An achievement or success." However, it has a negative connotation, as someone on an ego trip is usually self-obsessed.

establishment. (P.O.W.—Air Force) "The power structure of institutions (politicians, police, teachers, etc.).

F

far out. (P.O.W.—Air Force) "All-purpose expression of approval for an unusual experience. Used as exclamation. Now often used sarcastically to indicate disgust or boredom."

Fed. Federal narcotics agent.

flip / flip out. To perform an emotional cartwheel.

flower child. Youngster of the late 1960s who believed that love and beauty could overcome materialism and war.

As a footnote to this dry definition, here is an *alternative* definition prepared by John O. Clark, who was there when the term was coined and still has no trouble expressing himself in the argot of the Haight:

" 'Flower child': This is pure San Francisco, 1966 or 1967. There was a 'riot' and the National Guard was called—or was it just a whole bunch of cops? I dismember—so a whole bunch of teenyboppers and hippie-dippies, mostly zonked on acid or 'shrooms, went to the park where they gathered flowers. As I remember, daffodils and daisies predominated. Pictures appeared in the dailies of young girls reaching up on tiptoe, their firm, nubile young nipples almost bursting from their tattered, tie-dyed T-shirts . . . and their sweet damps practically embracing the butts of the assault rifles as they put daisies in the gun barrels, while the military formation sweated and wrestled with their hardons . . . I think that the term 'flower child' was birthed in a photo caption of one of the Haight-Ashbury foxes pouting at the soldier with a 'Don't you wish you could but you never will' smile as she stuffed a daf in his bang-bang."

flower power. The hippie notion of the power of natural beauty, and the belief that society could be changed through love and peace.

freak. (1) Drug user; one who

has freaked out. (2) Any member of the counter-culture ca. 1967. (3) An enthusiast: food freak, rock freak, beach freak, etc.

freak / freak out. (1) To become crazy on drugs; to have a bad or extreme drug experience. (2) To lose control of one's temper. (3) To shock or surprise, as in freaking somebody out.

freaky. Psychedelic; bizarre.

fuzz. The police.

G

ganja. Marijuana or hashish.

gas, it's a. (P.O.W.—Air Force) "Cool, great. Refers to an event. Ex: A favorite TV program might be referred to as 'it's a gas.' "

gay. (P.O.W.—Air Force) "Homosexual. Acceptable term by homosexuals."

get down. (1) To begin; to get down to it. (2) To have a good time: "Hey, let's party; let's really get down."

get into. (P.O.W.—Air Force) "Become absorbed or involved in something intensely, usually with a positive attitude."

get it on. To commence; to get going; to *get down*.

get it together. (P.O.W.—Air Force) "To get organized."

gig. Job.

goof on. (1) To laugh at or make fun of. (2) To mislead.

go straight. (P.O.W.—Air Force) "(1) Give up the use of drugs. (2) Return to an approved lifestyle."

granny glasses. Old-style wire-rim glasses with small lenses.

grass. (P.O.W.—Air Force) "Marijuana; dope, pot, reefer, weed."

groove. (1) To concentrate on, to meditate with. (2) To like; to enjoy. (3) A fine thing. "What a groove."

groovy. Good, nice, cool.

groupies. Young women who followed rock musicians with whom they tried to have sex.

guru. Spiritual leader; mentor; not just Indian gurus or spiritual teachers.

H

hairy. Thorny, worrisome.

hang me up. Keep me waiting; to not show up.

hang up / hang-up. (P.O.W.—Air Force) "(1) Dislike, a mental block. (2) Reoccurring problem, source of irritation or disappointment with no apparent solution."

Also, (3) a neurosis, quirk, or obsession.

The past participle, "hung up" or "hung up on," means to be obsessed or neurotically preoccupied with.

happening. (P.O.W.—Air Force) "Event."

hash. Hashish.

hassle. (P.O.W.—Air Force) "(1) Problem; troublesome or irritating situation or event, conflict situation. (2) To disagree, argue, or bother."

hay. Marijuana.

head. (P.O.W.—Air Force) (1) "Drug user; freak." Also, (2) an enthusiast in the sense that "Deadheads" are fans of the Grateful Dead. (3) The mind, as in, "That's where my head is at."

head shop / head store. Place for drug paraphernalia, psychedelic posters, underground comics, etc.

heat. (1) The police. (2) Police pressure.

heavy. (P.O.W.—Air Force) "Deep, complicated, meaningful. Bad or disgusting." The term lives on, among other places, in "heavy metal."

hemp. Marijuana.

herb. Marijuana.

hip. (1) (P.O.W.—Air Force) "Aware. Connotes understanding and familiarity with drug scene and/or the radical view of political activity." (2) To make aware; to inform: "She hipped me to the fact that there was some quick money to be made."

hippie / hippy. (P.O.W.—Air Force) "Predominantly middle-class white youth ranging in age from twelve to twenty-five; some drop out of society, do not work, take drugs, have long hair. Anybody with long hair is considered a hippy."

hold. To possess drugs; to "carry."

honky / honkie. (P.O.W.—Air Force) "Any white person, connotes racist."

hooch. Marijuana.

hooked. (1) Addicted to. (2) In love with.

hustle. (P.O.W.—Air Force) "Try to interest someone sexually. A way of obtaining money, or drugs, that is usually illegal or deceptive."

I

in. (P.O.W.—Air Force) "Socially acceptable within a group, usually a subculture, now used sarcastically to indicate disgust with attention to conforming."

-in. Suffix for an event of mass participation: be-in, sit-in, live-in, teach-in, smoke-in, love-in, etc. The suffix keeps finding new applications. In 1989 a headline in the *National Farmers Union Newsletter* read, "NFU Legislative Fly-In Is Set for June 17–20."

inner space. One's inner self, which some believed could be effected with drugs.

into. (P.O.W.—Air Force) "Involved, interesting, engrossed in, pursuing the study of. Ex: 'She's into astrology.'

—————— **J** ——————

Jesus freak. (P.O.W.—Air Force) "A young person who openly and publicly finds 'Salvation in God'—will tend to be evangelical."

jive. (1) Nonsense. (2) To joke with.

joint. Marijuana cigarette.

juicehead. One whose drug of choice is alcohol.

—————— **K** ——————

killer weed. Marijuana.

kilo. A kilogram of drugs, usually marijuana.

—————— **L** ——————

lid. A quantity of marijuana, usually one ounce.

lifestyle. (P.O.W.—Air Force) "A way of living according to some subcultures."

loco weed. Marijuana, but also applied to certain hallucinogens like peyote.

—————— **M** ——————

Mary Jane. Marijuana. The name is based on the letters M and J in marijuana, as well as being a play on the pronunciation, a rough translation from the Spanish, "mary-juana."

match box. A small quantity of marijuana, originally the amount that would fit inside a match box.

maxi. (P.O.W.—Air Force) "Meaning larger. Ex: 'maxi-coat,' a long coat of ankle length."

mike. One microgram—one millionth of a gram—of LSD.

mindfucking. (1) Doing bad things to the mind and spirit, as opposed to *mindblowing,* which is good. Examples of those practicing the former would be Charles Manson and Jim Jones, while the Grateful Dead and light shows characterize the latter. (2) Disinformation; lies; propaganda.

Movement, The. The general move to the left, and the specific move to stop the Vietnam War.

Ms. (P.O.W.—Air Force) "Women's liberation term which is an abbreviation meaning either 'Miss' or 'Mrs.'"

N

narc. Originally short for "narcotics agent" but extended to include any law enforcement person.

nitty gritty. The heart of the matter; the essence.

no way. (P.O.W.—Air Force) "Impossible."

O

off. To kill; to bump off.

old lady / old man. The steady woman/man in a man's/woman's life, even if the old lady/old man in question is only eighteen. This lives on in biker slang.

oregano. Marijuana. This term may be an acknowledgment of the fact that oregano was sometimes sold as the real stuff to the uninitiated.

out of it. (P.O.W.—Air Force) "To be out of touch with reality when under the influence of a drug, especially hallucinogens. To lack understanding and awareness, especially in a subculture."

out of sight. (P.O.W.—Air Force) "Wonderful or terrific."

overkill. Excessive and wasteful. Term borrowed from the Pentagon, where it was used for excessive nuclear capability.

P

pad. (P.O.W.—Air Force) "Place where one lives. Room or residence."

paraphernalia. An assortment of drug-related implements, including rolling (cigarette) papers, *roach clips,* and water pipes.

People, The. Everybody, it seemed, but "white moderates," the police, government bureaucrats, and hard hats.

pig. (1) Derogatory term for a police officer, or any power-

ful member of the establishment (Presidents Johnson
and Nixon were both pigs).
(2) The system itself became
known as "the pig" from
about 1970 through 1972.

Planet, The. The Earth.

plant your seed. Hippie motto
suggesting that the doctrine
of love and pacifism be
spread by example.

plastic. Insincere, phony, un-
real.

pot. Marijuana.

pothead. Marijuana user.

pounds, shillings, and pence.
LSD. "There were a bunch of
Englishers hanging around
the Haight in the sixties,"
says John O. Clark, who was
there, "so it was inevitable: L
with a line through, S for shil-
ling, and d. for pence, spelled
LSD."

psychedelic.   (P.O.W.—Air
Force) "Refers to a new social movement, including the
change in moral structure,
music, dress, and the arts."
It originally referred to something that was influenced by
hallucinogenic drugs—the intensely colorful and florid
"psychedelic art," for example.

pudding. The cosmic oneness;
the godhead—the state of

one who is into the pudding.

pull yourself together. (P.O.W.—
Air Force) "Secure, emo-
tionally clear conception of
one's self and relationship to
others and life in general.
Have everything or some-
thing clear in one's mind."

putdown / put down. (1) An insult. (2) To insult.

put-on / put on. (1) A joke or
prank. (2) To pull a joke on;
to tell a lie or mislead for entertainment (rather than deception).

R

rap. (P.O.W.—Air Force) "Conversation, usually about a
'meaningful' subject. A sort
of lecture or specific approach to a subject." This is
the term that was adopted
and applied to rap music in
the 1980s.

reefer. Marijuana. Clearly a
term from an earlier generation, given a great boost by
the reissue of *Reefer Mad-
ness,* a campy, shrill anti-
marijuana movie.

right on! (P.O.W.—Air Force)
"Exclamation of agreement
with importance or truth of a
statement. Means the same
as 'perfect.' "

rip off. (P.O.W.—Air Force). "Steal and or cheat. Mislead in order to get the upper hand."

rip-off artist. One who deceives for a living—a slumlord, confidence man, dishonest lawyer, etc.

ripped. High on drugs.

roach. The remains of a marijuana cigarette.

roach clip. Any device used to hold a *roach* while smoking it, so as not to burn one's fingers.

ruined. High on drugs.

S

scene. (P.O.W.—Air Force). "Place of action. An experience."

scuz / scuzz. Marijuana.

shades. (P.O.W.—Air Force) "Eye glasses—usually sunglasses."

shit. Marijuana.

shuck. (1) To deceive. (2) A phony person or thing; that which is bogus.

smashed. High on drugs.

smokables. Marijuana.

smoke. Marijuana.

soul. (P.O.W.—Air Force) "An inherent quality black people feel they have and whites rarely do. It implies an awareness and understanding of life and a naturalness of expression." *Newsweek* carried this definition in 1969: "In American Negro parlance, omnibus term for courage, sensitivity, humor, style, arrogance, and grace."

soul brother. (P.O.W.—Air Force) "Black person."

soul sister. (P.O.W.—Air Force) "Black female."

spaced / spaced out / spacey. (1) Dazed and distracted, often from drugs. (2) Goofy.

spliff. Marijuana.

split. (P.O.W.—Air Force) "Go. Leave or depart."

stash. (1) A secret supply, usually drugs. (2) To hide drugs.

stoned / stoned out. High on drugs.

straight. (P.O.W.—Air Force) "(1) Off drugs either at the time or permanently, or (2) not homosexual." Also, (3) outside the realm of *freaks* and *hippies*.

strung out. (1) To become ill (physically or mentally) because of drugs. (2) To be excitable, nervous, at wit's end. (3) To be addicted to drugs.

Summer of Love. Summer 1967.

swacked. High on drugs.

T

tea. Marijuana.

tell it like it is. (P.O.W.—Air Force) "To be open and honest. Withholding nothing about what one thinks or believes."

The Man. Person or persons in control, often applied to a police officer.

thing. That which compels; that which one concentrates on. "His thing is playing checkers."

together. Balanced; in harmony; calm and content. Some guy who has gotten his mental life in order has "gotten his shit together." This is also the together of the Beatles' "Come Together."

toke. (1) Marijuana. (2) To inhale the smoke of marijuana or hashish.

trash. Damage or destroy.

tribes. Those who were part of the movement, from the Gathering of the Tribes on January 20, 1967, on the Polo Field in Golden State Park.

trip. (1) Feelings under the influence of drugs, especially LSD. (2) Attitude or lifestyle—a power trip, for instance, or a guilt trip. (3) Any exceptional experience.

trucking. (P.O.W.—Air Force) "Walking—using legs to get somewhere." Used in the motto "Keep on Trucking," which was often displayed with a Robert Crumb cartoon featuring Mr. Natural.

tune in. To focus, zero in on, especially to the culture.

turn his/her head around. To change someone's mind; to arouse interest.

turn off. (P.O.W.—Air Force) "Disgust or repulse someone." Antonym of *turn on*.

turn on. (P.O.W.—Air Force) "(1) Get high on drugs. (2) Arouse sexually." Also, (3) to introduce someone to drugs or something new. (4) Anything that is exhilarating or sexually arousing.

U

underground. (P.O.W.—Air Force) "Unsanctioned by prevailing social attitudes; antiestablishment."

up. High, but not necessarily on drugs.

up front. (1) Honest, uninhibited, open. (2) At the head of a line or demonstration.

uptight. (P.O.W.—Air Force) (1) "In a state of tension. Worried, upset, or inhibited."

Also, (2) intimate with, close to, as in "tight with" or "up tight with."

V

vibes. (P.O.W.—Air Force) "Vibrations. Nonverbal expressions of thoughts or feelings."

W

wacky t'backy. Marijuana.
wacky weed. Marijuana.
wasted. High; under the influence of.
weed. Marijuana.
what's happening? (P.O.W.—Air Force) "Salutation meaning 'What is going on?'"
where it's at. (P.O.W.—Air Force) "The core of a situation or event."
Women's Lib. (P.O.W.—Air Force) "Women's liberation activist movement to secure equal rights for women."

wrecked. High; under the influence of.

Y

Yippie. (P.O.W.—Air Force) "Person associated with the Youth International Party, an eccentric group of hippies." (What is left out of the Air Force definition is that the Yippies were intensely political and opposed to mainstream politics.)

Z

z. An ounce of marijuana; from the abbreviation "oz." for "ounce."
zap. (P.O.W.—Air Force) "Emphasize in an unforgettable manner." Also, to hit figuratively—for instance, to zap with understanding and love.
zonked. (P.O.W.—Air Force) "Extremely high on a drug."

SOURCES

Wordheads and argot freaks who helped in the preparation of this glossary are Joel Makower, president of Tilden Press, whose own books include *Boom! Talkin' About Our Generation* and *Woodstock: The Oral History,* John O. Clark of Philo, California, who "majored" in all of this, and James Thorpe III, who watched it unfold. Material in the Tamony Collection was also most useful.

The Air Force list appeared in a number of newspapers when it was first released, including *The New York Times,* March 8, 1973. One of the few good articles to appear on the subject of sixties slang, "If You Think It's Groovy to Rap, You're Shucking," by Mike Jahn, appeared in *The New York Times Magazine,* June 6, 1971.

CRIME, PUNISHMENT, AND THE LAW

Words You Didn't Hear on *Hill Street Blues*

> "The slang—or, as it used to be called, 'cant'—of thieves, gypsies, vagabonds, and their fellows has enriched the English language and its literature since Shakespeare's time."
>
> —Geoffrey Nunberg in *The New York Times Book Review*, May 2, 1982

Most of the early works on slang in English were concerned with the cant of criminals. *The Tom and Jerry Flash Dictionary*, published in London in 1825, for instance, contained an elaborate slang which included no less than sixty orders of *coves*—or receivers of foreign goods—including *footpads, rumpadders, twirlers, maces, pab priggers, cadgers, dubsmen*, and *swaddlers*.

Then, as now, this is a rich area for the collector of slang. Today there are really four sets of slang associated with crime and punishment. The first is that of the criminal, the second is that of prison, and the third is that of the police. Those three are addressed in this chapter. The fourth is the slang of drugs, which is the subject of the next.

Although there are differences in these various slangs, they are all interrelated.

A

all day and night. A life sentence to prison.

armor. Weapons, to a convict.

B

baby raper. Inmate term for older convict who has committed a sexual offense against a minor or whose crime is unknown.

badge. A cop.

bag. (1) Police term for a uniform; to be sent back to the uniformed ranks after being a plainclothes officer is known as going back "into the bag." (2) To arrest, as in "bag him."

B&W / black and white. Police car. This term varies from city to city, as police colors change.

baton. Nightstick.

beagle. A detective.

beat. Diluted, as in a "beat drug," which has been cut.

beat the bricks. To get out of prison.

belch. To inform or testify.

bit. A prison sentence.

blaster. Gunman.

blotter. Police station-house ledger.

blue flu. A police sick-out; a job action in which police call in with false illnesses.

bolo. Police shorthand for "be on the lookout for."

book. Life sentence.

boost. To shoplift.

bottle baby. Derelict.

bounce. Police vernacular for brainstorm session.

bow-and-arrow squad. A police unit not allowed to carry firearms.

breakdown. Shotgun.

broom. Cop who keeps the station house clean and acts as "go-fer."

brownie. A traffic cop, in the eyes of the police who deal with crime.

bubs. The blue flashers or bubbles on the top of police cars.

bug. Police term for a criminal without compassion or empathy.

burn. To shoot.

bush gang. Prison gang that works outside cutting brush and doing other jobs. It has been termed a chain gang without the chains.

"buy you a suit." Phrase used to tell a police officer that there is a bribe forthcoming if a violation is overlooked. It is also phrased as "give you a hat."

C

cage. Prison cell.

canned. Imprisoned.

carry-out rape. Police term for abduction and rape.

chicken hawk. Child molester.

chill. Kill.

cold gun. A gun that has been worked on to disguise its origins, as opposed to a *hot* or stolen gun.

collar. To arrest.

cooping. Police sleeping or relaxing on the job.

cop killer. Armor-piercing bullets.

corset. Bullet-proof vest.

crib. In prison, one's cell.

crib burglar. One who breaks in and robs from homes and apartments.

cut. To attempt suicide behind bars.

D

daddy. Pimp.

dance hall. Execution chamber.

dead presidents. Money in bills: "Open your wallet and show me some dead presidents."

dead time. Time spent in jail that does not count against a sentence. For instance, time spent for contempt or not co-operating with a grand jury is often dead time.

deck. A pack of cigarettes to a prison inmate.

deuce-deuce. A .22 caliber gun.

Deuce, The. The block of Forty-second Street between Seventh and Eighth Avenues in New York City, to police and criminals alike. This may be the highest area of crime concentration in the nation.

devastator. An exploding small-caliber bullet.

digger. A pickpocket.

dinger. Burglar alarm.

dirty. Describing a bad prison reputation.

divorce. To police, a domestic shooting.

DMZ. Street or area of a city that demarks high-crime area from one with average or low crime rate. In New York City, the DMZ of the Upper East Side is Ninety-sixth Street. DMZ is an acronym for De-Militarized Zone.

dog house. Prison watchtower.

drive-by. Committing crime from a moving vehicle, such as a drive-by shooting.

drop a dime. Police term for calling in information on a specific crime.

drum. Jail cell.

E

85. Police slang/code for a girlfriend.

equalized. Armed.

eyeball van. Police term for surveillance vehicle with one-way glass.

F

fade the heat. To take responsibility, in prison parlance.

feero. Fire bug; an arsonist.

56. Police term for time off.

finger. (1) Police informer. (2) To identify someone as a suspect; to inform on someone.

fireworks. Gunplay; shootout.

fish. A new prisoner.

fix. (1) A stationary post for a police officer. (2) Trouble (to be in a fix).

flake. To plant false evidence.

flip. To turn on; to give evidence to the police or to prison authorities.

floater. Police term for a body found in water.

fly. To escape from prison.

fooled out. To make a mistake.

four-five. A .45 caliber gun.

four-to-four. Police beat from four in the afternoon until midnight, but which also may include time to unwind at a bar that closes at four A.M. In *One Police Plaza,* William J. Caunitz describes one of these shifts and adds, "The session lasted until four in the morning. Policemen's wives have dubbed these tours the 'four-to-fours.'"

freeway dancer. Police term for people who dash across major highways in the dark.

G

gat. Gun.

gauge. Shotgun.

gee. A guy in prison.

get busy. Street slang: to rob someone.

get paid. Street slang for committing a successful robbery.

get small. To get away; to disappear, especially as a suspect is getting away ("He got small in a hurry.")

G-joint. Federal prison.

gladiator school. Maximum-security prison.

glass beat / glass post. Police term for a beat with a lot of stores with large plate-glass windows.

gold tin. Detective's badge, as opposed to *tin,* which is the name for a uniformed police badge. To "get the gold tin" is to be promoted to detective.

go on the box. To take a lie detector test.

grounder. In his book *Close Pursuit: A Week in the Life of a NYPD Homicide Cop*, Carsten Stroud says that this term is used by the New York Police Department for "a homicide case that can be solved with relative speed and simplicity." The opposite of a grounder is a "mystery" or a "queer one."

H

hair bag. (1) Veteran cop to other cops. (2) a *perp*, especially since *Hill Street Blues*.

hard time. (1) Sentence with no parole in sight. (2) Sentence to hard labor.

heat. (1) Gun. (2) Pressure.

heeled. Carrying a gun.

he/she. Transvestite to the police.

hit. Shoot or stab.

hitch. Prison sentence.

hold your mud. Criminal talk for not blabbing to the police or feds when arrested; one who does not rat on others. In James Mills's *Underworld*

Empire a man is described as "an old-time crook, who holds his mud."

hole, the. (1) Solitary confinement. (2) The subway to an urban cop in a city with an underground.

horse. Person that smuggles money or drugs into prison. Also known as a *mule*.

horsemen. The Royal Canadian Mounted Police in Canada.

hot. Stolen.

house. Prison cell.

hugger-mugger. A man who, according to Joseph Wambaugh in *Echoes in the Darkness*, "picks on plain or homely women, turns on the charm and gives them some cuddles while he picks their purses."

I

IBM. For Italian Business Man, in the parlance of the FBI and other law enforcement groups. It refers to someone associated with the mafia.

in a crack. In trouble, especially in prison.

in-house lawyer. Inmate paralegal.

inside / outside. Inside and outside the walls of a prison.

in the free. Prison term for out of jail; on the street.

J

jacket. The reputation (good or bad) of a prisoner or inmate.

Jade Squad. Special police unit used to thwart the efforts of Asian crime syndicates.

jakes. Police term for uniformed police.

jocker. Aggressive homosexual male prisoner.

John Law. The police.

joint. Prison

jug. (1) To attempt to cut the jugular vein. (2) Jail; the *joint*.

juice. Good prison connections; penitentiary pull.

jumpouts. Teams of arresting officers who commonly jump out of hiding or out of a patrol car.

K

kazoonie. Passive homosexual male prisoner.

keep. Prison.

keeping six. Safecracker's code for a lookout; one who watches for the police and other interlopers.

K.G. (Police) Known Gambler.

kite. Letter to, from, or within prison; for example, "to float a kite."

klepto. Kleptomaniac.

knocked. Arrested.

Kojak light. Portable flashing red light that police can throw up on the roof of an unmarked car to mark it. The term comes from the television cop, Kojak, who used such a light.

L

lajaras. Hispanic street slang for New York cops. Carsten Stroud points out that the term derives from the name O'Hara.

launder. Legalize.

lay chickie. To act as a lookout.

lock down. To put in a maximum security cell.

loid. To open a lock with a credit card or other piece of plastic. The term predates credit cards and harks back to the time when burglars used thin strips of celluloid.

M

man, the. The warden.

mark. (1) Victim. (2) Someone who wants to be a gang member.

maxin'. Prison slang for serving

maximum time. By extension, hanging out, as one must do while serving a long sentence.

maytag. Prison slang for a male inmate unable to protect himself from homosexual rape.

Mirandize. To warn a suspect of his or her constitutional rights under the Supreme Court's Miranda decision.

mole. Inmate secretly working for the man.

money bus. Armored truck.

mooch. Target of scam.

mooner. Person who gives police a hard time and is believed to be most pesky during a full moon.

mug. (1) Rob and beat. (2) To take a police or prison photo, or *mug shot*.

mug shot. A police or prison photo.

mule. See *horse*.

mushfake. Contraband in prison.

mustard chucker. Pickpocket who, according to an article on criminals who prey on tourists in the *New York Times* (July 13, 1989), "sprays a victim with mustard. He apologizes profusely and helps to remove it while an accomplice steals the victim's wallet."

Mutt and Jeff act. Interrogation technique in which one cop is the bad cop (heavy and hostile) and the other good (good-natured and friendly).

O

off. Kill.

one-percenters. Term used by outlaw/outcast bikers (motorcyclists) to show that they represent the worst one percent of the population.

on the arm. A free meal or other item in police terminology. Writing in the *New York Times* (February 15, 1970), David Burham said that this expression "might be a play on the expression 'the long arm of the law.'" A character in Vincent Patrick's *Pope of Greenwich Village* says, "He wasn't that greedy at all. He was putting next to nothing into his pocket. It was all bar bills and seven-course dinners on the arm."

on the grain and drain train. To be in solitary confinement in prison. It comes from the old notion of "bread and water" or "grain and drain."

P

paper. (1) Parking ticket. (2) To issue a ticket. (3) Acid (LSD) in drug parlance.

paper hanger. Check forger to police.

patch. The proceeds of a crime that are given to corrupt police to keep from going to jail. A patch is much more costly than a simple bribe or payoff since it involves the total haul.

pavement princess. Prostitute.

perp. Perpetrator.

phony collar. Unjust arrest.

P.I. Prison Industries.

piddling. Crafting items out of matchsticks, toothpicks, and other humble objects in prison. An item in the Houston *Post* for March 23, 1989, speaks of a death-row inmate known for his piddling ability.

piece. A revolver.

place, the. Prison.

plant. Police stakeout.

pocket man. Criminal holding the money after a robbery or other crime.

pop caps. To open fire, in police parlance.

popcorn machine. Light(s) on top of a police car.

P.P. Short for "penitentiary pull"; influence in prison.

punch job. Safecracking in which the dial of the safe has been removed.

punk. Prison talk: (1) To sodomize. (2) Victim or willing partner in a homosexual arrangement.

put his papers in. For a policeman to retire.

R

rap. Talk, especially in prison.

rap sheet. Criminal record.

reefer. (Police) The six-button tunic worn by police in cold weather.

ride on. A drive-by shooting.

ride-out. Automotive scam in which the perp intentionally slams into the car of an apparently wealthy person in hopes of making an injury claim and getting a fat settlement.

roll. (Police) To take fingerprints.

roscoe. Gun. This term is dated, common to gangster movies of the 1940s, but still used with tongue in cheek. (There is a sizable slang vocabulary from these movies, which is still toyed with—among others, "shamus" for private eye, "mug" for man or his face, "big house" for prison, etc.

rough off. To steal; to rip off.

rounder. Street criminal who operates around bars, clubs, and hotels, selling drugs, setting up high-stakes poker games, etc. So called because they are always "around" to make the deals.

S

S&J. Sentence and Judgment.

S&W. Short for Smith and Wesson.

satch. Paper that has been impregnated with heroin or LSD and mailed into prison in an envelope.

Saturday night special. Cheap handgun.

screw. Prison guard.

SCUM. Semi-acronym for police Street Crimes Unit.

second-story man. Burglar.

shakedown. Search in prison.

shank. (1) A knife. (2) To stab.

shine on. To ignore, in prison parlance.

shiv. Knife.

shoe. Plainclothes detective.

short. Describing somebody with little prison time to do.

size the vic. To observe, or size up, a victim from a distance.

skell. Police name for a derelict or habitual drunk.

slammer. (1) Prison. (2) In illegal boiler-room sales swindles, the high-pressure salesperson who gets the mark to part with his money.

slim jim. Thin, limber strip of metal used by car thieves to yank open the lock on a car door.

smurfing. Money-laundering procedure by which currency is exchanged at various banks in amounts slightly less than those that must be reported to federal authorities. These amounts change, but when all transactions of $10,000 or more had to be reported, many transactions took place involving $9,999.

snitch. Informer.

songbird. Informer.

spit on the sidewalk. To commit a minor crime.

spitter. Police slang for a pickpocket.

squat. An intentional accident in which two cars bump each other so that a fraudulent injury claim can be made.

squeal. Complaint, in police parlance.

stall. Person who distracts a victim in a robbery. The "hook" is person who takes the money or goods.

staties. State police.

step back. Incarceration. A prosecutor may waive "step back" in certain arraignments. It comes from the words of judges who tell some defendants to step back and be escorted to prison.

stir. Prison.

stooge. A person working for the prison administration.

straight eight. Tour in which patrolman puts in eight hours with no overtime.

strapped. Armed, in the parlance of street gangs.

system, the. The entire corrections, jurisprudence bureaucracy; to inmates it is the enemy.

T

10/13. Police radio code for an officer in trouble who needs immediate help. This is part of a set of radio 10 codes: for instance, 10/6 stands for "Shut up, you're jamming the frequency," and 10/98 means "This car is ready for a new assignment."

throwaway. Clothing worn by a mugger and discarded immediately after committing the crime, to confuse pursuers.

throw bricks. Commit a felony.

tin. Policeman's badge; by extention, a policeman. See also *gold tin.*

trey-eight. A .38 caliber gun.

24/24. Prison slang for all day.

24/24 rule. (Police homicide) Explained by Carsten Stroud in *Close Pursuit: A Week in the Life of a NYPD Homicide Cop:* "It means that the most important hours in the investigation of any murder are the last 24 hours in the victim's life and the first 24 hours after the body has been discovered."

V

vic. (1) A duped customer, such as one to which a bogus drug has been sold. (2) A crime victim.

W

wagger. Flasher, to police.

Waldorf Astoria. Solitary confinement in prison.

walls. The joint; prison.

waste. Kill.

wired. (1) Carrying a recording device or microphone. (2) Armed.

yellow sheet. Same as *rap sheet*.

yoking. A form of mugging in which a male victim is grabbed from behind, put in a headlock, and has his wallet taken from his jacket pocket.

——————— **Y** ———————

yard hack. Guard in a prison yard.

SOURCES

The Tamony Collection greatly aided this glossary, as did the eagle-eyed Joseph C. Goulden, who scanned many a newspaper cop story for examples. Among other things, he sent along a ca. 1961 carbon of a piece he did for the Dallas *News* on South Dallas cop/perp slang. Russell Mott, Charles D. Poe, Edward O'Brien, and Suzy Nace were all of great help.

It should be noted that a particularly useful and fascinating glossary of police terminology appears in the back of Carsten Stroud's *Close Pursuit: A Week in the Life of an NYPD Homicide Cop* (Bantam, 1987).

10 THE DRUG TRADE

The Spacey Talk of the Junkie, Cokie, Druggie, and Pothead

". . . to which we must now add drugs."

—Anthony Burgess's reaction to the
old assertion that slang's chief stimuli
are liquor, money, and sex. The
London *Times Literary Supplement,*
December 5, 1986

There is little that is subtle about today's drug trade. The same is true about the slang used in that realm, which is at once direct, streetsmart, and composed of a vast collection of synonyms. For instance, in Esther and Albert Lewin's *Thesaurus of Slang* more than a hundred contemporary terms for marijuana are listed along with more than seventy for heroin.

A

Acapulco gold. Powerful Mexican marijuana.
angel dust. PCP.

B

babylon. The outside world. (This and the next term is a Rastafarian term used primarily by members of a Jamaican *posse.*)

back in the box. To be back in operation again after being arrested on a drug charge.

baldhead. Undesirable; outsider.

bank. Money. To say that one has bank is to say that one has a lot of money.

Barnes man. New York street slang for a major drug dealer. According to Carsten Stroud in *Close Pursuit: A Week in the Life of an NYPD Homicide Cop,* the term comes from the name of a famous Harlem dealer, Nicky Barnes.

basehead. One addicted to the freebasing of cocaine. In his autobiography, *Long Time Gone,* musician David Crosby described himself as a basehead for fifteen harrowing years of his life.

bazooka. (1) Cocaine paste or coke paste that is said to have an "explosive" effect on the user. (2) Synthetic drug.

beast. Police.

beat bag. Quantity of heavily cut (diluted) narcotics.

Belushi cocktail. A mixture of cocaine and heroine (and an obvious reference to the late comedian John Belushi, who was killed with such a mixture).

benz / benzo. Mercedes-Benz.

biker's speed. Methamphetamines.

bindle. Paper in which drugs are wrapped.

biscuits. Methadone.

bite. Arrest.

black tar. Potent Mexican heroin with a tarry look.

blast. A line or snort of cocaine.

blow. Cocaine.

blue sky. Heroin.

boat. Marijuana laced with PCP.

boom car. Drug dealer's car with loud, expensive stereo system.

Brompton cocktail. Mixture of cocaine, alcohol, syrup, and morphine.

bud. Marijuana. One expensive strain of California pot is known as "Mendo bud." This is a term that came into vogue during the countercultural era.

bule. Marijuana.

bullet. A line or snort of cocaine.

burn. To cheat; to sell bogus drugs. A source who knows about such things says, "A burn artist is a dope dealer who consistently sells catnip for pot, Accent for speed, coffee for heroin, etc. Don't take up the trade; you could get shot."

burn bag. Quantity of bogus drugs sold as real.

burner. Gun, usually a handgun.

burnout. One addled by and dependent on marijuana.

burros. Derogatory but common name given to people who carry cocaine and other drugs across the Mexican border on their persons.

bush. Marijuana.

buzz. High on marijuana.

C

cali. Marijuana.

candy. Cocaine.

cartwheels. Amphetamines.

catch a buzz. Smoking marijuana.

chasing the dragon. Smoking a mixture of heroin and cocaine.

chipper. Weekend junkie.

chippying. Light narcotic sampling.

clap. Shoot.

cocabucks. Cocaine money, in the same sense that oil money has been called "Petrodollars."

coke. Cocaine.

coke bugs. Nickname for cocaine hallucination in which bugs infest the user's body.

cokie. Cocaine user.

cold turkey. The act of completely and suddenly quitting drugs. The term is also used for getting off tobacco, alcohol, etc.

colly weed. Marijuana.

cooker. A receptacle in which drugs are heated before injection.

cop. To buy drugs.

copilots. Amphetamines, so called because of truck drivers who have been known to use them on long trips.

corn. Marijuana.

crack. Form of cocaine that is highly addictive, relatively cheap, and is smoked by the user.

crackhead. One addicted to *crack.*

crack house. Building in which crack cocaine is sold and consumed.

crank. Meth or methamphetamines.

cranny. Marijuana.

Crop, The. The agricultural side of the marijuana business. As one close observer writes from his rural northern California home, "When people in the Emerald Triangle speak of the Crop, they do it reverently, and they ain't talkin' about apples, grapes, or corn."

crystals. Methamphetamines in crystalline form.

cubes. Demerol.

D

deadhead. Heavy marijuana use.

detox. Short for "detoxification"; the process of getting off drugs, even if only temporarily.

dime bag. Ten dollars' worth of drugs.

doctor shop. To try to get drugs legally by prescription.

dose. LSD.

downers. Barbiturates. Any drug used to slow the nervous system. Sometimes used to bring user down from a high.

druggie. User.

dummy. PCP.

dust bunny. Person showing effects of *angel dust*.

E

early girl. Marijuana that comes in before the main crop.

eightball. One-eighth-ounce quantity of methamphetamines (*crank*).

eight-track. 2.5 grams of cocaine.

evil. Cocaine.

F

farm to arm. Describing an operation in which the same people grow, process, and sell a drug. For instance, a Mexican heroin grower who controls the pushers who retail it on the streets of Chicago.

fix. An injection of narcotics.

food. Marijuana.

freebase. (1) To purify cocaine with the aid of ether. (2) To smoke the pure cocaine thus produced.

G

ganja. Marijuana.

gate. House or apartment.

geek. Crack addict.

geronimos. Barbiturates.

gong. Gun.

H

H. Heroin.

hash. Hashish.

hash bash. Rally or event for the legalization of marijuana.

herb. Marijuana.

high beams on. High on cocaine.

his. Heroin sold in a straw. The powder is tapped into the straw and heat sealed at either end.

hit. A puff, injection, swallow, or snort that gets a drug into one's system.

hooter. Marijuana.

horse. Heroin.

hot shot. A very potent dose of heroin which may be lethal.

huffer. Person who inhales vapors from solvents and other chemical compounds to get high.

hustler. Seller.

I

ice. A smokable form of amphetamines that first hit the streets of Hawaii and California in the latter half of 1989. It is similar to *crack*, but the high lasts longer and would appear to be even more addictive.

ice cream habit. A state of minimal addiction; non-severe habit.

ily. Marijuana.

J

jab. To inject heroin into the blood.

jar wars. Controversy over drug testing which involves the use of urine samples.

Jim Jones. Marijuana cigarette dipped in PCP, from the name of the crazed cult leader.

jolt. Cocaine.

joy popper. Intermittent user of hard drugs.

juice. PCP.

juke. Holdup.

junkie. An addict.

K

kibbles and bits. A combination of the stimulant Ritalin and the painkiller Talwin. It is, of course, a reference to a heavily advertised dog food called Kibbles 'n Bits.

L

lid. One ounce of marijuana.

lit / lit up. Under the influence of drugs.

love boat / lovely. PCP.

luded out. Showing the effects of Quaaludes.

'ludes. Quaaludes.

M

marahoochie. Marijuana.
Maui Wowie. Marijuana strain that may or may not have come from Hawaii.
Medusa. Ethyl chloride.
morf. Morphine.
mother's helper. Valium.
muggle. Marijuana.
mush mind. Marijuana user whose mind has become muddled by it.
mushrooms. Name for innocent bystanders who sometimes get hurt or killed in inner-city drug shoot-outs.

N

nail. Hypodermic needle.
nemmies / nimbies. Nembutal.
nickel. Five dollars' worth of drugs.
nose candy / nose powder. Cocaine.

O

on the pipe. Freebasing cocaine. See *freebase*.

P

panic. Shortage of heroin. "There's panic in needle park."
paper. LSD.
perks. Percodan.
P-funk. A synthetic form of heroin that was first discussed for a national audience in front of the Senate Judiciary Committee in September 1989, hearings on new trends in narcotics.
posse. Jamaican gang often dealing in marijuana, crack, or both.
pothead. Regular marijuana user; one who has become addled by the weed.
pumping. Selling.
puppy. Gun.
purple hearts. Phenobarbital.

Q

quacks. Quaaludes.
quarter. Twenty-five dollars' worth of drugs.

R

rad weed. Marijuana.
ragweed. Inferior marijuana.
ratboy. Street slang for a human laboratory rat who is skilled at testing the strength of various drugs.
red devil. Seconal.

red flag. According to Carsten Stroud, this is a method of injecting heroin in which the needle is put in and is allowed to expand until blood is drawn into the bulb. This ensures a hit in the vein rather than in the muscle.

rings. Guns and bullets.

rock. Portion of *crack* cocaine.

rocket fuel. PCP.

roller. Police, from the fact patrol cars roll through open-air drug markets slowly.

rope. Marijuana cigarette.

R's and T's. A combination of the stimulant Ritalin and the painkiller Talwin.

S

shake. Useless or poor-quality leaves of a marijuana plant.

sinsemilla. (1) Seedless, as applied to marijuana, specifically the unpollinated female plants. (2) The name of the powerful northern California seedless.

skid-drop. A means by which a large load of drugs is landed from the air, by a cargo skid attached to a parachute. It avoids landing with the drugs.

smoke. Marijuana.

snow. Cocaine.

speedball. A mix of heroin and cocaine.

spliff. A joint or portion of marijuana.

square grouper. A bale of marijuana in south Florida.

stardust. Cocaine.

steerer. One who does not sell drugs but guides or steers potential buyers to places where they are sold.

stem. Glass pipe for smoking *crack* or *ice*.

step on. To cut or adulterate a drug, by doubling its weight (and halving its purity). If 15 pounds of a drug is stepped on twice, it becomes 60 pounds.

stick. Marijuana cigarette.

stick-up boys. Those who rob drug dealers.

strawberry. Prostitute who will trade sex for cocaine.

T

tab. A dose of LSD.

tea / tea 13. Marijuana. Why 13? In her trendy, punky *Modern English*, Jennifer Walters asserts that the number 13 alludes to the fact that M, for marijuana, is the thirteenth letter of the alphabet.

teeth. Bullets.

T-man. Federal narcotics agent.

tolly. Street name for toluene, a hydrocarbon solvent that is inhaled by *huffers*.

tool. Gun.

tootsie roll. Powerful form of Mexican heroin.

tracks. Marks left in the skin from continued injection of drugs into the veins.

trey. Three bucks' worth of drugs, often a half-inch vial of *crack*.

turkey. A fake capsule containing only sugar or chalk, but which is sold as a powerful drug.

———— **U** ————

uppers. Amphetamines. Drugs used to stimulate the nervous system.

———— **V** ————

viper. Marijuana smoker.

vitamin A. LSD.

———— **W** ————

water. PCP.

weed. Marijuana.

white Christmas. Cocaine.

white snow. Powder cocaine.

wisdom weed. Marijuana.

works. Drug user's equipment.

———— **Y** ————

yellowjackets. Barbiturates.

Ye Olde Peruvian Marching Powder. Mock elegant nickname for cocaine.

———— **Z** ————

zombie. Heavy marijuana user.

SOURCES

Esther and Albert Lewin's *Thesaurus of Slang* (Facts on File, 1988) was most useful in the preparation of this listing, as was *Modern English* by Jennifer Walters. An anonymous Californian helped authenticate some of this, Charles D. Poe located many newspaper references, and the Tamony Collection provided many examples. Virginia Scallis also contributed.

11

FANTASY, THE FUTURE, AND SCIENCE FICTION

Coming to Terms with Parallel Worlds

". . . listen to a fan's speech. It's a foregone conclusion if he uses words such as faned, fapan, fanac, sercon, Neffer, vombic, fout, slan, neohood, grok. By the way, a female fan is a 'fanne.'"

—From "The amazing World of the Fen," San Francisco *Examiner*, October 13, 1968. Most of these science fiction terms are now archaic.

Most slang concerns itself with the real world, of what is or what was. However, there is a small corner of the slang universe reserved for what will be or could conceivably be. It is the realm of science fiction, futurism, and fantasy, and it generates its own odd terminology. Here is a smattering from all three of those nether worlds.

_____ **A** _____

ALF. Acronym for Alien Life Form. Presumably the Alf of television fame was named with this science fiction acronym in mind.

APA / -apa. (1) It stands for Amateur Press Association or Amateur Press Alliance, which are cooperative efforts to publish *fanzines,* or in this case, *apazines.* As one versed in APA ways explains, "Minac [minimum activity] is generally two pages per issue. Each author pays to print his pages, and the O.E. (official editor) collates and distributes the APA when each issue is ready." (2) As a suffix, the term is used in constructions like "Bobapa" for an APA where all discussion relates to Bob.

apazine. See *APA.*

B

BEM. Acronym for the Bug-Eyed Monster of science fiction. The bible of BEM's is *Barlowe's Guide to Extra-Terrestrials,* by Wayne Barlowe and Ian Summers, which contains such fine examples as the Abyormenite, Denu, Ixtl, Pnume, Thrint, and Unhjinian.

big crunch. The hypothesized contracting of the universe by implosion and the flipside of the "big bang" of creation. The general estimate is that if it takes place, it is still some 110 billion years off.

biosoft. Software that can plug straight into a jack that goes into a person's head, to give them, for example, fluency in Spanish or an understanding of electronics. This term is associated with *cyberpunk* science fiction.

Boswash. Futurists' term for the emerging supercity sprawling between Boston and Washington. For those who believe the city will stretch from Portland, Maine, to Portsmouth, Virginia, the name is Portport. The Chicago to Pittsburgh supercity has been called Chipitts, and the sprawl from San Francisco to San Diego, Sansan.

C

CE. A close encounter. A CE3 is a close encounter of the third level, celebrated in the film *Close Encounters of the Third Kind,* which according to this scale is a contact with a UFO and its occupants. CE2's involve UFO's that interact with the environment, and CE1's are encounters that are close and detailed enough to rule out misinterpretation of some other stimuli.

character. The playing piece that most people use in role-playing games. "You enter these games through the persona of a character," says writer and fantasy-game designer Mike Stackpole. "If you play well, your character will develop into a 'real' person who will leave you no doubt about how he or she would handle a situation."

chit. Playing piece in role-playing games.

-con. A science fiction convention expressed as a suffix. Examples include Worldcon, Lunacon, Swampcon (in Baton Rouge), Amigocon (El Paso), Onceuponacon, Kublacon, Deepsouthcon, Mythcon, Loscon (Los Angeles), Okcon (Tulsa), Armadillocon (Austin), and Pretty Goodcon. The names of these conventions underscore the urge to pun and play with words that is at work in organized science fiction fandom. See also *noncon.*

crudzine. "A worthless fanzine," according to Robert Runté's *Fanspeak Glossary.*

cyberculture. Society served by automation.

cybermetrician. Person with a highly advanced level of rapport with computers.

cyberpunk. A science fiction movement led by a group of young writers who—according to Michael Dirda, writing in the *Washington Post*— "share a liking for hard-edged, high-tech, razzle-dazzle visions of the future, especially a grim future where computers, drugs, and cybernetics rule." The dust jacket on the recent edition of Rudy Rucker's 1982 novel *Software* contains this claim: "The astonishing cyberpunk novel that started it all." By most accounts the best example of the genre is Bill Gibson's *Neuromancer.*

Cyberpunk has its own sublingo. See *biosoft, cyberspace, derms, flatline, meat puppet, razor boy/girl,* and *sensetapes.*

cyberspace. Worldwide computer network that facilitates data transmissions and exchanges. Hackers/cowboys use special techniques to break through security and steal data.

cyborg. Human fitted with electronic parts.

cybot. Cybernetic robot; a robot capable of making decisions.

D

D&D. The game Dungeons & Dragons.

derms. Dermal patches that introduce drugs into a person's system, a term with ties to *cyberpunk*.

D.M. Dungeon Master; in *D&D,* person who designs adventures for others to engage in.

dozmo. Irritating or boorish science fiction fan.

drobe. One who attends science fiction conventions in costume.

E

earth grazer. Asteroid that comes close—that is, within several million miles—of Earth.

egoboo. Ego boost in the world of science fiction.

encounter. In the realm of *ufology,* one of three levels of extraterrestrial contact. See *CE.*

ETI. Acronym for ExtraTerrestrial Intelligence.

exobiota. Extraterrestrial life.

exosociology. Futurists' term for that aspect of sociology dealing with extraterrestrial civilization.

F

faaan. A fanatical science fiction devotee. Written as faaan, it is often called "triple-A fan."

fanac. Fan activity ("fan" and "activity"—pronounced FAN-ac) in the realm of science fiction. A prime example of fanac is publishing a *fanzine.*

fandom. The science fiction subculture.

faned. Fan editor for short.

fannish. Relating only to science fiction fans; of the realm.

fanzine. A blend of "fan" and "magazine," these are simple science fiction periodicals which may be stenciled or photocopied.

fen. Plural of "fan." Some say that this term is obsolete, but it still shows up in print.

FIAWOL. Fandom Is A Way Of Life; science fiction initialism for one of the two camps of *fandom.* The second camp is represented by the idea of:

FIJAGH. Fandom Is Just A Goddamned Hobby.

fixed pie. The view of the earth's future that contends there is a known limit to the planet's resources.

flatline. To be slain while hacking into a system in *cyberspace*. This is the most severe form of dealing with an intruder.

FRP. Fantasy role playing. Expert authority Michael Stackpole says, "This is the generic term used to describe all of the role-playing games, though purists stick to RPG for that designation."

FTL. An acronym for Faster Than Light (travel).

--------- **G** ---------

GAFIA. Getting Away From It All. "To gafiate means to abandon science fiction and return to the mundane world," writes Michael Dirda in the *Washington Post*.

gamer. One who plays role-playing games.

G.M. Game master, the director of role-playing games. A definition given by Chaosium, Inc., a distributor of such games, says that the G.M. "is one player who acts as the story's narrator and coordinator, describing the game world to the players, presenting the evening's objective, and controlling the actions of all the bad guys."

Golden Age. The period in which some of the greatest science fiction writers (Arthur C. Clarke, Isaac Asimov, and Robert A. Heinlein) were writing their classics. The 1940s and early 1950s.

grok. To be, to love, to understand, to have cosmic awareness, etc. The verb is Martian and comes from Robert A. Heinlein's *Stranger in a Strange Land*. The term has spread outside the realm of science fiction, where it is still used but considered passé.

--------- **H** ---------

hard science / hard s.f. Science fiction that is hardware intensive or in which the magic and fantasy obey the laws of science. With the advent of the *New Wave* of the 1960s, hard science fiction was deemed to be conservative and "Old Wave."

Heroic Fantasy / Heroic Fiction or **H.F.** A genre of fantasy fiction that mixes monsters, barbarians, and pretty women. It is also known as *S&S*.

hibernaculum. Place where a human is put into artificial hibernation for travel into deep space.

High Frontier. Term characterizing space as vast human habitat.

Hugo. The most famous award in the world of science fiction, it is awarded by the World Science Fiction Convention and is voted on by members of that convention. It is named after Hugo Gernsback, the "father of modern science fiction."

hyperspace. Space containing more than three dimensions. A realm in which vehicles move faster than light. It was made popular in the movie *Star Wars*.

———— **I** ————

ish. In the world of science fiction literature, this means issue and is often used as a suffix. *Nextish,* for instance, is the next issue of a *fanzine*.

———— **L** ————

LGM. Little green men.

lifeboat ethic. The moral code based on the belief that an individual or nation can justify not aiding less fortunate individuals or nations because of widespread shortage and deprivation. Some believe that holding onto this "ethic" will lead to wars of redistribution.

light sailing. A means of spaceship propulsion in which a giant sail is used to catch powerful solar winds.

———— **M** ————

Martian Statue of Liberty. An idea that first appeared in Arthur C. Clarke's *Profiles of the Future*. The inscription on the base of this imaginary structure reads: "Give me your nuclear physicists, your chemical engineers, your biologists and mathematicians."

meat puppet. In the realm of *cyberpunk,* a person who has had a neural cutout so they do not have to be conscious of what is happening to their body. Generally used to describe prostitutes, who use the cutouts to be "elsewhere" while their johns thrill themselves.

megacharacters. Characters in role-playing games who have become "too tough" and possess many weapons and powers.

monster fodder. A role-playing-game term for characters who are often used as guinea pigs to test traps and other hazards.

monty haul. Derogatory term for a role-playing game in which there are incredible rewards for trivial actions. It is a play on the name of Monte Hall, host of the once-popular *Let's Make a Deal* television quiz show.

moontel. Lodging on the moon.

mother ship. Term used in science fiction and UFO writing for a large spaceship from which smaller craft emerge.

munchkin. Derogatory role-playing-game term for immature players who dwell on boring war stories.

mundane. A person with no knowledge of science fiction; nonfan.

————— **N** —————

Nebula. The second most famous award in the world of science fiction (after the *Hugo*). It is awarded by and voted on by members of the Science Fiction Writers of America (SFWA).

neofan. A new science fiction fan who sometimes displays excessive enthusiasm.

New Wave. Label for the "soft" science fiction of the 1960s, which deemphasized science and technology and emphasized values, politics, sociology, psychology, and social experimentation.

nextish. See *ish.*

noncon. A "nonconvention"—a science fiction gathering that is too small to be a convention.

normals. Fantasy gaming for characters without special powers who must constantly be rescued. Akin to *monster fodder.*

NPC. A Non-Playing Character in fantasy gaming. "The players may interact with this character, in most cases to resort to combat, hence initiating role playing," says Michael Stackpole, who adds, "munchkins kill NPC's."

————— **P** —————

parallel world. (1) Science fiction setting/premise in which the world is presented as it would be if a key historical or biological event had gone differently. (2) A universe similar to ours but in another spacetime.

parsec. A parallax second, which is the equivalent to 3.26 light-years.

Planet X. A tenth planet in the solar system, which was once suspected but not proven. It is now used in a mocking, tongue-in-cheek context. Futurist Ralph Hamil has this to say about a name for Planet X: "Over the years, astronomers have postulated a 'Hades' and a 'Oceanus,' among other names suggested for the hypothetical planet. 'Charon' and 'Proserpine' are other alternatives from science fiction." Martin Kottmeyer adds that "Nemesis" is the hypothetical planet involved in dinosaur extinction theories.

propars. Futurists' blend word for *pro*fessional *par*ents.

—————— **R** ——————

railway thinking. That way of thinking about the future in which events repeat themselves.

ramscoop. A spacecraft that operates on hydrogen, which it scoops up in space and converts to energy.

razor boy/girl. A cybernetically augmented thug in the world of *cyberpunk*. The name comes from the addition of razor-blade claws (retractable or not) in the fingers. Augmentation includes eye replacement for sighting, direct computer links, etc.

RPG. Role-Playing Game. Literature from Palladium Books of Detroit, distributor of the "megapopular" *Teenage Mutant Ninja Turtles* game, defines an RPG in its sales literature this way: "An [RPG] is not a traditional board game. In fact, it has no playing board, no deck of cards, no spinner, nor even playing pieces. Instead the players have a book of rules with background information about adventure in a fictional world." See also *FRP*.

rules lawyer. Derisive role-playing-game term for a player who memorizes rules so carefully that he or she can cite verbatim specifics in arguments.

S

S&S. Short for Swords and Sorcery, a genre of fantasy fiction that mixes monsters, barbarians, and pretty women. It is also known as *H.F.*, *Heroic Fiction* or *Heroic Fantasy*. The Conan the Barbarian series epitomizes this science fiction format.

saving roll / saving throw. The use of dice to simulate fate in role-playing games.

sci-fi. What science fiction is called outside the world of science fiction. "Sci-fi"—pronounced "sigh-fi"—is used by fans with irony. Science fiction fans say "science fiction" or *s.f.*

sensetapes. A *cyberpunk* equivalent of videotapes, which allows the user to get the sensations of actors within the teleplay. Most tapes represent very rich, upper-class life situations so the hopeless can experience what they will never know in life.

sercon. Science fiction fan term for *ser*ious and *con*structive.

SETI. Search for Extra Terrestrial Intelligence.

s.f. Short for "science fiction," although some insist that it stands for "speculative fiction" or "science fantasy." The faithful say "s.f." rather than "sci-fi" and pronounce it "ess-eff."

skiffy. Sci-fi.

slash and hack. Term used in role-playing-game circles for the play of beginners whose characters turn into traveling butchers who kill monsters and take treasure. Also known as "shoot and loot" or "trash for cash."

smof. *Fannish* word created from acronym of Secret Master Of Fandom. Defined by an insider: "Mysterious and shadowy, but not as much as they might like, smofs supposedly run fan groups and put on conventions. It has either complimentary or pejorative connotations, depending on usage."

solo. Role-playing game that can be played by one person working against a programmed text.

space opera. A science fiction story written especially for action and excitement—intergalactic adventure. It is comparable to calling old-fashioned cowboy movies "horse operas."

spaceship ethic. The moral code based on the concept that the earth is a large vehicle or spacecraft whose survival depends on cooperation by the passengers.

splatterpunk. S.f./horror genre/ movement that unites the nihilism of punk with hyperviolent action.

suitcase war. One waged by people leaving small thermonuclear devices in other people's countries.

system hacker. A role-playing-game participant who uses loopholes and words like "sometimes" in the rules to do outlandish things. "You can generally see them coming, and can modify situations to disallow most of their nonsense," says Mike Stackpole.

---------- **T** ----------

tachyon. Theoretical particle that fuels much science fiction in that it moves faster than light and cannot go any slower.

terraforming. Reengineering the atmosphere or terrain of planets to make them ready for human habitation.

Third Industrial Revolution. That which frees us from the confines of Earth. The first two freed us from physical slavery and repetitive tasks.

Titanic analogy. False perception of the earth as "unsinkable," in the sense that the *Titanic* was regarded as unsinkable before it sank.

transphotic. Describing faster-than-light travel.

Trekker. *Star Trek* fan. In his *Fanspeak Glossary* Robert Runté points out that this term is used for more restrained or older fans, while the next, *Trekkie,* tends to be used for the more fanatical or young fan.

Trekkie. Fan of the *Star Trek* phenomenon, two television series, five movies, books, etc.

twitcher. Fantasy gamer who is so excited by a subject that he explodes with energy and chatter, given to long, one-sided conversation.

---------- **U** ----------

ufology. The study of unidentified flying object (UFO) reports.

uforia / ufomania. Zest for

UFO's and/or conviction that aliens are visiting our world.

W

waldo. Mechanical hands.

white hole. The hypothetical vehicle from which matter and energy emerge after being sucked into a black hole.

wild card. Futurists' term for an event that defies conventional forecasting; for instance, the emergence of AIDS.

X

zenology. The study of extraterrestrials.

SOURCES

Earthlings who helped with this glossary are writer and game designer Mike Stackpole, futurist Ralph Hamil, the mathematical Martin Gardner, and book editor Michael Dirda. Many of Stackpole's definitions have been quoted in their entirety, especially those from his memos on game and cyberpunk terminology. Martin Kottmeyer of Carlyle, Illinois, read the original version of this glossary and made important suggestions for its improvement.

The second edition of Robert Runté's *Fanspeak Glossary* (which is sold by the author care of: P.O. Box 4655, Postal Station South Edmonton, Edmonton, Alberta T6E 5G5), and a fanzine glossary produced by Mike Gunderloy, editor of *Factsheet Five* of Rensselaer, N.Y., were very useful in decoding s.f. talk.

12 FOOD AND DRINK

Words and Phrases to Fill a Doggie Bag

"Ah, the menu—what contortions of language it embodies, what culinary sleights of hand it conceals, what glories of the kitchen it celebrates and how mysterious it can be."

—Stanley Dry in *Food & Wine* magazine, March 1984

English is a liberal language that seems predisposed to welcoming words from other languages. One can make a game of coming up with strings of these immigrants. Think of an intensely masculine, hungry, highly qualified public advocate, and you have your basic *macho ombudsman extraordinaire* who, when hungry, may *nosh* on *dim sum*.

The point at which we speakers of American English are most open-minded would seem to be when we are most open-mouthed. We devour words like *pasta, empanadas, souvlakia, quiche lorraine, havarti, caldo verde, tabbouleh, yakitori,* and *osso bucco.*

The reason for this linguistic liberalism, which has been especially strong since World War II, is simple. Some things are better said with a word or phrase that is or approximates the original. A wok is a wok, and to call it "a shallow pan used for quick stir frying" is to define rather than describe it.

Because of this international stew, a large amount of new food terminology is neither English nor American slang. There is not the same need for a native slang as there was in the earlier part of the century, when there were rich food slangs for the soda fountain, diner and lunch counter, mess hall and lumber camp. These slang terms involved were colorful and not very appetizing. As John F. Mariani explains about lunch counter slang in his *Dictionary of American Food and Drink*, ". . . the vitality of lunch-counter speech—*cat's eye* for tapioca, *baby* for glass of milk, *jerk* for ice cream soda, and *Adam and Eve on a raft* for fried eggs on toast—had a raciness about it that many people sought to put an end to in the 1930s."

Another factor in all of this has been the rise in processed store food and fast-food restaurants. In a world of bottled salad dressings and nationally franchised drive-in restaurants, we get new terms like *Green Goddess* and *Big Mac,* but these are carefully selected product names and not slang. *Junk food* is a slang term, and people in the fast-food business would just as soon lose the adjective "junk."

Here is the slang of food and drink—some old, some new—all in use.

A

A.C. American cheese.

all the way. A sandwich served with all the fixin's; lettuce, mayo, onion, etc.

amateur night. (Drink) To heavy drinkers, this is New Year's Eve.

apron. (Drink) A bartender.

B

B&B. (1) Bed and breakfast. (2) Bread and butter.

back. (Drink) On the side. "Scotch, soda back," would be straight scotch with soda water on the side.

banger. (Drink) Straight booze, usually vodka, on ice, which the bar customer bangs ceremoniously on the bar before downing.

barfly. (Drink) One who spends much time at a bar drinking.

barkeep. (Drink) Bartender.

beergoggles. (Drink) Perception influenced by the consumption of alcohol. "He was handsome, but I was wearing beergoggles."

behind the stick. (Drink) To tend bar.

big three. In the burger realm, McDonald's, Burger King, and Wendy's.

binder. Constipating food.

bite. Small meal or snack.

blind pig. Long-established but still relevant name for a tavern that opens after the legal closing hour in the city in which it is located.

black. Black coffee.

bootie food. Food that goes right to the butt.

booze. (Drink) Liquor, an old slang term that is as commonly used today as it ever was.

booze cruise. (Drink) Short boat trip on which there is plenty of music and drinking.

bouncer. (1) Bad check to a restaurant. (2) Person employed to keep order in a bar or nightclub.

bowl of red. Chili con carne.

branwagon. The drive toward healthier eating, an allusion to both bran (as in oat or wheat) and bandwagon.

brewpub. (Drink) A bar/restaurant where beer is brewed on the premises.

brewsky. (Drink) Beer.

brown bag. (1) Paper bag or wrapping for a meal. (2) To bring one's lunch in a brown paper bag; as in "Let's brown bag it tomorrow and go to the park."

bucket o'blood. (Drink) Tough bar or saloon.

bug juice. Noncarbonated fruit drink.

Bullshot. (Drink) Vodka and beef broth.

burger. Hamburger.

burger joint. Place where the specialty is hamburgers.

buzzmaker. (Drink) A particularly potent mixed drink, often a *shooter.*

C

carryout. Place that sells food to be taken from the premises.

C.B. Cheeseburger.

chaser. (Drink) Hard liquor thrown back after a beer or other less potent drink.

chicken-fried. Describing a flour-covered steak or other piece of beef that has been cooked in deep hot fat, in the manner of fried chicken.

chilly. (Drink) A beer.

chocoholic. Person with a passion for anything chocolate.

chow down. To eat.

chugalug. (Drink) To drink without pausing to finish a gulp.

church key. (Drink) Beer-can opener. This term is at least thirty-five years old and should have been eliminated by the pop-top can, but it is still heard.

cooler. (Drink) (1) A wine concoction, usually combining wine, carbonated water, and fruit juice. (2). A bouncer—one who throws unruly patrons out of bars and clubs.

crispy. (Drink) Hungover.

D

dagwood. Enormous sandwich from the multilayered constructions of Dagwood Bumstead of comic-strip fame.

damages. The bill in a restaurant.

deli. (1) Delicatessen. (2) In the style of a delicatessen, such as deli-sized sandwiches.

demi-veg. Part-time vegetarian.

doggie bag / doggy bag. A bag provided by restaurants to hold a patron's leftovers. Despite the face-saving name, the contents of a doggie bag are usually destined for human as opposed to canine consumption.

do lunch. Have lunch.

D.Q. Short for Dairy Queen.

E

early-bird special. Restaurant meals that are reduced in price for those who are seated early.

easy over. See *once over easy.*

86. To be out of something—"Eighty-six on the lemon pie." This is one of the few survivors of an elaborate restaurant code that obtained before World War II. For instance, "95" stood for a customer leaving without paying, and "400W" stood for maple syrup.

empty calories. Term used to describe foods with little nutritional value.

F

fast food. Food that is cheap, standardized, and quickly dispensed. Most fast-food restaurants are chains with plenty of parking.

fat farm. Camp or resort where one goes to diet and exercise.

fatidis. The inability to pass a Dairy Queen without stopping. Pronounced feh-TI-dis.

fat pill. A pastry or other food that is very high in calories and seemingly has the effect of a pill taken to make one fatter.

fern bar. Establishment characterized by light wood, hanging plants, and good illumination.

five B's. Name used in parts of New England for Boston baked beans and brown bread.

flight. (Drink) Three different samplings (2½ ounces) of wine offered for a flat price. Trendy way of getting a sip of three expensive wines.

fluff and fold. In restaurant parlance this is an injunction to take special care of a patron or tableful of patrons.

foodie. The food trendy of the eighties; one who was quick to discover *grazing*, talks about "food as fashion," and is among the first to try out new restaurants.

free-range. Describing a chicken or other fowl that is raised outside rather than in a closed coop. These birds are preferred by people who have ethical problems with the treatment of fowl in factory-like coops. Free-range eggs are the eggs laid by these fowl.

frickles. Fried pickles, a dish with a following in parts of the South.

frontloading. (Drink) Drinking a lot in a short period of time before going to an event where liquor will not be served, such as the ballet.

full house. Lettuce, tomato, and mayo.

G

garbage. Restaurant adjective for that which is left over from one dish and used in the next. It is not as nasty as it sounds: a *USA Today* article on the new California cuisine featured a restaurant specializing in "garbage salads" (based on leftover shrimp, avocados, etc.).

getting stiffed. Waiter/waitress term describing a party that leaves no tip or a very small tip.

G.J. Grapefruit juice.

gorp. A "trail mixture" of peanuts, raisins, candy, and grain. It has been claimed that the term began as an acronym for "good old raisins and peanuts," but many would side with William Safire, who thinks that the acronym story is bunk. Safire has written, "To me, the word seems formed like Lewis Carroll's creation of *chortle* by combining *chuckle* with *snort; gorp* is a wedded *snort* and *gulp*."

grazing. Ordering a series of small entrée portions rather than one large entrée. One can graze a meal's worth at a single restaurant or at several.

greasy spoon. Restaurant at the low end of the scale in terms of food, cleanliness, and decor; a dive.

greenhouse look. Restaurant or bar with immense windows and lots of greenery.

grinder. Sandwich served on Italian bread sliced sideways. This is one of a number of names for the same thing, with this one being popular in parts of southern New England. Other names, in other regions, include *hero, hoagie, Italian, torpedo, submarine,* and *wedge*.

ground hog. (Drink) Today as always, the preferred nickname for a steam-operated steam still.

H

happy camper. In the context of bars and restaurants this term refers to one who is intoxicated.

happy hour. (Drink) Period before dinner during which bars attempt to promote themselves, often with reduced drink prices.

hero. Sandwich served on Italian bread sliced sideways. Known also as a *grinder, Italian, submarine,* etc.

hoagie. The same thing as a *hero, submarine, torpedo,* etc.

hold. To withhold in a restaurant order: "Roast beef, hold the gravy."

hooter. (Drink) Same as *shooter.*

hopping. Moving around in search of food, restaurant hopping; drink, bar hopping; or companionship, table hopping.

hush puppy. Deep-fried cornmeal dumpling.

I

inhale. To eat quickly, as if one is breathing in air.

in the ozone. Restaurant term describing a table where the patrons have had too much to drink.

in the trees / in the weeds. Describing a kitchen that is running way behind.

Irish sweetener. (Drink) Alcoholic substance added to coffee—often Irish whisky or brandy.

Italian. Long sandwich served on Italian bread. In the upper northeast it is often pronounced "eye-talian." Known also as *hoagie, torpedo,* etc.

J

jigger. (Drink) Bar glass holding 1½ ounces of liquor and used for measurement.

junque food. So-called adult fast food, a $7.95 hamburger touted as "our deluxe, gourmet burger."

K

knock back. (Drink) To drink aggressively.

L

lite. Low in calories; lighter than normal.

lo-cal. Low in calories.

long list. (Drink) A restaurant's full listing of wines in stock.

long neck. (Drink) A beer bottle with a long neck. There is a certain bravado associated with carrying one around a bar, especially a Lone Star long neck in Texas.

M

mayo. Mayonnaise.

meat market / meat rack. Singles' bar where the primary objective seems to be to get laid.

medley. Upscale *menuese* for a mixture or combination, as in a medley of baby vegetables.

megadiner. One of the new breed of diners that can seat as many as 500—in contrast to the classic forty-seaters built in the 1930s through the 1950s.

menuese. Derogatory term for the overblown descriptions of simple food found in some menus. Here is an example from a real menu:

Fresh Fruit Salad—transported in a pineapple boat for the highest vibration and your transmutation with yogurt on the side for accent or dressing sprin-

kled with coconut. . . $6.35
mud pie. An ice cream concoction that is intensely chocolate.
munchies. Craving for food, usually junk food.
mystery meat. Food, usually from an institutional cafeteria, that defies identification.

N

neat. (Drink) Straight liquor, not on the rocks.
nibbling. (Drink) Sipping slowly.
nightcap. (Drink) Drink taken late at night.
nosh. To munch or snack; a Yiddish-Americanism.
noshery. Delicatessen or snack bar where one goes for appealing food.

O

O.D. To overeat; from the drug initialism for "overdose."
O.J. Orange juice.
once over easy. To turn over and cook lightly on the other side, usually applied to fried eggs. Eggs can also be "medium—over hard" and other variations.

on the rocks. (Drink) With ice.
on wheels. Said of a restaurant order that is to go. Sometimes stated as "put wheels on that."
open dating. Products with an easily read date telling when it was packed and when it must be pulled from the shelf.

P

pig out. To overeat. Also *pork out*.
pit stop. Place where one goes for food and a rest room on a car trip.
pork out. To overeat, to *pig out*.
pot luck. (1) Meal made of what is on hand. (2) A dinner to which everyone brings a dish.
power breakfast / power lunch. A meeting at which policy makers discuss business or politics over food.

R

rabbit food. Raw vegetables.
repeaters. Beans.
rinse. (Drink) See *Chaser*.
roach coach. Small truck selling prepared food; common around industrial areas where there are no cafeterias.

rocks glass. (Drink) Old-fashioned glass.

Rocky Mountain oysters. Testicles of bull or other male animal which have been breaded and fried.

roots and berries. Derogatory characterization of natural foods and/or vegetarianism.

S

scarf. To eat quickly. The term is often used in connection with fast food.

shooter. (Drink) (1) Straight *shot* meant for consuming in one gulp. (2) House drink that is usually sweet and easy to consume quickly. These shooters are common to summer beach bars and often feature a fruit liqueur such as DeKuyper Peachtree Schnapps, or Southern Comfort, or tequila. These drinks often have names that are as wild as their formulas. Writer Joe Goulden brought back a copy of the *Beachcomber* free newspaper from the Delaware coast a few years ago which contained a "shooter survey" rating such libations as the Blood Clot, Midnight at the Oasis, 57 Chevy with Hawaiian Plates, Sex on the Beach, the Russian Quaalude, Deep Throat, the Chocolate Virgin, and Daphnie Divine's Deluxe Dixie Daiquiri.

shopping list menu. Menu that not only tells you what is available, but what went into it, including the garnish ("garnished with a sprig of spring parsley," for instance).

short dog. (Drink) (1) Single can of beer. (2) Small, cheap bottle of wine.

shot. (Drink) A small, measured quantity of liquor—usually two ounces, give or take a half ounce.

shot glass. (Drink) Small vessel for measuring liquor, usually 1½ or 2 ounces.

sinker. Heavy, dense version of dish, especially baked goods. (The term is likely to bring back the thought of a particularly bad example. In the author's case it was a heavier 'n lead stack of blueberry pancakes served to him in Maine, where they are called "sinkas.")

smothered. Covered.

splash. (Drink) A small amount of water or soda, as in "bourbon with a splash."

spritzer. (Drink) White wine and soda water.

sproutsy. A vegetarian.

spud. Potato.

stack. A pile of pancakes or toast.

sticks. Food sliced into long sticklike shapes—fried mozzarella sticks or batter-dipped zucchini sticks, for instance.

stinking rose. Garlic, among garlic lovers.

straight up. (Drink) Without ice.

submarine. Sandwich served on Italian bread sliced longitudinally. Known also as a *hero, Italian, hoagie,* etc.

suds. (Drink) Beer.

sunny side up. Eggs that are fried with their yolks up and fully cooked on one side.

surf-n-turf. Generic name for meat and seafood on the same platter.

swill. (Drink) Beer.

T

table from hell. Term used in the restaurant business for a table of people who are drunk and abusive.

T&T. (Drink) Tanqueray and tonic.

tater. Potato.

Tex-Mex. Type of food that is influenced by innovations on either side of the Texas-Mexico border.

three-martini lunch. Codeword for the excesses of expense-account dining. It has recently become emblematic for the kind of common business lunch that began to erode with growing health consciousness; however, such lunches are still not uncommon.

to go. Food that is taken out of the restaurant for consumption elsewhere.

torpedo. Sandwich served on Italian bread sliced sideways. Known also as a *hero, hoagie, Italian,* etc.

trash fish. Cheap, unpopular whitefish.

tube steak. A hot dog.

twist. (Drink) Twist of sliced lemon or lime peel.

U

Umbrella Room, The. A sidewalk food cart: "Let's grab a quick lunch at The Umbrella Room." This term was acquired in New York City by Joseph C. Goulden, who reports that it is popular there.

V

veggies. Vegetables.
veggy. Vegetarian.
vegucation. Education about vegetarianism.

W

watering hole. (Drink) A bar.
wedge. Sandwich served on Italian bread sliced sideways. Known also as a *hero, hoagie, Italian,* etc.
western. Omelette (or a sandwich containing an omelette) filled with ham, green pepper, and onions.
wet dog. (Drink) Description used for a bad wine with a chemical smell.
wolf down. To eat quickly.

Z

zapper. Microwave oven.
zip-code wine. (Drink) A wine-trade term for a French wine from a shipper who has an impressive address but whose grapes do not come from that region.
zombie food. Unacceptable food that has been brought back to acceptability with the aid of irradiation or other sterilization techniques.

SOURCES

Phyllis Richman, *Washington Post* food critic, was most helpful, as was the food file in the Tamony Collection, and ever-helpful Charles D. Poe. Gary Shipper also contributed.

13

MEDICAL SLANG

___

Words You Don't Want to Hear from Your Hospital Bed

"The range and number of these [slang] terms suggests the extensiveness of the verbal aggression towards patients among medical personnel. These terms are all used 'backstage,' never in the presence of a conscious patient."

—From "Not Sticks and Stones, But Names," by Lois Monteiro, in *Maledicta 4*, Summer 1980

There are two medical languages. One is the highly technical, Latinate tongue that has been called *medicant*. In this tongue a headache is *cephalalgia*, sweating is *diaphoresis*, and vomiting becomes *emesis*. It is also stuffy and bureaucratic: measurements and characteristics become parameters, centimeters come out as "sawntimeters," and doctors and nurses become providers (turning patients into consumers). As one critic writing in the *New England Journal of Medicine* put it, it takes English and turns it into something that is "impressive, intimidating, and incomprehensible."

It poses those very questions that we as patients must grapple with: would we, for instance, be better served if we were told we had leprosy or Hansen's disease? Unless we are hypochondriacs, wouldn't most of us prefer to hear that we "just have a simple rash" than hear it in Latin, a case of *pityriasis rosea?* And what of the medical pronoun "we," as in "we treat this with rest and aspirin"? Some see this as the mark of a partnership between patient and doctor ("we will beat this one"); others see it as the doctor's way of saying that the medical profession (the collective use) is of one mind on this matter.

But there is another level of communication working here: blunt, irreverent, and not meant for public ears. It is pure slang—the slang of doctors, nurses, and hospital technicians.

A

albatross. Chronically ill patient who will remain with a doctor until one of them expires.

angel lust. Male cadaver with an erection.

Aztec two-step. Diarrhea acquired in Latin America.

B

baby catcher. Obstetrician.

bag. To administer an oxygen mask.

banana. Patient with jaundice.

big C. Cancer.

blade. Surgeon.

blue blower. Patient with severe lung disease.

blue pipe. Vein.

bounceback. Patient who keeps returning to the hospital.

box. To die.

BRAT diet. Common prescription for infant diarrhea: bananas, rice, apple sauce, and toast.

bronk. To undergo bronchoscopy.

buff up. To ready a patient for release.

bug juice. Antibiotics.

bugs in the rug. Pubic lice.

C

C&T ward. Place where comatose patients are placed in a hospital. It is short for "cabbages and turnips."

cath. To catheterize.

code azure. Message to other medical professionals to do nothing extraordinary to save a very ill patient who will die shortly no matter what is done. It is the opposite of the official Code Blue, which mobilizes the staff in an effort to save someone.

crock. Complainer.

D

deep fry. Cobalt therapy.

Delhi belly. Intestinal upset acquired overseas.

doc. Doctor to a doctor. For instance, firms that help M.D.'s with the financial side of their practice are known as "doc-watchers."

doc-in-the-box. Small medical facility, usually in a shopping center, where one can go for treatment without an appointment.

domino transplant. A rare organ transplant in which a person is given a new heart and lungs.

DOW. See *M.I.*

dowager's hump. Manifestation of osteoporosis.

Dr. Feelgood. A doctor who is indiscriminate about prescribing drugs.

duck. Portable urinal for bedridden male hospital patients. Before these were made of plastic, they were known as glass or porcelain ducks.

dump. Patient that nobody seems to want.

dwindles, the. Advancing old age.

F

fanger. Oral surgeon.

fascinoma. An interesting disease.

finger wave. Rectal exam.

flatline. To die.

fluids and electrolytes. That which is consumed at happy hour.

G

gasser / gas passer. Anesthetist.

gomer. A complaining, irksome patient. Medical lore holds that this began as an acronym for Get Out of My Emergency Room. However, William Safire has suggested that it may have come from the Scottish dialect word "gomeral" for "simpleton."

gone camping. Describing a patient in an oxygen tent.

gone to _____ . Hospital euphemism for a death; for instance, a member of the staff at a Virginia hospital reports that it is "gone to Chicago" where he works.

gorked. Anesthetized.

grapes. Hemorrhoids.

H

hole in one. A gunshot wound in

the mouth or other bodily oriface.

hospitalitis. Malaise of patients who have been in the hospital too long.

———— **I** ————

ivy pole. Rack from which intravenous equipment hangs.

———— **J** ————

jungle rot. Fungus infection of the crotch area.

———— **K** ————

knife-happy. Describing an overly enthusiastic surgeon.

———— **L** ————

liver rounds. A staff party, so called because of liver-damaging alcohol.

lunger. Patient with obvious lung disease.

———— **M** ————

Melody Hill anemia. Drunk on cheap wine. The name of any cheap wine can be inserted before the word anemia.

M.I. Normally this stands for "myocardial infarction," but a Florida M.D. explains that some acute M.I.'s are not admitted to hospitals as "hospitals use M.I. to mean 'monetary insufficiency.'" An alternative initialism is *DOW*, which stands for "deficiency of wallet."

molar masher. Dentist.

Montezuma's revenge. Diarrhea, especially when touched off by foreign food or a trip to a lesser-developed nation.

Mount Saint Elsewhere. Inferior hospital for welfare charges and the terminally ill.

———— **N** ————

not even in the ball game. Confused senile patient.

———— **O** ————

oids / roids. Steroids.

old-timer's disease. Alzheimer's disease.

organ recital. A hypochondriac's medical history.

O sign. Comatose patient with mouth open wide. See also *Q sign*.

———— **P** ————

pan. To pass out bedpans.

pink puffer. Patient breathing rapidly due to lung disease.

pit, the. The emergency room.

player. Same as *gomer.*

plumber. Urologist.

PMSB. Acronym for Poor Miserable Son of a Bitch. Explained by a neurologist in this sentence: "This PMSB comes in complaining of a thousand things, and rightfully so!"

PPPP. Diagnostic initialism for a patient in bad shape: "particularly piss-poor protoplasm."

preemie. Premature infant.

psychoceramic. Same as a *crock.*

Q

Q sign. An *O sign* with the patient's tongue hanging out—a worse prognosis.

quad. Quadraplegic.

R

rear admiral. Proctologist (*Maledicta* editor Reinhold Aman has noted that this term was given a boost when President Carter was operated on for hemorrhoids by Dr. William Lukash, who held the rank of Rear Admiral.)

reeker. Smelly patient.

red pipe. Artery.

S

scope. To undergo endoscopy.

shadow gazer. Radiologist.

shrink. Therapist or psychologist.

SICU. Pronounced "Sick-U." Short for Surgical Intensive Care Unit.

soufflé. A patient who has jumped or fallen from a high place.

stirrups. Apparatus used when women are given "internal" exams or are delivering a baby.

T

tern. Intern.

Thorazine shuffle. The slow, lumbering gait of psychiatric patients who have been given large doses of phenothiazines.

three P's. Term some doctors use to refer to the Pill, permissiveness, and promiscuity.

three-toed sloth. Patient with diminished capacities, usually from long-term alcoholism.

tubed. Died, as in going down the "tubes."

train wreck. A patient with several serious medical problems.

_____ V _____

vegetable garden. Ward for those in comas.

vitals. Pulse, blood pressure, and other vital signs.

_____ W _____

ward X. The morgue.

whale. Grossly obese patient.

witch doctor. Specialist in internal medicine.

wig picker. Same as *shrink*.

_____ Z _____

zap. To administer electroshock therapy.

SOURCES

Thanks to Dr. P.B.P., Dr. F.M., Reinhold Aman, and Dr. Aman's journal *Maledicta,* which contained the following: "Milwaukee Medical Maledicta" by Sue Ture (*Maledicta* 8, 1984–85), "Not Sticks and Stones, But Names," "More Common Patient-Directed Pejoratives Used by Medical Personnel" (*Maledicta* 7, 1983), by Lois Monteiro (*Maledicta* 4, no. 1, Summer 1980), "Common Patient-Directed Pejoratives Used by Medical Personnel," by C. J. Scheiner (*Maledicta* 2, 1978). Barry Reicher also helped.

14 | MENTAL STATES

Cutting with a Dull Tool

"But the first time I heard that idea, it was from the eminent prosecutor, Mister Shanley, and when Richard Shanley says something, and it sounds good to me, I start wondering if maybe all of a sudden I'm not traveling with a full seabag anymore."

—From George V. Higgins's *The Judgment of Deke Hunter*

Slang dotes on mental illness, oddness, and offness. There are scores of slang synonyms for mental aberration and various states thereof. Without leaving the D's, we have *daffy, dippy, dotty, dingy,* and *dingaling,* and the B's include *bananas, beany, birdy, buggy, bugs, bughouse,* and *bonkers.*

This lexicon is cruel, yet paradoxically kinder than the proper language of psychiatry. To be branded as loopy or wifty seems less dire than being labeled neurotic or psychotic. In fact, the trend seems to be toward metaphoric description as opposed to a single word. There is nothing new about this. People have had bats in their belfries, snakes in their heads, and bees in their bonnets for generations, but what is new is that we seem to be in the midst of a bumper harvest of metaphors for being a bit "off."

These have certainly been influenced by what have been termed "Westernisms" or "ruralisms," folksy bucolic similes and metaphors along the lines of "steeper than a cow's face," "dumber than a barrel of hair," "as useless as tits on a boar hog," and "long as a Texas lie."

Here is a contemporary collection of slang expressions that all mean more or less the same thing. The trick here is to come up with a new metaphoric way of saying that same thing.

B

No **beans** in his or her pod.
Belt doesn't go through all the loops.
Gone around the **bend.**
Bow is unstrung.
Brain is stuck in first gear.
Two **bricks** shy of a load.
A **bubble** off of plumb (or out of level).
Missing a few **buttons.**

C

Car isn't hitting on all cylinders.

D

Dealing with a **dead battery.**
Missing a few dots on his or her **dice.**
Temporarily **disconnected.**
All of his or her **dogs** aren't barking.
One **doughnut** shy of a dozen.
Dow-Jones average is off a few points.

Cutting with a **dull tool.**

E

Over the **edge.**
Elevator doesn't run to the top floor.
Running on **empty.**
Enchiladas have lost their chili.

F

Fishing without bait.
Not playing with a **full deck.**

G

Has a **guest** in the attic.

H

Hat is on too tight.
Has had his/her **hat** blocked with him/her still in it.
Off his/her **hinges.**
Playing **hockey** with a warped puck.
Nice **house,** nobody home.

K

Not **knitting** with both needles.
Has a **knot** in his or her kite string.

L

A **leak** in the think tank.
A **low-watt bulb.**

M

Missing a few **marbles.**
Too much **motor** for his/her axle.
Puts **mustard** on his/her Fruit Loops.

N

Nuttier than a squirrel's breakfast.
Nutty as a fruitcake.

O

Has only one **oar** in the water.
Overdrawn at the memory bank.

P

Cuts out **paper dolls.**
Half the **pickets** are missing from his/her fence.
Somebody blew out his/her **pilot light.**

Somebody pulled his/her **plug.**

Q

Running two **quarts** low.

R

Driving in **reverse.**
Rice Krispies don't snap, crackle, and pop.
Off his/her **rocker.**
Not present at **roll call.**
Has a **room** for rent.

S

A few **sandwiches** shy of a picnic.
A **screw** loose.
In one too many **scrimmages** without a helmet.
Has all of his/her **shit** in one sock.
Splinters in the windmills of his/her mind.
On the highway of life, he/she is a **stalled vehicle.**

T

On his/her **team,** they're one player short.
A few **termites** in the attic.
Is out of his/her **tree.**
Runs a **typewriter** without a ribbon.

_____ **U** _____

Off in the **upper story.**

_____ **W** _____

One **wheel** in the sand.
Not **wrapped** too tightly.

SOURCES

Robert D. Specht, Joseph C. Goulden, James W. Darling, and Joseph E. Badger all helped with the compilation of this list. The best list of Westernisms that the author has seen was compiled by David McQuay and appeared in the *Denver Post* of August 25, 1985. Chicquita, Larz Cohen, and Melissa Baker also contributed.

15 | NAUTICAL SLANG

At Sea with the Language

" . . . every seaman, whether naval, Merchant
Marine, or yachtsman, knows that when he steps
aboard a vessel he is stepping into another
existence and wishes it to remain that way."

—Gershom Bradford, author of
The Mariner's Dictionary, quoted in the
St. Petersburg *Times*, December 9, 1984

What distinguishes nautical slang from other slang is that so much
of what was once specialized slang and jargon is now standard
English. From *stem* to *stern*, from *port* to *starboard,* dozens of
terms are now—and have long been—found in conventional dictionaries along with the notation of *naut.*

Much of this slang and terminology came ashore long ago. The
author spent three years in the U.S. Navy in the early 1960s, where
he was well-indoctrinated in the slang of the sea. Imagine my
surprise when I came out of the Navy and found nautical images in a
brokerage house where I went to work for a year. There people
routinely *jumped ship,* produced *boilerplate,* and went *full speed
ahead.* . . . trying, of course, not to go *overboard* in the process.

This is not to say that this traditional slang is safe from the
onslaughts of verbal reform. During the 1970s the Navy—the

United States Navy—attempted to purge itself of its traditional slang. The shipboard mess was officially renamed "enlisted dining facilities," the galley of yore became a "kitchen," and the brig became a "correctional facility." In deference to the genderless society, the Department of Defense ruled in 1979 that a ship would be an *it* and not a *her* and that it would be *crewed* and not *manned*.

In 1984, a good year to lash out against such things, then-Secretary of the Navy John F. Lehman, Jr., condemned "the bureaucratization of naval language" and ordered all naval facilities to return to traditional use by January 1, 1985. Halls were once again *passageways,* and toilets became *heads.*

Without replaying all of the traditional terms, here is a selection of today's un-"reformed" nautical slang, whether it be from the USN or the World Cup.

A

airdale. Any person in the air (aviation) department aboard an aircraft carrier. If this was once derogatory—an Airedale is a dog, after all—it is used with some pride by those in the air wing of a carrier.

all hands. The entire crew of a ship.

anchor. Lowest ranking man or woman in the class at the U.S. Naval Academy.

ash can. Depth charge.

B

battlewagon. Battleship.

beach, the. Ashore, whether it be Cannes or Norfolk.

belay that. Stop that.

bellhop. Sailor's term for a Marine, especially one in dress uniform. Sometimes stated as "seagoing bellhop."

big chow. Meal served before a big day in the Navy; for instance, before a major aircraft carrier attack.

Big Portsmouth. The Navy's prison at Portsmouth, N.H.

bilge. The proper meaning of this term is that portion of a ship below the water line. The slang use of this term refers to (1) bad food and (2) bad information. At the U.S. Naval Academy it means (3) to flunk out. Annapolitan Bill O'Neill reports that there is a gate at the Naval Academy known as the bilge gate, which is "one small gate that lads being bounced out of the academy pass through; hence no middie will walk out that gate, though civilians use it. A middie will step into the roadway and stroll out the big gate instead."

bilge rat. Boiler technician or other below-decks sailor.

bilge water. Soup.

bird farm. Aircraft carrier.

bird hatching. Fathering more than one child; term coined by Admiral Hyman Rickover.

black shoe. A member of the regular seagoing Navy, as opposed to naval aviators who are allowed to wear brown shoes.

bluejacket. Sailor.

blue shirt. Aircraft handler on an aircraft carrier.

blue-water sailor. Boater who heads for the open seas, as opposed to those who stay close to the coast.

boat pox. Gelcoat blisters on Fiberglas boats.

boomer. (1) Submarine with nuclear missiles. (2) Member of the nuclear-powered Navy.

boot. Sailor fresh from boot camp.

brightwork. Brass that must be polished.

brig rat. Prisoner serving time in the brig, a naval prison.

bunk. A sailor's bed.

C

can. Destroyer; short for *tin can*.

captain of the head. Sailor in charge of cleaning toilets.

cat. The catapult used to launch planes on an aircraft carrier.

Charlie Noble. Smokestack of a ship's galley.

Cinderella liberty. A Navy or Marine Corps pass that expires at midnight.

coasties. Members of the Coast Guard.

coffee grinder. Winch for controlling yacht sails. Also simply known as *grinder*.

conn. Control of the ship. An officer of the deck on a Navy vessel will "take the conn" when taking responsibility for the ship's course and speed.

Crabtown. Annapolis, Maryland.

Crotch, the. The U.S. Marine corps.

crow. The sleeve insignia eagle that marks petty officers in the U.S. Navy. To get one's crow is to get a promotion to petty officer.

cumshaw. That which is obtained by bribery or other illegal means.

D

dead horse. A debt, to a Navy man.

deck ape. Enlisted sailor assigned to deck or gunnery duties.

deep six. To throw away or kill, as in "deep-sixing a project." Its traditional meaning is "to drown," alluding to a person who is six fathoms deep.

Dilbert dunker. Contraption of the modern U.S. Navy used in training to simulate the action of an airman ditching at sea.

dolphins. The U.S. Navy submariner's badge.

Dutchman. A plate covering a crack or other imperfection.

E

easy. Carefully.

end on. Head on.

F

fender belly. Term for a fat, potbellied sailor, usually a "lifer," such as an old Navy chief petty officer.

field day. Day, or portion thereof, set aside for cleaning up a Navy vessel or base.

fish. Torpedo.

flat top. Aircraft carrier.

fouled. Jammed or obstructed.

four-oh / four-point-oh. Outstanding; used to express the highest degree of admiration. It comes from the highest rating—4.0—that one can achieve on a Navy fitness report.

four-oh sailor. Human perfection. In John Barron's *Breaking the Ring,* a character defines a four-oh sailor as "a guy who can walk on water without getting his shoes wet."

four striper. Navy captain.

Freshwater Navy. The Coast Guard.

G

galley yarn. A shipboard rumor.

geedunk. Navy/Marine term for ice cream, candy, junk food, etc.

Gertrude. Underwater telephone, used for communication between submarines.

Gitmo. Guantanamo Beach, Cuba; specifically, the U.S. Navy base there.

glory hole. Quarters for chief

petty officers aboard Navy ships.

gouge. (1) To cheat. (2) The answer or solution.

grinder. (1) Large winch for raising and lowering sails. (2) Person positioned just behind the mast who controls such winches. A 1984 article on the crew of America's Cup entry *Liberty* in *USA Today* termed this the "most brutal physical position" on a twelve-meter yacht. (3) A Marine Corps parade ground.

gummer's mate. Dental technicians.

H

hash mark. Stripes worn on the sleeves of Navy enlisted men, representing years of service. Each stripe signifies an enlistment.

head. (1) Toilet. (2) Compass heading, as in the query, "Quartermaster, where is your head?"

heavier metal. A larger, more powerful warship—a cruiser is heavier metal to a destroyer crew.

holiday. An imperfection; a spot left unfinished or uncleaned.

Hollywood shower. Full-length shower; a rarity on most Navy vessels, where freshwater conservation measures are normally in effect. A line from Tom Clancy's *The Hunt for Red October:* "A Hollywood shower is something a sailor starts thinking about after a few days at sea."

hook. The anchor.

hooligan. Not seamanlike; something that has been sloppily slapped together.

hot bunk. The use of the same bed by more than one sailor, who move in and out of that bunk as their watches (shifts) change.

huff duff. High frequency direction finder (HFDF).

I

Irish pennant. Loose rope or loose thread on a sailor's uniform.

J

jarhead. Member of the Marine Corps to a sailor—who is likely to be called *swabbie* in return.

joe. Coffee.

jump. To leave; to jump ship is to leave without permission.

jury rig. To repair or put together in an emergency; to

slap together. After a dis-
masting, a makeshift mast
may be jury-rigged.

_____ **K** _____

keel haul. To punish. It is an
allusion to the long-outlawed
practice of punishing a sailor
by dragging him by rope
under the keel of the ship.

_____ **L** _____

lay day. A day off from racing,
such as can be requested by
either boat during the America's Cup.
liberty. Overnight leave, save
for _Cinderella liberty._
liberty hound. One who finagles
extra time off; one who takes
all the time off allowable.

_____ **M** _____

mast. Ship captain's hearings to
which sailors are brought and
punished for minor infrac-
tions.
mat. The main deck of an aircraft carrier.
**mating dance of the lead-
bottomed money-gobblers.**
Phrase used to describe the
positioning of boats for the
start of the America's Cup
and other major races.

Med, the. The Mediterranean
Sea, in the parlance of the
Navy's Sixth Fleet.
Mickey Mouse rules. Petty rules
and regulations. In his marvelous book on nautical
terminology, _Salty Words,_
Robert Hendrickson writes,
"One theory holds that
World War II U.S. Navy Military Indoctrination Centers,
or MIC's, where undisci-
plined sailors were re-
strained, gave their initials to
this expression for petty
rules.
monkey fist. Knot put at the end
of a heaving line, often with a
small piece of lead or other
weight in the middle of the
knot to allow it to be thrown
easier.
mosquito boat. Motor torpedo
boat or PT boat.
mothballs. In reserve.
mousing. Lashing across a
hook to keep it from slipping.
mule. Handler on the flight
deck of an aircraft carrier.

_____ **N** _____

navy shower. Water-conserving
practice in which a sailor
wets down for a few seconds,
turns off the water and
lathers up, and then enjoys a

few more seconds of fresh water to rinse off. It is preferable to have a *Hollywood shower.*

nuc. Sailor in the U.S. Navy who serves aboard a nuclear sub or other nuclear-powered vessel.

O

O.D. Officer of the deck in the Navy. The O.D. is in charge of the ship and the representative of the captain.

old man, the. The captain.

P

padre. Chaplain in the Navy.

painter. A rope in the bow of a boat used to tie it to a dock or another vessel.

pipes. Boatswain—bos'n.

pitman. Same as *sewerman.*

purple shirt. Member of an aircraft carrier flight-deck fueling crew.

Q

quarters. Living spaces on a ship.

R

rates. Deserves, USN.

razor blades. A scrapped ship that has presumably been converted to razor blades.

red lead. Ketchup.

red shirt. Emergency crew member on the deck of an aircraft carrier.

reefer ship. Supply ship with refrigeration facilities.

rubber duckie. Inflatable rubber boats that are towed behind ships to confuse radar-guided missiles; a decoy.

S

screw. The propeller.

scuttlebutt. (1) Drinking fountain. (2) Gossip and rumor.

sea gull. (1) Navy term for one who follows the ship or fleet—applied to spouses and prostitutes alike. (2) Chicken served on a Navy vessel.

seaweed. Spinach.

secure. To put away or tie down.

sewerman. Crew member on a large sailboat who is in charge of sails below deck—or the sewer—where new sails must be unpacked and repacked during a race.

shellback. Sailor who has crossed the equator; hence one with some experience.

Sherwood Forest. Missile room on a U.S. submarine.

ship over. To reenlist in the Navy.

sick bay. Medical area on a Navy ship.

six-pack license. License that allows a civilian to commercially captain a boat with no more than six passengers on inland waters.

skins. Waterproof oilskin clothing.

skunk. To a submariner, an unidentified surface contact.

skylarking. Goofing off, Navy style.

slop chute. (1) A ship's garbage chute. (2) Canteen where beer is sold.

snipe. Navy seaman working below decks in the engineering department.

soup. Fog.

splice the mainbrace. To have a drink; head off for happy hour. Although this term dates back to the British Navy and the era of wind and sail to indicate a ration of grog, it is used playfully today by people conscious of its anachronistic quality.

stamps. Mail clerk on a Navy ship.

striker. Sailor training in specific area; trainee.

stripes. An officer in the Navy,

because of the gold stripes worn on the dress uniform.

swab / swabbie / swab jockey. Common seaman.

T

tadpole. Frogman not yet fully qualified, such as one still in training.

tin can. Navy detroyer.

tin fish. Torpedo.

two-foot-itis. The mock disease that infects recreational boat owners who are always looking for a vessel that is two feet longer than the one they have.

U

under the gun. Under armed guard.

V

vulture's row. The island area of an aircraft carrier where mechanics, plan pushers, and others concerned with flight operations congregate during deck landings.

W

W.E.T. Weekend training, in the Naval Reserves.

white-blue-white. Marine summer dress uniform: white cap, blue tunic, and white trousers.

_____ X _____

X.O. The executive officer, or second in command, on a naval vessel.

_____ Y _____

yellow sheet. An aircraft spotter on an aircraft carrier. They control *blue shirts*.

yeoman. A Navy petty officer with clerical duties.

_____ Z _____

Z-gram. The terse, direct style of memos and orders pioneered by Admiral Elmo Zumwalt during his tenure as Chief of Naval Operations.

SOURCES
Bill O'Neill, Dick Dana, James Darling, Charles D. Poe, and the Tamony Collection were all of help in compiling this glossary.

16 | PENTAGONESE

Fort Fumble Speaks

"Pentagonese. (World War II to Modern; all
Services) s. A peculiar artificial language
developed by the aborigines of the Puzzle Palace
for the express purpose of confusing the troops.
It is extremely difficult to translate into English."

> —From *A Dictionary of Soldier Talk*
> by Col. John R. Elting, Sgt. Major Dan
> Cragg, and Sgt. Ernest Deal

"Perhaps no institution has twisted the mother
tongue more systematically . . . than the Defense
Department. Not only do Defense officials tend
towards a particularly leaden bureaucratic patois,
often called 'Pentagonese,' but military secrecy
requirements also generate a dense thicket of
evasive phrasing and arcane code words."

> —David C. Morrison, the *National
> Journal*

It was born of three unholy influences: (1) the bureaucracy which it
is at one with, (2) secrecy, which is its lifeblood, and (3) the need to
obfuscate, especially useful in dealing with the Congress. The fact
that its business is killing people tends to produce euphemisms for
much military activity, as George Orwell noted in his classic "Politics and the English Language."

In the time of emergency, Pentagonese can be useful in making a
war sound like anything but, or, as the late Charles McCabe of the
San Francisco *Chronicle* once defined it: "a non-lingo in which
murder can be made to mean salvation."

There was a time during the darker days of the Vietnam War when the Pentagon created terms to make the adventure sound like a Boy Scout hike. The $34 given to families of South Vietnamese civilians killed by mistake were officially called *condolence awards,* and gross bombing errors were seldom termed anything more incriminating than *navigation errors, misdirections,* or *technical errors.* Defoliants that could kill plants fifteen miles from where they were dropped were termed *weed killers* ("the same as you buy in the hardware store at home," said an American official in 1966). Terms like *routine improvement of visibility in jungle areas* and *resources control* gave it the sound of a 4-H conservation effort.

Here is a sampling of what it sounds like today and how it translates into plain English. To get the full effect, read it in conjunction with the chapter on bureaucratese and think of it as a bureaucracy with enough nuclear firepower to knock the earth off its axis.

A

ABC. The Pentagon's 1988 acronym list gives three translations: (1) American-British-Canadian. (2) Argentina-Brazil-Columbia (the ABC countries), and (3) Atomic, Biological, and Chemical.

(This underscores the extent to which Pentagonese is dependent on acronyms. The aforementioned 1988 is, as the *Washington Post* termed it, "449 jam-packed pages of Pentagonisms.")

across the river. Washington, D.C., especially the White House and Congress.

air breathing. Describing a missile or other airborne delivery system that requires the intake of air for fuel combustion and therefore must remain within the earth's environment. The term is used to distinguish these systems from those that are rocket propelled.

air support. Bombing.

antipersonnel. Killer, in the sense that an antipersonnel weapon is meant to destroy people rather than equipment.

B

backpack nuke. A nuclear device that can be carried by a single person.

balloon goes up, the. A major war starts.

Beltway bandit. High-priced consultant or consulting firm. The name contains an allusion to the Beltway, an interstate highway which goes around the city of Washington. (See also Chapter 18)

blue top. Press release, from the traditional DOD press-release forms which have blue tops. To "blue top it" is to put out a press release.

bogsatt. Acronym for Bunch Of Guys Sitting Around the Table—a particular form of decision making.

boomer. Ballistic-missile submarine; one with nuclear weapons.

brilliant pebbles. A defensive technology that would employ thousands of small satellites floating in space to home in on incoming enemy missiles and detroy them.

broken arrow. An accident or mishap involving nuclear weapons.

burn me a copy. Make a Xerox copy.

C

C-cubed. Communications, command, and control.

chairman, the. Chairman of the Joint Chiefs of Staff.

Code 3. As explained by former Assistant Secretary of Defense John G. Kester in his article on Pentagonese in the *Washingtonian:* "A high-ranking official—used in messages to designate rank of an expected visitor, as in 'I have a Code 3 on board.' Code 1 is the President; Code 6's are too common to mention."

code word. Extra-secret; more secret than top secret.

collateral damage. Civilian damage from a nuclear strike.

cubed out. Bona fide Pentagon slang for filled to capacity.

D

dense pack. A cluster of intercontinental missiles in hard silos.

dirty battlefield. Combat zone obscured by smoke and dust.

It is a term used in the context of automated "smart" weapons that may not work as well in such an environment.

D.O.E. reaction. Acronym for Death of Earth; Armageddon; Doomsday.

dog-and-pony show. Formal presentation aimed at gathering support for a system or issue. Visuals (usually projected on a screen), handouts, and large graphs are essential to a true dog-and-pony show.

E

Early bird. Name of a compilation of military-related news clippings distributed early each morning for the edification of those who work at the Pentagon.

ejecta. Debris thrown by the explosion of a missile.

escalate. Since the 1960s, to intensify, to wage a wider war. In 1966 the national commander of the Veterans of Foreign Wars, Andy Borg, called for a "big and fast step-up of the U.S. war effort in Vietnam." The UPI's Dick West termed it a "horrible blunder" because, as every hawk and dove knew, you don't step up a war, you escalate it.

event. Nuclear explosion or accident.

F

feasless. Without feasibility.

first strike. A nuclear surprise.

footprint. The area of destruction left by a nuclear weapon.

Fort Fumble. The Pentagon itself.

fourth medium. War in space—after the first three martial media: land, sea, and air.

fratricide. The tendency of one incoming warhead to destroy its companions on detonation.

G

GCD. General and Complete Disarmament, a term that first emerged from arms control talks in the 1960s.

gigaton. A measure of nuclear destructive power which is equivalent to a billion tons of TNT.

go-go. From the acronym Government-Owned, Government-Operated. A facility not in the hands or ownershp of an outside contractor.

ground zero. (1) The point at which a thermonuclear weapon makes its impact. (2) Snack bar in the center of the courtyard in the middle of the Pentagon. It is of course an allusion to meaning (1) in that the center of the Pentagon would be the prime target in a missile exchange.

H

hard. Protected—a hard target is one that has been covered with earth and concrete.

heavy bead. The biggest of the big ticket items in the annual Pentagon budget.

he/him. (1) The enemy. This is one of the surest ways in which one distinguishes the military mind from the public mind. The rest of them say "they"; the Pentagon says "he." An example culled from reports on the Vietnam War in the Tamony Collection: "I don't believe the enemy has any great capability to assume any general offensive in the near future. He has been hurt and hurt badly. He is tired . . ." (2) The President of the United States.

horror stories. Term for public disclosure of parts rip-offs, such as paying $9609 for a simple wrench and $900 for a plastic cup.

humint. Human intelligence, as opposed to that which is gathered electronically, or *sigint* for signal intelligence.

I

Indians. Staff members.

J

jam. To interfere with. Electronic jamming is the purposeful impairing of the enemy's electronic systems.

K

kill-jamming. To impair the ability of an aircraft's electronics and communications while a second plane comes in for the kill.

kneecap. The NEACP (National Emergency Airborne Command Post) jet plane that sits in waiting to get the President out of Washington when enemy missiles are headed toward the city.

L

Langley. The CIA, which is based in Langley, Virginia.
Leprosy Effect. An ill-fated program or weapon that taints everything associated with it.

M

MAD. Mutual Assured Destruction; the theory that neither superpower will attack the other because retaliation would be fatal.
Mark 1 Mod 1. The earliest version of something; usually a weapon.
megadeath. A million dead.
MFR. Memorandum For Record; a written memo recalling what went on at a given meeting.
milicrat. Blend of "military" and "bureaucrat."

N

NOFUN. (Acronym) No First Use of Nuclear weapons.
NUTS. (Acronym) Nuclear Utilization Targeting Strategy; a theory/strategy based on the idea that military targets, and not cities, will be targeted in a nuclear exchange.

O

offload. Unload.
onload. Load.
overkill. More destructive ability than plausibly required.

P

Peacekeeper. The MX missile.
Pentagoose Noose. Nickname for the *Pentagram News*, distributed within the building.
physics package. Thermonuclear bombs named kindly.
program. Almost anything. More than thirty years ago Senator Stephen Young defined a Pentagon program as any assignment that took more than one phone call to complete.
Puzzle Palace. The Pentagon itself; *Fort Fumble*.

R

retool. To do it over.
revolving door, the. The practice that allows military officials to leave the Pentagon for corporate jobs with defense contractors.
rug rank. Higher ranking; an officer who rates a rug on his or her floor.

R.V. Reentry vehicle; the cone-shaped package that carries a nuclear warhead to its target.

S

sanitize. To edit out; to censor.

scare book, the. Nickname for the periodic report issued by the Secretary of Defense which is entitled *Soviet Military Power.* It is so called because of its tendency to focus on the extent of Soviet military strength. Scare books are usually released to coincide with the Pentagon budget request.

scenario-dependent. Dependent on a chain of events.

search and destroy. Pure Pentagonese for destroy and search.

Secdef. Short for "Secretary of Defense." The *Washington Post* reported in 1988 that there was a sign in the top man's military airplane on his private cabin that read "Secdef and Mrs. Carlucci."

second strike. Retaliatory attack in the wake of a retaliatory strike.

selected. Promoted.

selected out. To be let go or fired.

sigint. signal intelligence, or that which is gathered electronically rather than by spies *(humint).*

sign off on. To sign or initial; to pass along. To approve something without assuming responsibility for it; to not disagree with higher authority.

SIOP. The plan for nuclear war; the initials stand for Single Integrated Operational Plan. Peace has been described as a "benign pre-SIOP environment."

soft. Vulnerable, not protected from nuclear attack; a city, for instance. "Soft targets" are people.

southside basing. The idea that U.S. missiles could be nestled against the southern side of deep western mesas to protect the missiles from Soviet missiles.

T

Tank, the. The Joint Chiefs of Staff Conference Room, also known as "the Gold Room," after its decor.

thermal radiation. Name for nuclear heat moving along the ground at the speed of light.

At the source the temperatures are equivalent to those at the center of the sun.

threat tube. The path of an incoming missile.

three-humped camel. That which results when the three services work jointly on a project.

ticket puncher. Someone who undertakes an assignment (*e.g.,* combat) because it looks good on a resume, or because its absence will look bad.

Triad. Code name for U.S. nuclear response—submarines, land-based missiles, and long-range bombers.

tube. Same as *threat tube.*

U

unk-unks. Unknown unknowns, factors considered (or not considered) in deciding on new weapons systems. "Things we not only don't know about, but don't even know we don't know about," is how John G. Kester defined them in his article "How to Speak Pentagonese" (*Washingtonian,* February 1982).

W

weapons system. Weapon. At some moment in the past it became unfashionable to call a weapon a weapon, and even the simplest tool of combat—up to and including a portable potty—became a system.

whiz kid. Derogatory term for a systems analyst or senior Department of Defense staff.

window. Gap or opening. A "window of vulnerability" is a defensive gap that would allow an enemy first strike.

wiring diagram. An organizational chart.

Y

yellow stuff. Small tractors, earthmovers, etc., used in military operations.

SOURCES

Among the many attempts to decode the language of the Pentagon, the best was John G. Kester's February 1982 *Washingtonian* article. The Tamony Collection provided many examples, as did the Washington *Star* files at the Washingtoniana Room in the Martin Luther King Library in Washington. Joseph C. Goulden, James Thorpe III, and Charles D. Poe provided much help.

17

PERFORMING SLANG

Terms from Out of the Green Room

"The newspaper that transmogrified American slang . . ."

—*Variety*, described in *The New York Times*, November 10,1987

Show business slang is influenced by special forces. For starters, there are these two:

1. *Yinglish* (a term coined by Leo Rosten for the combination of Yiddish and English) which has long been the argot of many in show business.

2. The trade weekly *Variety* has not only influenced show-business talk, but the total body of American slang. Many *Variety*isms have lost their currency, like *passion pit* (for a drive-in movie lot) and *gams* (female legs), but others are still very much with us.

However, other influences pale in comparison to the overall impact of television. It has had a singular impact on language in general, and in the process, has taught us its own internal lingo. What's more, television lets us in on the slang of the rest of show

business. Legitimate theaters have had Green Rooms for generations, but it was not until the goings-on in the Green Room became a
topic of conversation on the *Tonight Show* that we all became aware
of it.

What helps distinguish television from the rest of show business
and other fields of endeavor is its compulsion to air its internal
business. For this reason terms like these routinely pop up in
television conversation: *segues, ratings periods, lavalier mikes,
booms, wipes, fills, rim shots, pans, minicams, voice-overs, feeds,
simulcasts, laugh tracks, promos, overnights, outtakes, remotes,
spin-offs, residuals, teleprompters,* and so much more. Most of us
know, for example, that if we ever got a call out of the blue from 30
Rock or Century City for a guest-host shot, the thing to do would be
to immediately call AFTRA and the William Morris Agency.

We are, in fact, treated as if we were all part of "the business" (as
opposed to the movies, which is "the industry"), and addressed as if
we really cared if the station we're watching is an *indy,* an *affiliate,*
or an *O & O* (owned and operated by the network), or that some
executive has decided that it sounds better if a *repeat* is called an
encore presentation. Newspapers don't tell us what went on in the
composing room, magazines don't report their "front of the book"
meetings; but television revels in the off-camera. "As I was telling
Johnny during the break . . ." says one guest, and another tells us
for the 110th time that he's never been in a Green Room that was
actually green. There is so much on-camera chat about the Green
Room that it has entered American mythology, with many of us
believing that it is the place where all the really funny lines are
spoken and all the really good gossip is traded.

A glossary:

A

above the line. The cost of a
movie before the camera begins to roll. Compare with
below the line.

actcom. Action comedy, in tele-
visionland. The actcom has
been defined as a sitcom that
starts with a disruption of the
status quo and then follows

the central character's action as he or she tries to bring things back to normal. By this definition, *I Love Lucy* was the prototypical actcom.

AFTRA. Pronounced "af-tra," it stands for the American Federation of Television and Radio Artists.

ankle. To quit or depart. A term from *Variety.*

arcs. TV scriptwriter's term for a villain who stays on for a string of episodes rather than one show.

B

B-. Second-rate, as in B-material or the B-western of yore.

back end / back-end money. Reference to the final profits in a film after all expenses have been met.

backer. Investor.

bankable. Describing a star whose presence in a film virtually guarantees investors and audiences.

below the line. Describing the actual costs of producing a movie.

billing. Order in which actors' names appear in ads, on marquees, and in film credits.

Black Rock. CBS corporate headquarters in Manhattan, from the dark gray color of the building.

bloom. A sudden flash of light on television from light reflecting off objects.

blunting. In television, competing with a show on another network by programming a similar show on your network, say running a movie musical against a music special. Compare with *counterprogramming.*

boffo. Box office hit. A term from *Variety.*

bofs. In the record business, albums that feature "the best of."

break. Moment at which a motion-picture distributor breaks even and starts to amass profits.

buck. In Hollywood, $100,000. William Safire may have been the first to report that when a movie mogul says "ten bucks" he is talking about a million dollars.

Business, The. Television; as contrasted with motion pictures, which are termed *The Industry.*

bye-bye. Broadcasting term for phrases beginning with words like "We now take you to . . ."

C

chop socky movie. Karate and kung fu movies as a genre. A term from *Variety.*

counterprogramming. Offering different television programming in an effort to attract a different audience—for instance, programming a comedy against a news special.

crash TV. Quasi-sports shows emphasizing sex and violence. The pioneer examples of the genre which *Newsweek* has typified as "rough, tough and rotton": *Roller-Games* and *American Gladiators.*

crawl. The rolling of credits at the beginning and/or end of a television show.

creep. Same as *crawl.*

crossover artist / crossover star. Performer who can move from one realm to another, such as from country and western recording to pop music or the movies.

D

dish. Ground terminal that receives satellite signals.

docudrama. Fictionalized depiction of a personality and/or event.

dramedy. Dramatic comedy in television—*M*A*S*H* and *All in the Family* are classics of this genre.

drive time. Radio broadcast periods during which commuters are in their cars. Compare with *housewife time.*

drooling. Unrehearsed conversation used to fill out time allotment in radio and television.

E

ear candy. Light, syrupy music billed as "easy listening."

elevator music. The same thing as *ear candy.*

F

flagging. The diagonal shift of the top portion of a television picture, causing the picture to bend to the right or the left.

flash and trash. Derogatory name for local news specials during ratings periods which tend to feature especially sexy or violent topics.

flop sweat. Nervous reaction to failure or impending theatrical doom.

flyover people. Television term

for the people who live in between New York and L.A.,
the two cities in which the
vast majority of television
shows are produced.

four-walling. Renting a theater
for the showing of a movie.
Under such an arrangement
the renter pays all expenses
but takes all the box-office
receipts.

front end. Money made before
or during the production of a
movie, as opposed to money
from profits determined later,
the *back end*.

G

gaffer. The chief electrician on
a movie set. This term and
grip are slang that has long
appeared in movie credits.

golden gater. In Hollywood, a
script that is so bad that it is
suicidal; akin to jumping off
the Golden Gate Bridge.

gorilla. An enormous hit
(movie, play, record); a
blockbuster.

Green Room. Place in which actors, actresses, television-
show guests, etc., wait to go
on.

grip. Technician/handyman on
a movie set. Hollywood's version of the Broadway stage-
hand.

gross player. Movie actor who is
a big enough star to be able
to act for a percentage of a
film's gross income.

H

hammer. A handyman on a
movie set.

hammock. To program a weak
television show between two
strong ones.

heat. In Hollywoodese it is
either (1) talent or (2) word of
mouth.

HINT. Acronym for Happy
Idiot News Team, or Happy
Idiot News Talk, both inside
references to the encourage-
ment of banter and chit-chat
between segments of the local TV news.

hoofer. Dancer.

house nut. The operating and
overhead expenses of one
who shows a movie. It must
be overcome before a profit
can be posted.

housewife time. Name for the
period from ten A.M. to three
P.M. in radio. Compare with
drive time.

I

idiot cards. Cue cards, or sheets of cardboard on which a performer's lines are written.

Industry, The. The motion-picture business; Hollywood. Compare with *The Business*.

indy. Independent television station.

indyprod. Hollywoodese for "independent producer."

in the can. A movie that has been shot but is still not ready for distribution.

K

key grip. The head of the grip department, which on a motion-picture set is in charge of setting camera equipment and devices that control shadows.

kidvid. Television or home video for children.

L

lavaliere. (1) A small microphone used in television which fits around the person's neck or can be clipped to the person's lapel or dress. (2) To attach a microphone:

"Lavaliere the lady for the cooking demo."

legs. Strength and longevity at the box office.

M

major. one of the top distributors of movies (Universal, Columbia, Paramount, etc.).

mike sock. Foam rubber sleeve that fits over the business end of a microphone. It helps cut down on the extraneous sounds created by wind, heavy breathing, and the like.

MOR. Middle of the road. That which appeals to middle-class, middle-aged Americans; light rock, for instance.

MOS. Man on the street; target for quick interviews.

N

nix. To refuse, ban, overrule. A term from *Variety*.

nonpro. Person outside the movie industry.

nostril shot. Unflattering camera angle on television.

numbers. Receipts in Hollywood. A movie that is grossing a lot is said to have "good numbers."

O

O & O. A station that is owned and operated by the network, as opposed to an affiliate.

oater. Movie western, from the oats that horses eat. A vintage term from *Variety* which still comes into play when someone plans to film a western.

overnights. The overnight ratings in television.

P

payola. A term from *Variety* for an illegal payoff made to get air time for a record.

people meter. Device for registering-in home response to television.

personality. One who plays themselves on radio or television. A man who does a music and talk show for commuters on their way to work is known as a "morning personality."

phoner. (1) Radio talk-show interview conducted by telephone. (2) A false—or phony—plot device, whether it be in Hollywood or on Broadway.

points. Percentage of ownership in a movie or play.

Q

Q. Recognition. It comes from TV-Q, a system that rates actors by their recognition by television viewers. One gets more money if one has a high-Q.

R

riggers and juicers. Crew of electrical assistants who work on a movie set to set up and control lights.

rim shot. Comic punctuation from a drummer, it comes immediately after the punch line of a joke.

S

scrambler. Device used to keep cable-television subscribers from getting pay stations and events without paying for them. A decoder is required to unscramble a scrambler.

scrim. (1) To soften the intensity of a light. (2) A screen or curtain used to create the effect of mistiness on stage or on the screen.

segue. (1) To move from one thing to another. (2) Transition, as in "That was a nice segue." Pronounced "seg-way," the word is Spanish.

shock jock. Radio disc jockey whose speciality is off-color material and general irreverence and rudeness.

sitcom. Situation comedy. A term from *Variety.*

skitcom. Comedy format in which the star or stars shows up in unrelated comedy skits. As this is written, the "Queen of the Skitcom" is Fox's Tracy Ullman.

slasher movie. As defined by film critic Roger Ebert, "movies starring a mad-dog killer who runs amok, slashing all of the other characters."

sleaze TV. Talk shows featuring sex, gore, and sensationalism. The same thing as *trash TV.*

slot. Time period in television programming.

special. Anything not in the normal television schedule of programs. Television commonly puts its mistakes and visual typos into prime-time "bloopers" packages and calls them specials.

splatter movie. In which there is a lot of blood and gore.

stretch. An actor reaching or working hard to fit into a part, as opposed to a natural fit. This term has become part of a common talk-show question—"Was that a stretch for you or did it come easy?"

stunting. Television tricks used to hook an audience at the beginning of the year or during a rating period. The tricks include special two-hour episodes, guest appearances, and tie-ins with other shows.

superstation. A local television station that has been distributed to cable systems nationwide via satellite.

─────────── **T** ───────────

talent. Performer, as in "Do we need limos for the talent?"

30 Rock. Headquarters of the National Broadcasting Company, which is at 30 Rockefeller Plaza.

toilet. A second-rate or small-time nightclub or comedy club, in the parlance of stand-up comics.

topline. To get top billing in a play or movie.

topspin. Momentum in Hollywood.

trades, the. The magazines and newspapers that serve the entertainment industry.

trash TV. Talk shows featuring sex, gore and sensationalism. The same as *sleaze TV*.

turnaround. In Hollywood, the dropping of a project by one studio, thereby making it available to another.

_____ **U** _____

up-front exposure. Money put up to get a film started, regardless of whether it is actually made.

_____ **V** _____

voice-over or VO. Describing a commercial or other television item on which the voice of an announcer is heard but the person is not seen.

_____ **W** _____

weeper. Sad movie.

wide / wide break. Exposure for a movie. A film that opens "wide" is likely to debut on close to 2000 screens.

wipe. (1) To bring one scene in on top of another on film or television. (2) To fire a person.

wrangler. In Hollywood, a person who is in charge of animals that will appear in a film.

_____ **Y** _____

yawner. Boring show. A term from *Variety*.

SOURCES

The Tamony Collection provided special help in preparing this collection, as did several columns by William Safire which originally appeared in *The New York Times*, and many clippings provided by Charles D. Poe. Cydney Erickson-Feinstein also contributed.

18

POLITICAL SLANG— CONGRESSIONAL VERSION

The Lingo of the Hill People

"Most of what is said in Congress sounds like a foreign language and requires an interpreter . . . Congress becomes so entangled in vocabulary that people often have to work past midnight to figure out what they're doing."

—Susan Trausch writing in the *Washington Post*, March 16, 1986

A

A.A. Administrative Assistant. The top staff aide in a congressional office. Very few people on the Hill actually ever call someone by their full title, but tend to refer to Congressman Smith's A.A. or the senator's *L.A.*

affair. fund-raising event. Congressional affairs range from bull roasts to fancy dinners, and the cost of admission to one of them can range from $10 to $1000.

are they in / are they out? Questions asked to determine if Congress has reconvened (in session) or adjourned (out of session).

Atari Democrats. Those who foresee a bright future in high technology and electronics. The term was coined by Elizabeth Drew of the *New Yorker,* who alluded to the electronic game and computer company. It lost some of its appeal in 1983 when Atari cut its U.S. work force and moved those jobs to Taiwan.

B

Boll Weevils. Nickname for conservative southern Democrats—pests who keep the pressure on the Democratic majority.

bomb thrower. Anyone who will not compromise.

bundling. The practice of a PAC (political action committee) giving an elected representative a bundle of smaller checks as opposed to one large one.

bunk. (1) Meaningless oratory designed to impress one's constituency. (2) Politics viewed with a cynical eye.

C

casework. The business of dealing with the problems of constituents. It is a constant in the workings of a congressional office and commands a major portion of staff time.

caseworker. Staff member whose prime responsibility is constituent problems.

caucus. (1) A meeting of party members in either house to elect leaders and set the legislative agenda. (2) Any informal gathering of lawmakers working on a course of legislative action. (3) A group that meets regularly to monitor and advance the interests of a specific group.

Christmas tree bill. A bill that has been adorned with extra, often unrelated pieces of legislation.

clean bill. A new version of a bill, replete with a new number, prepared after a committee has reworked the original. It allows the bill to move on its own rather than having each revision voted on individually.

cloakroom. A large room just off the floor of either chamber which serves as a combination communications center and meeting place. Each party has a separate cloakroom off the floor of either house.

closure. The same as *cloture*.

cloture. Process by which debate can be limited in the Senate without unanimous consent. When invoked by roll-call vote, it limits each senator to one hour of debate.

coattail. The ability of a presidential candidate to help win seats in Congress for members of his party.

D

dark side of the moon. The House of Representatives in contemporary Hill slang.

"Dear Colleague." Traditional salutation used in letters in which one member asks another for support or cosponsorship of a bill. Defined deftly in Sue Grabowski's *Congressional Intern Handbook* as "hustle" in the form of a letter.

demagogue it. To take a dramatic, grandstanding position on an issue without necessarily supporting or believing in the position; to mislead with spirit.

district work period. Congressional recess.

doorkeeper. Person who has various duties ranging from announcing the President's arrival in Congress to the control of gallery passes.

dove. Legislator who is specifically against military intervention by the U.S. and generally against increased military spending of any kind. The dove's opposite number is the *hawk,* and a well-known Congressional watering hole is the Hawk & Dove.

duck. A pest or nuisance, such as a lobbyist.

E

Everest committee. Any congressional team organized to investigate something just because, like Mount Everest, it's there. "I hear tell," Will Rogers once wrote, "Congress is a mite concerned with its members' tendency to form a committee at the drop of a hat. But everything's all right now. Congress has just announced it's forming a committee to investigate."

executive session. A meeting closed to the public and the press.

F

filibuster. To delay or stop action on a bill in the Senate through constant talking. It is a time-honored technique which is almost always employed by a minority to defeat a measure favored by the majority.

floor. The working area of the Senate or House chamber.

freshman. A newly elected member serving his first term. In the House, freshmen regard themselves as a class, as in the freshman class of the 100th Congress, and elect class officers.

G

gag rule. Any special rule that limits the debate on a bill.

-gate. The common congressional suffix for scandals since Watergate, as in Koreagate and Irangate. The original scandal was named for the Watergate apartment complex where the incident that first announced the problem took place. Also popular is the -scam suffix, as found in ABSCAM, Contrascam, and Debatescam. The original name was the FBI code name for its foray into the realm of congressional ethics. ABSCAM stood for AraB SCAM, a reference to the front group for the operation, the bogus "Abdul Enterprises."

gavel-to-gavel. The period from the moment either house convenes until the moment it adjourns.

gerrymander. To design or redesign a congressional district to unfairly favor the party in power by taking advantage of traditional voting patterns.

ghost senator. Sometime slang for a strong Administrative Assistant.

ghost speech. A speech that is never delivered but appears in the *Congressional Record* or the printed record of a committee.

goat. Derogatory slang for a constituent.

goat food. Shameless political posturing.

goo-goos. Forces of and for *go*od *go*vernment. The League of Women Voters is a perennial source of goo-gooism. Although the term sounds intensely defamatory, it is often used with a certain degree of affection.

grassroots. The folks back home; people who are not in the business of politics.

gray ghost. A senator's or representative's chief staffer.

greenies. Environmentalists. Derived from West Germany's Green party and the international Greenpeace movement.

Gypsy Moth. Republican moderate. According to William Safire in his *New York Times Magazine* column on language, the term was created by Rep. Lawrence DeNardis (R.-Conn.) who said that the gypsy moth was as much of a nuisance in New England and the Great Lakes as the *Boll Weevil* is down South.

H

hawk. One who tends to favor military intervention and increased military appropriations. Compare with *dove*.

head count. The supposed lineup of votes for a bill, amendment, or confirmation.

Hill, the. (1) Congress. (2) The neighborhood surrounding the U.S. Congress.

hit list. A group that has been targeted for removal, whether they be members of Congress or federal employees. The group may be legislators who the White House would like to see defeated in the next election or a group of government officials the administration would like to get rid of.

hopper. The box on the House clerk's desk where bills are placed on introduction. In the Senate bills are introduced by verbal announcement.

hustings. Where election speeches are made.

I

influence peddler. Lawyer, lobbyist, or anyone ese who seeks special privileges from Congress for his clients. The term, which entered American political slang in the early 1950s, is reserved for those who are paid for their skills.

J

junket. Derogatory term for an expenses-paid trip made by a member of Congress. A trip is a junket if paid for by public funds or by a special interest group.

L

L.A. Legislative Assistant, the person in a congressional office who is in charge of legislation.

lame duck. (1) Name for an incumbent member who has lost an election but whose term has still not run out. (2) Adjective applied to Congress after November elections and the convening of a new Congress in January.

lawyer's bill. Any bill that, if enacted, would create a lot of confusion and litigation.

Leadership, The. How Congress refers to its officers and ranking committee members.

leaning. Status of a legislator who is still uncommitted on a major upcoming vote but tending—or leaning—toward one side or the other.

leg counsel. Short for legislative counsel.

limousine liberal. A wealthy political liberal.

logrolling. Horse-trading vote to get important—or pet—bills passed.

love fest. Label slapped on any overt display of bipartisan cooperation.

L-word. Liberal, especially in the context of the negative notion of one soft on crime, drugs, and wasteful government spending.

M

McGovern Democrat. Term that has come to mean a liberal whose beliefs are so far to the left that the person is out of the mainstream of American politics. It is a reference to Senator George McGovern and his 1972 candidacy, in which he strongly opposed U.S. policy in Southeast Asia.

MEGO. Acronym for My Eyes Glaze Over; bored. Common Washington response that has become a fond bit of Hill shorthand.

must list. Legislation that must be passed during a session. For example, the Senate Majority Leader might have two items on his must list at a given moment.

N

nonpaper. A briefing paper that is circulated around the Hill but does not carry the author's name.

O

oilies. Nickname for oil industry lobbyists.

Old Guard. Originally applied to the conservative element in the Republican Party, it is now used for any long-established group—for instance, old-guard southern Democrats.

omnibus bill. Any piece of proposed legislation that deals with a variety of subjects.

one-minute. A speech lasting no more than sixty seconds, which a member of the House can make on any topic before the official start of business.

orange pouch. Marked mail sack for expedited delivery to member's home district or state. Also known as "gold bag."

other end of Pennsylvania Avenue, the. One of the ways that Congress refers to the White House, and vice versa.

over on the floor. Reference to the chambers where the two houses meet.

P

PAC. Acronym for Political Action Committee.

pigeonhole. To kill a bill by keeping it in committee and not reporting it to the larger body. The term comes from the cubicles—or pigeonholes—in the old congressional desks.

platform. The principles that a political party stands for during an election.

pork. Funds from the *pork barrel.*

pork barrel. Nickname for the Federal Treasury into which legislators "dip" to finance projects for their home districts. The process of lining up locally popular projects, such as special highway extensions, is known as "pork barrel politics."

postcard pressure. Collective impact of constituent mail, with special reference to the printed postcards that are often in the arsenal of special interest groups.

posture. (1) To make an obvious bid for attention on an issue without really doing anything. For instance, to make an abstract attack on government corruption. (2) Military preparedness.

public trough. Where consultants, corporations, and

other members' constituents feed greedily.

pump priming. The process of using federal funds to stimulate the economy, whether it be the national economy or a local one.

R

railroad. To push or jam a bill through Congress.

revenue enhancement. Hill talk for taxes when one does not want to mention taxes. Another euphemism cropped up in 1982 when a tax increase was proposed and was described as "updating the revenue mechanism." Still another: "closing loopholes."

robo. (1) A form letter members use to answer some of their constituent mail. These letters are generated by a robotype machine which also provides a facsimile signature. (2) The robotype machine itself.

S

safe seat. Incumbency that attracts no more than token opposition.

safety net. Level of established financial support for individuals through Social Security, Medicare, Welfare programs, and Veteran's Assistance.

Sagebrush Rebels. Informal but cohesive band of western legislators whose major concern since the late 1960s has been local control over the millions of acres of federal land that lie west of the Rockies.

seatwarmer. A senator or representative who has been appointed by a governor to fill a vacancy, with the understanding that he or she will *not* run in the next election.

six-pack Republican. Sometimes known as "Joe Six-Pack Republican." Populist GOP member or candidate.

sleaze factor. That component of an administration, political party, etc., which is corrupt, unethical, controversial, scandal-ridden, or otherwise under a cloud.

smoking gun. Metaphor used at either end of Pennsylvania Avenue for unequivocal guilt, as if one has walked in on a man with a smoking gun in his hand standing over a bullet-ridden body. Just before the Senate report on the Iran-contra affair was released in 1987, Senator David Boren (D-Okla.) was quoted as saying, "There's no smoking gun."

Squish. Nickname for an uncommitted conservative.

stump. To travel around giving political speeches. The term derives from the speech from the stump of a tree, one given on the road, usually in a small town.

————— **T** —————

three I's. Three countries with large natural constituencies among the American population: Ireland, Israel, and Italy.

tie the President's hands. Words commonly summoned when a legislator decides not to challenge the administration, as in "I won't tie the President's hands on this one." It is more commonly invoked during foreign policy debates.

towered. Drunk. This term showed up in the weeks following the rejection of John Tower as Defense Secretary, as in "Let's go out and get towered."

tree huggers. Environmentalists who come to Congress to lobby their cause.

————— **W** —————

war chest. Campaign kitty; funds held in reserve by an incumbent to fend off future challengers.

whip. (1) Member of each party in each house who is charged with the responsibility of rallying the party to pass or defeat a piece of legislation. The position amounts to that of assistant party leader. (2) To act as a whip; such as "whipping the Ohio delegation."

winger. A person of the far right or left.

SOURCES

A number of sources contributed to this glossary, including years of reading about Congress in the *Washington Post*, the *Congressional Record*, and *Roll Call*.

19 | REAL ESTATE

Vocabulary to Go with a 3 br./ CAC/WBFP

The real estate business is fueled by contracts, liens, easements, and the like—legal paperwork. This guarantees that much real estate jargon sounds identical to legal jargon. On the other hand, there is the fancy-smancy real estate sales talk that turns a covered parking space into a *porte cochere,* a covered patio into a *lanai,* and can turn any corner with a sink and a stove into a *kitchenette.*

Somewhere in between legalese and the bloated language of the sales brochure lies real estate slang. It sounds like this:

A

alligator. Investment property whose income does not cover insurance, mortgage, and taxes. The presumption here is that an alligator "eats" capital.

anchor. Major element around which a shopping center or mall is built. Depending on the size of the develpment, an anchor might be one or more major department stores, a supermarket, or a large discount store.

ARM. Acronym for Adjustable Rate Mortgage.

B

balloon. A final payment on a loan or mortgage that calls for an unusually large amount of money. It is one that has ballooned at the end.

binder. Payment that keeps a property from being sold for a specified period of time.

birdbath. Paved area that holds water (even though it was not meant to).

boilerplate. Time-tested language in deeds, leases, and other agreements.

buydown / buydown mortgage. Arrangement under which a buyer is allowed discounted, below-market interest rates for the first few years of a long-term, fixed-rate mortgage.

C

CAC. Real estate ad abbr. for central air-conditioning.

catslide. Term that is used in some parts of the South for a style of house that is called "salt box colonial" or "salt box" in the rest of the country.

CC&R's. Covenants, Conditions, and Restrictions—the limitations placed on deeds.

choke point. Point at which mortgage interest rates prompt strong resistance by potential home buyers. The choke point for most consumers is about thirteen percent.

clear title. Ownership without a *cloud*.

cloud. An outstanding encumbrance, such as an unpaid tax lien.

condo. Condominium.

crank. Refinancing an existing mortgage obligation.

creative financing. Nonconventional loan.

D

dockominium. A marina which is run like a condominium, with each member owning his or her own slip.

downstroke. Seed money for an investment.

E

earnest money. Cash used to bind a sale.

ego pricing. Describing a situation in which a seller demands too high a price for a property because of the value he or she places on improvements and decor.

empty-nesters. Couples with grown children who no longer live at home.

F

Fannie Mae. Federal National Mortgage Assocation.

first. A first mortgage, used to distinguish it from a *second*.

fizzbo. Realtor's pejorative term for "for sale by owner."

front foot. The property line that joins the street, body of water, public way, etc.

front money. Down payment.

G

garbage fees. Exorbitant but legal fees charged by lenders at settlement.

gazump. Raising the price of a property after a deal has been struck (but no contract has been signed). This term, current in America, originated in England, where it has been a major factor in the real estate market. The Sunday *Telegraph* for April 5, 1987, cited "the problems of gazumping as a major cause of one in three buyers' purchases falling through after an offer has been accepted."

Ginnie Mae. Government National Mortgage Association.

grandfather. To allow a flaw or violation to remain. It comes from the grandfather clause, a provision in a new law or a regulation that exempts those in existing property.

H

handyman special. In need of repair. This term has been applied to houses in such dire and dilapidated condition that it is now something of a joke.

hard money. Money put into improved ownership or equity. Compare with *soft money*.

haver. Person who owns (has) a property that will satisfy a buyer's needs.

_____ **I** _____

inside lot. Lot that is not on a corner.

_____ **J** _____

junior/junior lien. Claim against property that can only be exercised after a prior claim has been settled.

_____ **K** _____

kennel. Substandard house; a dog.

kicker. Loan surcharges.

kiddy condo. Condominium that is bought by parents for a child to live in while in college.

knockdown. Structure built from preassembled components.

_____ **L** _____

LULU. Acronym for Locally Unwanted Land Use.

_____ **M** _____

Maggie Mae. Mortgage Guaranty Insurance Corporation.

mall. v. To build a large regional shopping center. The development of many of these malls over the last twenty years has been referred to as the "malling" of America.

meeting of the minds. Mutual agreement at the time of contract.

mingling. Term for those who share properties—apartments, condos, house—to help pay for the cost of housing.

monkey. Mortgage, sometimes phrased as "monkey on the house" or "monkey with a long tail."

_____ **N** _____

NIMBY. "Not in my backyard." Rallying cry of those who oppose halfway houses and nuclear waste dumps.

_____ **O** _____

open house. Period when a property can be viewed without an appointment.

P

pink house syndrome. Term for the tendency of some people to do something to their home to make it more saleable, but which actually makes it harder to sell—such as painting it pink.

PITI. Initialism for principal, interest, taxes, and insurance, used to express the monthly payments on a property.

podmall. Small convenience-oriented shopping center serving a neighborhood; a *strip* center.

points. Fee charged by lender for making a loan. Points are over and above the cost of interest, and one point is equal to one percent of the mortgage amount.

puffing. "Misleading but not wholly untrue statements that are sometimes made to sell real estate," according to Thomas and Charles F. Hemphill in their *Essential Dictionary of Real Estate Terminology.*

Q

qualifying. Process by which real estate agents eliminate nonbuyers and concentrate on those eager and able to buy.

R

railroad flat. Apartment set up with one room after another so that you have to pass through one room to get to the rest.

redlining. Lending policy that prevents loans in certain areas. It is an illegal tactic used to thwart racial integration in housing.

rehab. Rehabilitate.

S

sandwich / sandwich lease. Three-party rental agreement between landlord, the original tenant, and a tenant who is subletting the property.

second. A second mortgage on a property that already has a mortgage, known as a *first*.

soft money. Money put into interest. Compare with *hard money*.

starter home. Cheap, low-end home.

strip. v. To build a small community shopping center; a

convenience *mall.* "Stripping" is "malling" on a smaller scale.

T

teaser rate. A first-year mortgage rate that is below the going rate, also known as a "starter rate." They are offered to make adjustable-rate mortgages more attractive.

U

upgrades. Improvements.

W

WBFP. Woodburning fireplace. One of many common real estate abbrs. that provide a language of their own. Most are easy, but some are puzzlers for the uninitiated: ROW, RHFP, BBHA, and FHW respectively stand for "right of way," "raised hearth fireplace," "baseboard hot air," and "forced hot water."

Y

yield. To surrender or give up a property.

Z

zero lot line. Describing a portion of a property where there is no yard; where the edge of the building is the edge of the property.

SOURCES
Gina Cressey helped with this chapter.

20

SEX, THE BODY, AND BODILY FUNCTIONS

R-Rated Terms You Probably Won't Find in Your Collegiate Dictionary

"You can hardly assert that their inclusion would ruin the morals of the multitude?"

—Eric Partridge asking one of the editors of the *Oxford English Dictionary* in 1947 or 1948 why the words *cunt* and *fuck* were excluded. They have since been installed. From the London *Times Literary Section*, November 28, 1975.

First came sexual euphemism. There was a time when Dr. Thomas Bowdler brought us a cleaned-up edition of Shakespeare's works in which a "gipsy's lust" became a "gipsy's will." And there were the writers of the last century who could not bring themselves to write words like *trousers* and *breeches* and settled for terms like *inexpressibles* and *unmentionables*.

Slang of the most forthright kind came forward to replace all of this. It was there all the time, but this was center-stage stuff. Linguistically, we let it all hang out, and modern speakers and writers held nothing back—"today an asterisk in a book is as rare as a virgin

194

in life," said one startled critic not that long ago. When the smoke cleared, all the old dirty words and their hyphenated variations were in standard dictionaries, and Hollywood started vetting scripts by making sure these words were included, not excluded. (Is it my imagination or is there a law that requires all movies made after 1965 to have the word *asshole* in the dialogue?) Small town theaters offered X-rated movies with titles like the redundant *Sluts in Heat*, and couples went shopping for sexual toys as if they were out to buy a Cuisinart.

Of late, however, it has become apparent that the words that the Federal Communications Commission used to call the "big six" (those that could not be used on the radio: piss, fart, shit, fuck, cock, and cunt) will always be with us and for all intents and purposes are no longer slang, but part of standard dictionary English. Many of them have little or nothing to do with sex or elimination anymore but are what kids used to call "curse words."

Modern sexual slang, on the other hand, does not make the dictionary and tends to be more of a throwback to euphemism than four-letter-word directness. We hung on to some of the Victorian urge to euphemize. In 1990 it is still common to ask a woman visitor if she "would like to powder her nose," and there are those who call a graveyard a "garden of remembrance." Euphemism has made the universe a little less perilous and harsh. Without a little euphemism, strikes would be harder to avert, fights would be harder to avoid, and parents would be dumbstruck when it came to explaining "the birds and the bees."

Here are a number of the terms—old and new—that are part of today's sexual slang. By its nature it is a sampling. One could make a list of more than a hundred of the coded terms used only in personal classified ads, and several hundred nicknames for the penis.

A

adult. Dirty; sexually explicit.
ass bandit. Homosexual, male.

B

bag. Condom.
bazongas. Breasts.
B.C. Birth control.
bearded clam. Female genitalia.
beauty spot. Female genitalia.
bed hop. To sleep around.
belly ride. Copulation.
bi/bicycle. Bisexual.
big brown eyes. Nipples and areolas.
big daddy. Penis.
blow your top. Achieve sexual climax.
blue steeler. A particularly virile erection.
boner. Erection.
boobs. Breasts.
bouncy-bouncy. Sexual act.
box tonsils. (Collegiate) To kiss passionately.
breeder. Homosexual term for a heterosexual.
buckets. Breasts.

C

cakes. Buttocks.
catcher's mitt. Diaphragm.
Coney Island whitefish. Condom.

cork. Tampon.
crack of heaven. Female genitalia.
cum. Semen.
cut. circumcised.

D

daisy chain. Three or more people linked sexually at the same time.
diddle. (1) To copulate. (2) To play with sexually.
D.O.M. Dirty old man.
dry run. To bring to climax without undressing.
dyke. Homosexual, female.

E

ear sex. Phone sex.
eleventh finger. The penis.
enema bandit. Homosexual.
exhaust pipe. The anus.

F

family jewels. Male genitalia.
fern. Female genitalia.
fish skin. Condom.
flesh session. Copulation.
French letter. Condom.
French tickler. Condom.
fun bags. Breasts.

G

Garden of Eden. The female genitalia.

getting your plumbing snaked. One of a number of terms for sexual intercourse in the "getting your" genre: getting your drain cleaned, getting your rocks off, getting your ashes hauled, etc.

glove. Condom.

go over the mountain. Achieve sexual climax.

group grope. Orgy.

G spot. An erotic zone or point of passion. Originally a specific spot on the upper vaginal wall and named for its discoverer, German gynecologist Ernst Grafenberg, it is now used generically.

H

hide the salami. Copulate.

hobble. To have sex.

hobbler. Slut.

hooters. Breasts.

horizontal bop. (Collegiate) Copulation.

horse. Condom, specifically a Trojan (from Trojan horse).

Hudson River whitefish. Condom.

hump. To copulate.

hung. Describing a well-endowed male; big. Often stated in simile form as "hung like a bull," "hung like a rabbit," etc.

J

jo-bag / jolly bag. Condom.

Johnnie. Penis.

joy hole. Female genitalia.

K

knob. Penis.

kosher. Circumcised.

L

labonza. Buttocks.

lay your cane in a dusty corner. To copulate. This metaphor implies the participants may be old.

lech. Lecher.

les. Lesbian.

love juice. Semen.

lubie. Lubricated condom.

M

Magnum. Oversized condom or penis.

Manhattan eel. Condom.

maracas. Breasts.

marital aid. Sexual toy such as a vibrator or dildo.

Maypole. Large penis.

McQ. Quickie, from the Mc of McDonald's of fast-food fame.

Mount Joy. Female genitalia.

Mr. Happy. Penis.

mustache ride. Oral sex. In this regard sideburns are "thigh ticklers."

_____ **N** _____

nookie. Sexual intercourse.

nooner. Sex at noon. (Incidentally, the sentence "Sex at noon taxes" is a palindrome, a word or sentence that reads the same forward and backward.)

_____ **O** _____

O. Orgasm.

one-eyed wonder. Penis.

one-night stand. One-time sexual encounter.

OTR. "On the rag"; menstruating.

over the shoulder boulder holder. Bra.

_____ **P** _____

parallel parking. (Collegiate) Copulate.

parsley patch. Pubic hair. By extension, "to take a trip around the parsley patch" is to have sex.

Peter, Paul, and Mary. Ménage à trois.

plug. Tampon.

pluke. To have sexual intercourse.

pood. (Rhymes with "wood") Penis.

pop one's cookies. Ejaculate.

porking. Copulation.

Port Said garter. Condom.

propho. Condom.

prunes. Testicles.

pud. Penis.

punchboard. Promiscuous female.

_____ **Q** _____

quickie. Fast sexual interlude.

_____ **R** _____

racks. Breasts.

raincoat. Condom.

Roman. A person with a proclivity for orgies, used in personal classified ads.

roto rooter. Penis.

rough rider. Ribbed condom.

_____ **S** _____

safe. Condom. This is an old term meaning "to have sex with birth control" but given a new meaning in the context of "safe sex."

shoot your wad. To achieve sexual climax.

shower cap. Condom.

shtup. To copulate.

skin. Condom.

slam. (1) Sexual intercourse. (2) Female genitalia.

snatch. Female genitalia.

stern-wheeler. Homosexual, mate.

strange. Sex with a stranger or out-of-towner, as in "Got me some strange."

switch hitter. Bisexual person.

T

T&A. Tits and ass.

tatas. Breasts.

threesome. Sex involving three people.

titty shake. Topless bar.

tongue wrestle. Deep kissing.

tonsil hockey. (Collegiate) Deep kissing.

toys. Sexual aids and pleasure enhancers.

trouser trout. Penis. By extension, "fishing for trouser trout" is masturbation, while "fishing for brown trout" is anal intercourse.

tube steak. Penis.

T.V. Transvestite.

twig. Vibrator with a slender business end.

U

udders. Breasts.

V

Venus mound. Female genitalia.

W

wall job. Stand-up sex.

W/E. Well-endowed, in the code of the personal classifieds.

wide on. Female version of *hard on;* aroused.

X

XXX. Particularly graphic and explicit depiction of sex.

Y

Y, the. Crotch, female. By extension, "eating at the Y" is cunnilingus, oral sex.

SOURCES

This collection was aided with material found in the journal *Maledicta,* the *Journal of Verbal Aggression, Playboy,* the Tamony Collection, and *Modern English* by the pseudonymous Jennifer Blowdryer (Last Gasp Press, 1985). Important help came from Robert T. West, Charles D. Poe, Leonard R. N. Ashley, Reinhold Aman, and Amanda Feinstein. Scott Callis also contributed.

21 | SPORTS SLANG

Introductory Jockese

"What am I supposed to believe when some TV announcer talks about a nose guard making a key tackle? Come on. A nose guard is a piece of equipment.
"And what is this nickel defense? I used to know a guy named Floyd Nickel. Pretty good athlete. You don't suppose? No, no. He went into auto insurance."

—Michael Kernan in the *Washington Post*, September 11, 1982

Sports slang is in a class by itself. It is so vast and extensive that its terminology is counted in the thousands. I authored a baseball dictionary in 1989; it contained more than 5000 terms, of which the vast majority were slang. But that is baseball. What about a pastime as humble as marbles? (About the only thing that the author excelled at as a kid.) I have begun a collection of marble terms because they are fast becoming archaic and will soon be "lost," and have already come up with more than 300. There are more.

Given this state of affairs, a compromise has been struck and a sampling of slang from various sports has been compiled. Each term has been labeled for the sport it comes from. Those terms that apply to a number of sports are labeled "basic jock talk."

A

airball. (Basketball) Shot that misses the rim of the basket.

aircraft carrier. (Basketball) the big man; a driver whose dominance can make a team a winner.

alley oop. (Basketball) A high lobbed shot-pass that is tipped in by a player near the basket.

also ran. (Horseracing) Describing a horse that finishes out of the money—that is, comes in fourth or worse.

armchair quarterback. Fan of televised sports who thinks he has most of the answers, not restricted to football or even sports (one can, for example, be a political armchair quarterback.)

audible. (Football) Play that is called verbally by the offensive team after it has positioned itself over the ball.

B

barnburner. (Basic jock talk) An exciting contest.

bases drunk. (Baseball) Bases loaded.

bathtub. (Skiing) Mark left in snow from a fall on the seat of the pants; a "sitzmark."

beanball. (Baseball) Pitch aimed at a batter's head.

bedposts. (Bowling) The 7–10 split.

bench warmer. (Basic jock talk) Player who is seldom brought into the game.

bird cage. (Basic jock talk) Protective face mask.

blitz. (Football) A massive attempt by the defense to penetrate the offensive line and ground (tackle) the quarterback.

boards. (Basketball) Backboards.

bogie. (Golf) One stroke over par.

bomb. (Football) An extremely long pass.

boogie. (Basketball) To drive fast.

book. (Basic jock talk) (1) To run fast; to *boogie*. (2) Data on an opponent.

bootleg. (Football) Any play in which a man carrying the ball pretends to give it to a teammate, then hides the ball on his hip and takes off.

bow. (Basketball) Elbow.

bucket. (Basketball) A field goal.

bulk up. (Basic jock talk) To add to muscle size by exercise and weight lifting.

bump and run. (Football) For a

pass defender to bump into a potential receiver (which is legal) to upset his balance and then run alongside him.

burn. (Basic jock talk) To score or beat.

burner. (1) (Basic jock talk) Pinched nerve. (2) (Football) Speedy wide receiver, who can "burn" the opposition.

buttonhook. (Football) Forward pass play in which the receiver runs downfield and then stops to turn evasively (hook) toward the passer.

C

camp. (Basketball) To establish oneself, such as "camping in the *paint*."

card. (Basic jock talk) Scorecard.

cellar. (Basic jock talk) Last place.

cement. (Skiing) Heavy, wet snow.

chalk talk. (Basic jock talk) Strategy session with a blackboard.

charity stripe. (Basketball) The foul line.

cheap shot. (Basic jock talk) Unsportsmanlike conduct.

check. (Hockey) To impede the progress of an opponent by use of the body (body check),

or the stick (poke check, or stick check).

cherry pick. (Basketball) To remain near the basket while play is at the other end of the court in hopes of getting a long pass and an undefended basket.

chops. (Boxing) The jaw.

coast to coast. (Basketball) Taking a rebound and singlehandedly taking it to the other end of the court for a basket.

combo coverage. (Football) Defensive football in which man-to-man and zone defense are combined.

cookie monster. (Bowling) A 5–7–10 split.

cords. (Basketball) The net below the rim of the basket. A quotation by Dave De-Busschere displayed at the Basketball Hall of Fame in Springfield, Mass., says, "It's kind of nice to get out there and make a couple of shots and hear the cords sort of talk back to you when you make a good jump shot."

counter. (Football) A play that goes in the opposite direction of its original movement.

cousin. (Baseball) A pitcher that a batter usually finds he can hit well.

crackback. (Football) Blocking maneuver by a pass receiver who runs downfield and then turns around to clear out the man covering him.

crawling. (Football) An attempt by a ball carrier to advance the ball after he has hit the ground.

cup. (Basic jock talk) A hard cup-shaped device for protecting the male genitals.

D

deef. (Tennis) Default.

dish. (Baseball) Home plate.

divot. (Golf) A piece of sod cut and lifted out of the ground by the clubhead.

does windows. (Basketball) Can dunk the ball.

dog it. (Basic jock talk) To play lackadaisically; to goof off.

dogleg. (Golf) A sharp turn on the fairway.

downtown. (Basketball) Deep. A three-point shot will come from downtown.

Dutch 200. (Bowling) Rolling a 200 game with alternative strikes and spares.

E

eagle. (Golf) Two strokes under par.

eat the ball. (Football) For a potential passer to hold onto the ball and be tackled (for a loss of yardage) rather than throw it.

elbow. (Basketball) Corner of the painted area under the basket. A player may shoot from the elbow.

enduro. (Basic jock talk) Endurance race.

F

fade. (Football) To gradually move backward or laterally.

favorite. (Basic jock but also common to horseracing) Team or entry in a contest who seems to be more likely to win.

finger roll. (Basketball) A basket that is made as the ball rolls off the tips of the shooter's fingers.

flanker. (Football) An offensive player set into a position beyond the end before the ball is put into play.

flats. (Football) The areas on either extremity of the line of scrimmage and extending about five yards into defensive territory. A "flat pass" is one thrown into this area for short yardage.

flow. (Football) The direction in which the players are moving after the play has begun.

footer. (Basketball) Big, slower player.

free trip. (Baseball) Base on balls.

furniture. (Tennis) Racket frame.

G

good hands. (Basic jock talk) The ability to catch a ball.

graveyard. (Bowling) Low-scoring lane.

gridiron. (Football) The field itself, from the appearance of its horizontal lines, which are spaced five yards apart.

gun shy. (Basic jock talk) Overly cautious, especially after an injury.

H

Hail Mary. (Football) A pass thrown into the end zone into a crowd of receivers and defenders. This is a desperation play commonly attempted in the last few minutes of a game by a team that is losing.

hangtime. (1) (Basketball) The duration of the time a player spends in the air—or hangs—while driving to the basket.

(2) (Football) The time a kicked ball hangs in the air.

hat trick. (Hockey) Individual feat of scoring three or more goals in a single game.

hawg. (Fishing) Big bass to a bass fisherman ("bassin' man.")

homebrew. (Basic jock talk) Locally bred player.

host. (Basic jock talk) To be the home team.

hot dog / hotdog. (Basic jock talk) (1) One who shows off. (2) To show off.

I

iceman. Hockey player.

inside. (Football) The interior line; between the tackles.

in-your-face. (Basketball) Describing a disrespectful or disdainful style of play.

iron man/woman. (Basic jock talk) One who chooses to play though injured.

J

jam. (Basketball) To dunk.

jock. (Basic jock talk) (1) An athletic supporter or jockstrap, for short. (2) An athlete. (3) Describing that which is athletic in nature, such as a "jock school" or "jock [fraternity] house."

K

keeper. (Football) Offensive play in which the quarterback holds onto and runs with the ball rather than passing it or handing it off.

key. (Basic jock talk) To watch and take one's cue from a player on the other team.

keystone. (Baseball) Second base.

kill shot. (Football) Extremely aggressive tackles of a severity that means the man tackled will have to be aided from the field. Lawrence Taylor of the New York Giants defined the term on the eve of Super Bowl XXI in 1986: "A kill shot is when snot's coming from his nose and he's quivering on the ground."

L

laugher. (Basic jock talk) Lopsided victory; a blowout.

leader board. (Golf) Scoreboard on which the rankings of golfers in a tournament are listed.

leatherman. (Baseball) A good fielder; one who uses the leather in his glove to advantage.

lock. (Basic jock talk) A certainty.

M

moguls. (Skiing) Washboard ridges created by other skiers' skiing at an angle.

Monday morning quarterback. Sports fan who has all the answers the day after the game.

mulligan. (Golf) Unofficial free shot.

N

nickel defense. (Football) Strategy in which an extra defensive back is put in the backfield to defend against a pass. The term alludes to the fact that there are five (a nickel) defenders rather than four.

nose bleeder. (Basketball) Player who can go high in the air for rebounds.

nose guard/tackle. (Football) A guard or a tackle who stands in front of—or nose to nose with—the opposing center during certain plays.

nutmeg. (Soccer) To push the ball between the defender's legs, run around him or her, control the loose ball, and continue dribbling. It is very embarrassing to a defender to be nutmegged.

O

110 percent. (Basic jock talk) Extra effort.

P

paint. (Basketball) The free-throw lane, usually painted a different color than the rest of the court floor.

palm. (Basketball) To hold a ball in your hand, usually for show.

paste. (Basic jock talk) Defeat.

physical. (Football) Rough or dirty. A team that is "very physical" is very nasty.

pigskin. (Football) (1) The football. (2) Relating to football, as in "pigskin preview."

pit. (Football) The area along the line of scrimmage where the two lines clash.

pluggers. (Football) Line-backers.

poodle. (Bowling) To roll the ball into the gutter.

punch on. (Basketball) To score on a defender.

R

red dog. (Football) Defensive play in which the linebacker crashes through the line to kill the offensive play before it begins. In an earlier time this was known as "rushing the passer."

redshirt. (Football) A college player who has been withheld from competition for a year so as to extend his eligibility to play.

ref. (Basic jock talk) Referee.

ringer. (Basic jock talk) Illegal player.

ring his bell. (Football) To hit someone hard in a contact sport.

rookie. (Basic jock talk) A first-year player; a novice (an apparent corruption of "recruit").

roostertail. (Snowmobile) The snow thrown up behind a racing snowmobile.

run-and-gun. (Basketball) Describing an open style of play in which direct assaults are made on the basket.

S

sack. (1) (Football) n. A tackle of the quarterback behind the offensive line, usually as the result of a *blitz*. (2) (Football) v. To tackle the quarterback. (3) (Baseball) A base.

sandwich. (Football) To trap an offensive player between two defenders.

second effort. (Basic jock talk) Sudden display of power and determination by an individual or team following a setback.

second wind. (Basic jock talk) A renewal of energy after a period of exhaustion.

shirts vs. skins / shirts 'n' skins. (Basic jock talk) Means of distinguishing one team from another in pickup games: one team wears shirts while the other is bare-chested.

shoestring. (Basic jock talk) At or near ground level. Catching any ball just as it is about to hit the ground is a "shoestring catch," and a "shoestring tackle" in football is one made just above the knees.

shovel / shovel pass. (Football) A forward pass tossed underhand.

skyhook. (Basketball) A high hook shot taken from an altitude above the level of the basket.

snakebit. (Basic jock talk.) A team or individual athlete that seems to attract an inordinate amount of bad luck.

southpaw. (Basic jock talk) Left-hander, originally a baseball term but now used in all sports.

spearing. (Hockey) The illegal use of a stick to poke another player.

spike. (1) (Baseball) To slide with one's baseball shoes, or spikes, high so as to hurt the man on base. (2) (Football) To celebrate a touchdown by slamming the ball into the ground of the end zone.

spread, the. (Basic jock talk) The number of points by which one team is believed to be better than another for the purpose of wagering. If the spread is 5, it means that the stronger team is favored by 5 points.

stick-um. (Football) Sticky substance that a pass receiver puts on his hand to hold onto the ball.

stutter step. (Football) Shuffle or quick step that is used to deceive a defender by giving the illusion that the runner is about to stop or turn. It is also used by pass receivers trying to stay inbounds as they catch sideline passes.

suburbs, the. (Basketball) Distance from the basket. To take a shot from the suburbs is to take a long shot.

sudden death. (Basic jock talk) Contest in which a tie is broken by the first person or team to score.

suicide squad. (Football) Special team used for kickoffs, so called because members of such teams are more likely to suffer injuries.

suit up. (Basic jock talk) To dress to play.

sweep. (Football) An attempt to carry the ball around the defensive end.

swivel hips. (Football) Attribute of a player who is particularly hard to catch and tackle.

T

taxi squad. (Football) Reserves who can be activated on short notice to replace others who are injured.

tenant. (Basketball) Player who tends to stay too long in the shooting lane (where one is allowed only three seconds.)

thin. (Basic jock talk) Said of a team without reserve players.

tools of ignorance. (Baseball) The catcher's paraphernalia.

touch. (Football) Game in which tackling is forbidden and a player is considered "down" when he or she is touched below the waist.

traveling. (Basketball) Illegal movement by a player with the ball.

triple-double. (Basketball) Single game performance in which a player gets double figures (10 or more) in terms of points, rebounds, and assists.

turkey. (Bowling) Three consecutive strikes.

turnover. (Football, basketball, etc.) The loss of possession.

U

ump. (Baseball) Umpire.

W

waggle. (Golf) Wrist flexing which causes the club to swing back and forth.

walk-on. (Basic jock talk) A player who shows up for a try-out on a college team who has not been recruited. A walk-on is drawn to the school by academics and does not have an athletic scholarship.

wallyball. Volleyball played on a squash court.

wave, the. (Spectator sports) The visual effect of a human wave or surge created as fans rise quickly to their feet as the swell passes through their section of the grandstand.

white knuckler. (Basic jock talk) A close game; one that goes down to the wire.

wiff. (Golf) To miss the ball entirely.

wig-wag. (Football) Hand signals, as opposed to instructions brought into the huddle by a player.

wildcard. (Basic jock talk) Made famous by professional football, it is the designation for a team that makes it into playoffs without having finished first in its division or league.

Wimby. (Tennis) Wimbleton.

wind sprint. (Basic jock) A short run.

Y

yips. (Golf) Pressure that affects a player; usually referred to as "the yips." To choke.

Z

zebra. (Basic jock talk) Referee in any sport in which that person is distinguished by a striped shirt.

zip. (Basic jock talk) A score of zero.

Zoning. (Tennis) Excellent play.

SOURCES
Webster's Sports Dictionary (Merriam-Webster), Tim Considine's *The Language of Sport* (Facts on File, 1982), and Harvey Frommer's *Sports Lingo* (Atheneum, 1979) are just a few of the many sources of more sports slang. The Tamony Collection pays particular attention to sports. Cathy Sanders also contributed.

22 | TEEN AND HIGH SCHOOL SLANG

Along with a Smattering of the Collegiate and Skateboard Jargon

"One cannot keep up with slang, especially the slang of the young, which is designed to be unintelligible to adults, and, once decoded, since today's young reject history, has turned into vapour or unspeak."

—Anthony Burgess writing in the London *Times Literary Supplement*, December 5, 1986

"I can take a phrase that's rarely heard. Flip it, now it's a daily word."

—Rap musician Rakim, quoted in the *Los Angeles Times*, August 29,1988

What links the generations is that much teen slang tends to be about the same things. Today there are a host of words for *cool*—including *cool*—and another batch for *geeks* and *dorks*—including *geeks* and *dorks*—just as there was for the class of '57. Other terms, including *groovy* and *funk*—which now mean "stodgy" or "out of it"—now mean the opposite of what they did to the Woodstock generation.

What was once *barfing* or *losing one's lunch* has emerged into a rich vocabulary of vomit. When *USA Today* wrote about teenage slang in 1988, a fourteen-year old reader wrote to say that she knew

53 different terms for blowing rainbows. Some terms that were once reserved for the young have now slipped into quasi-standard English—for instance, *hassle* (as in "that is too much of a hassle for me"), *put-down*, and *uptight*.

What all of this proves is that the slang of the young is mercurial, unpredictable, and somewhat allergic to print. If a noted linguist is quoted in the papers as saying that *bad* no longer means "good," the term seems to come back with a vengeance. If teachers start using a term, it is likely to either die or have its meaning change radically.

In other words, if you are a teenager and need this list, you're in trouble.

One final point. College slang tends to be an extension and embellishment of basic teen, so this glossary serves as a decoder for higher education as well. Apparently, if your parents were your *rents* in high school, they are likely to be your *rents* in college too.

A

abusak. Elevator music, a blend of "abuse" and "Muzak."

ace-high. The best.

acid. Steroids.

agro. Mad; pissed off.

aggresso. To act assertively; an act of aggression.

aggro. Great; good.

airhead. (1) One who is empty-headed, dumb. (2) Someone who is out of it.

This term dates from a time when many of today's teenagers were infants, but it still hangs on.

air mail. Garbage thrown out the window.

arbuckle. Dingbat.

ass out. In trouble.

attitude adjustment. High on drugs or booze.

awesome. (Pronounced "aah-some") Great; good; okay. This term is passé in some circles, current in others. Can be elevated to "totally awesome" or "mega-awe-some" for emphasis.

B

B. Frisbee: "Let's play some B."

bad. Good. People keep saying

that this term is verging on the edge of the archaic, but it just keeps hanging on.

bag. Kill; stop.

bail. (1) To cut a class; bail out. (2) To put something down: "bail that!" is used like "screw that!"

bail out. To leave.

bake. To smoke marijuana.

baked. Really stoned.

bald. Bad; terrible.

bank. Cash; money itself. This is a term that is common in rap music lyrics.

b-boy / b-girl. Rap music devotee. The *b-* in these terms stands for "beat."

b-boy stance. Defiant pose typically taken by crossing both arms across the chest. This is a term and posture common to rap music.

beat. That's terrible.

beef. A butt fall in skateboarding.

betty. A hot girl.

biftad. A preppy. A 1988 article in the San Francisco *Chronicle* on local high school slang reports that it is from quintessential preppy names, as in "Say, Biff!" "Yes, Tad?"

biscuit. Easy.

bizotic. Bizarre + exotic = weird.

Black & Decker. A real grind; a power tool (to which it is a punning reference).

blow it out. Forget it; let's move on.

boarder. Skateboarder.

boarding. Riding a skateboard.

bogue. Smoke a cigarette.

bogus. Phony; bad.

bonzai. Large or massive.

boogerhead. Nickname for a friend—affectionate.

book / book it. To move fast; to run like crazy, as in "He's really book'n 'round the bases."

boom. A stereo, especially a car stereo.

boot. To vomit.

bowhead. A Texas teen defines this one as a bouncy cheerleader type who "ignores her intelligence, is superficial, and wears bows in her hair."

box. (1) Large portable stereo tape-radio combination. (2) Large woman.

boxie. Bleached blonde. See *loxie*.

brainiac. Intelligent student.

brick. To be scared, as in, "We saw their front line and bricked." Probably from the expression "to shit a brick" as an indication of fear.

buff. Muscular; tough.

buggin'. (1) Being upset. (2) State of relaxation.

bummer. A bad break; a nasty experience. This term has been in use since the days when it was used to describe a "bad trip."

bump'n. (Pronounced "bum'-pun") Of the highest quality; such as clothes or music. Sometimes extended to "bump'n like a mug" for emphasis.

bum-rush. To come in; to break down the doors—a common rap term.

bunk. Uncool.

burly. A hard thing to accomplish.

burn. (1) To be put down. (2) A put-down, as in, "What a burn dad."

burn-out. One who abuses drugs or alcohol.

burnt. Terrible; tough; strict.

bus head. What one looks like after a long school field trip or away game.

bust. (1) v. To be in trouble, such as getting busted by one's parents over homework. (2) v. A rude insult, commonly stated as "bust you out." (3) n. A good shot; especially in basketball.

buttons. Remote control device for TV.

buzza. What's up?

buzz crusher. A killjoy.

C

caj/cas. Casual.

cameo. A type of haircut popular among young black males. The hair is trimmed short on the side and flat or angular on top.

cap. To put down; to insult.

cashed. Used up; finished.

catch one. To get drunk on beer.

checking. Pulling down another's outerwear boxer shorts from behind as a surprise.

check you later. Bye.

cheesehead / cheese meister. A jerk.

cheesy. Phony.

cherry. Something good; cool.

chick with a stick. Girl jock, presumably a reference to softball and field hockey.

chief. Form of address applied to virtually anyone.

chill / chillin' (1) v. To clam down; to become cool; to relax. (2) adj. Calm, cool, or laid back. (3). v. To stand up for a date. This is a term common in rap music lyrics.

chill out. To settle down; to quiet down; to get cool.

chill with you later. See you later.

chilly. With it; in tune with the times.

chilly most. Someone who is very cool; a paragon of chill.

chuborian. Fatty.

click. A clique.

clockin'. Bringing in; acquiring.

clueless. Describing someone who doesn't know what is going on, who doesn't have a clue.

Clydesdale. A stud; good-lookin' guy.

cob. Not cool; stupid.

cool. One of a number of words for this. It is a term that has displayed remarkable staying power.

costing. Expensive, as in shoes that look "costing."

cozy. Dull or lacking in interest. This same definition fits for the adjectives precious, special, and quaint.

crankin'. Excellent, especially in music.

creepers. Thick-soled black shoes.

crew. One's circle of friends.

crewby. Crew; that is, rowing, jock.

crib. Home.

critical/crit. Cool.

crush'n. That which looks good, especially clothes.

cujette. Female version of *cujine*.

cujine. Cousin; same as *homeboy,* but in an Italian neighborhood.

cut down on / cut on. Insult.

D

d. Bad.

daddylac. An expensive car that has been given to a young driver by his or her parents.

dag. To slow down, especially on a skateboard.

Deadhead. Grateful Dead fan.

death. To be very appealing; to die for.

decent. Excellent.

decorate your shoes. To vomit.

def. Outstanding; terrific. This is a common term in rap music lyrics.

An article in *The New York Times* ("Words to Rap By," August 22, 1988) quotes Robert Farris Thompson, a professor of African and Afro-American art at Yale University: "The rappers are saying 'def' derived from 'death' meaning terrific . . . when in the forties boppers said: "You kill me, you send me to heaven.""

deffest. The best; the coolest.

dexter. Nerd.

digithead. One who studies too much, or more specifically, works too long in front of a computer.

digits. Telephone.

dippin'. To listen in on somebody else's conversations for the purpose of obtaining gossip.

dipstick. Idiot; jerk; loser.

dis/diss. To show disrespect; to harass. This term is common in rap music lyrics. It is commonly believed to have been clipped from "disrespect," although some teenagers insist that it is short for dismiss.

ditz. Female airhead.

ditzy. Silly or goofy.

dog. (1) To intentionally ignore. (2) To criticize or bother. (3) To work hard, as in "dog it." (4) To crumble under pressure, in skateboard talk. (5) To have sexual intercourse. (6) To beat up.

donnez-moi un break. Give me a break. Explained by a sixteen-year-old from Connecticut: "It's a French-class thing. Anyone with a minimal French background will recognize 'give me a,' and they assume that 'break' means

break. 'Break' is French for station wagon; however, it makes a cute joke expression."

dooky. Excrement, as in "He smells like dooky."

dope. Great; superb—a common rap term.

do the do. Have sex.

double bagger. Person so ugly he or she needs two bags over his or her head instead of just one.

drain the main vein. For a male to urinate.

drive the porcelain bus. To throw up into a toilet.

drop some iron. To spend some money.

du. Hairstyle, from hairdo.

dual. Good.

duckets. Money.

dude. (1) Originally a guy, but now genderless. This term is a tricky one because a dude can be applied to someone who is especially well-dressed or, cynically, to one who is a mess. (2) A form of address, as in, "Hey, dude."

duker. Massive bowel movement.

dweeb. Loser; nerd; person who one would not want to have to share a locker with.

_____ **E** _____

eat chain. Drop dead; short for "eat a chain saw."

egg. To smash raw eggs on a car, house, or other large object.

express. In the mood to party.

_____ **F** _____

faced. Put down; having lost face.

face paint. To fall off a skateboard onto one's face.

fan (it). Forget it; let's not do it; pass. One father, Walt Gianchini, says that his daughters are likely to say "Let's fan on that" after he has suggested something like a Sunday picnic.

fat. Nice; good.

fetus. A real loser.

fierce. Terrific.

file. Dangerous.

fired up. Excited.

fire on (someone). To hit or punch.

flail. To do poorly on or fail a test; to mess up.

flake. To miss an appointment or not show for a date.

flamin'. To become infuriated, mad.

floppy disk. One who studies too much.

flu. Same as *fresh.*

fly-boy/fly-girl. Attractive young man/woman.

for real even? Are you serious?

fresh. Fine; very good. When a writer for the Detroit *News* discussed this term in a 1985 article on teenage slang, he said, "Possibly the most difficult new slang term to define, 'fresh' can encompass an individual's attitude, a state of mind, a mode of dress, or an enlivening influence or situation." It is a term of approval; common in rap music lyrics.

front. (1) To confront. (2) To put up a front.

full hank. Nerd.

full of acid. Describing a well-built guy who looks like he is on steriods.

fully-on/fully. Perfect; the best possible.

funk. Someone who thinks he or she is cool, but definitely is not.

_____ **G** _____

gag. Valley girl, from "Gag me with a spoon."

gangsta. A person in a gang.

gank. Flirt.

gay. Not cool; totally stupid.

geed. Looking good.

geek. Loser, nerd. A rare perennial in the ephemeral realm of teenage slang. "Geekoid" is used in some circles.

gel. To relax.

generic. Dull; out of it.

get horizontal. To lie down (alone or with someone else).

get naked. Not what it seems, but rather, a way to say "let's go."

getting off with your bad self. Obviously feeling good about something that you have done.

get up! Good job!

get yours. Defined in a collection of teenage slang in the June 19, 1988, *Newsday* (Long Island) Sunday magazine as "A friendly greeting used when you see a guy or girl together and you know one of them; then you yell 'Get yours,' meaning go for it."

gimp. A loser.

girly-mon. Effete or weak man, from the *Saturday Night Live* bodybuilders Hans and Franz, who say "girly man" in a German accent.

glitterbag. Flashy female given to shiny clothes, hair piled high with Aqua Net, and gum chewing.

gnarly. Disgusting, gross. But in some circles and in some sit-

uations it also means good, cool, hip.

god box. Remote control device for TV.

godly. Cool.

goob / gooker. Nerd, loser. But "to gooker" is to spit through one's two front teeth.

good answer! Cool, good—from the *Family Feud* television quiz show.

gooey. Girlfriend.

gorpoblorcho. Imaginary chemical used by chemistry teachers.

G.Q. or Q. Nice clothes, from the fashionable men's magazine *Gentleman's Quarterly*.

granola. One who dresses and shares the preferences of the 1960s. This term has gotten a significant boost from the *Bloom County* Bohemian character Lola Granola.

grill. Face, from the grill of a car. "How'd you'd get that scrape on your grill?"

groovy. Stodgy, old-fashioned; 1960ish. But also sometimes used in its original sixties context.

ground. To punish by keeping at home, as in "I'm grounded for the week because of my report card."

guidette. Female *guido,* who is likely to use much hairspray to keep her hair piled high and poufy. See also *glitterbag.*

guido. Male characterized by slick hair, gold jewelry, a hairy chest (exposed), acid-washed jeans, and a fondness for Bon Jovi music. A sixteen-year old from the Bronx says that although this started out as a stereotype of "cool" Italian-American guys, it now includes any group or nationality—for example, Greek and Jewish guidos.

gumby. An unintelligible person.

guns. Muscles.

gutter wear. Very hip, punky clothing.

H

hack. To get rid of undesirable people quickly.

ham. Any alcoholic beverage.

hang. Relax; hang out.

happy camper. Someone having fun, although this is often phrased in the negative, as "not a happy camper."

hard. Tough; authentic—a common rap term.

hardcores. Tough courses.

hard way to go. Sympathetic response to somebody's sad story.

harsh. Strict; bad.

headbanger. Heavy metal fan.

heifer. Fat girl.

hein. Person who is ugly and/or possessed of a rotten personality.

hella-. Prefix for "very," as in "hellacool" for very cool.

hellified. Super.

hellish. Horrible.

hello. I heard that.

high jack. To take something trivial, almost borrowing.

hip-hop. Catchall for rap music, rapping, break dancing, graffiti, and playing records. The language heard in rap lyrics has been called "hip-hop slang."

hippy witch. Girls who dress in black and wear sixties style clothing.

hittin' / hit'n. That which tastes good.

hit up. To ask someone where they are from.

ho! Great; good-looking; "Look out world!" A seventeen-year-old informant says that this term got a boost from the movie *Biloxi Blues.*

ho / hoe. A slut, and an obvious play on the word "whore."

holler at / hollerat. Talk to.

holmes / homes / homie. Deriva-

tions of *homeboy/homegirl*
which mean the same thing; a
common rap term.

homeboy / homegirl. Friendly
term of address for someone
from the same neighborhood
or school; a neighborhood
friend.

hook. Catch on.

hook-up. To begin a relationship.

horn. Telephone.

hosebag. Slut.

hot. Extremely appealing or
good-looking; very cool.

house. (1) To have a major success; to bring down the
house—a common rap term.
(2) To steal.

house ape. Small child.

hubba. Stupid.

hype. Great.

hyped. Full of energy.

I

I heard that. I agree.

illin'. Stupid; un-chillin'. This
term is common in rap music
lyrics.

iron pimp. School bus.

it ain't all that. You're overstat-
ing; don't exaggerate.

it rules. It is awesome.

Izod. Preppy guy or girl.

J

jacked. Happy.

jack shit. Nothing, as in "I'm
doing jack shit."

jack up. To kick in the rear end.

jam. In the world of rap, a concert, party, record, good time,
etc.

jammin'. Music that sounds
good.

jank. All-purpose noun.

jingus. Bogus.

joanin'. To insult publicly, as in
"They were joanin' me about
my car." When this term was
reported by the *Washington
Post* in 1987, it was suggested
that it might be derived from
Joan Rivers, but a number of
readers wrote to point out
that the term was an old one
which was common in the
black community when
Rivers was waiting for her
first break.

jockin'. For a girl to hang on a
guy.

johnny. Cop.

juco. Junior College.

juicer. Steroid-user.

juke. (1) Elude. (2) To make a
direct hit.

jump his/her bones. To have sex
with. Almost always phrased
conditionally, as in "I'd like
to . . ."

junks. Basketball shoes, especially expensive ones.

K
---

keystone. Describing the police.

kick back. To relax.

kickin' it. Doing something, even if it's just hanging out.

kill. Really good.

killer. (1) Good, like killer shoes. (2) A very tough course, especially in college.

L
---

lame. (1) State of boredom. (2) Stupid or nerdy.

lame time. Dull party.

lampin'. Hanging out, as one does when standing around a lamppost.

lardo. Fat person.

later. So long; good-bye.

law, law. I don't believe it.

left hanging. Stood up.

let's cruise. Let's go.

like. To say. This linguistic development was enough to net an article in *The New York Times* ("For 'Teenspeak,' Like Another Meaning for the Multipurposeful 'Like,'" August 25, 1988).

living large. Doing well in rap talk.

load. Car.

loaf. A fat person.

loft. Skateboard hang time.

loose. A senseless, daring act.

lop. A nerd or dork.

lost between the bells. Late for class.

lost in the sauce. Out of it.

loxie. A natural blonde, like Goldilocks, but unlike a *boxie,* who gets it out of bottle.

lunchin'. Characteristic of one who is out to lunch.

M
---

magnet. (1) A *dweeb* that won't even move from his/her seat; a "gluebottom." (2) A school or school program created to attract students so that racial or enrollment imbalances can be corrected voluntarily.

major. Extremely important.

mall crawler. Teenage girl who spends almost all of her spare time at the mall.

mega-. Prefix of emphasis, along with *mundo-*.

melba. Odd or unusual.

mellow up. Calm down.

mental. Describing any strange person.

mess 'em up. Good luck; the equivalent of "break a leg."

mess up. To screw up; to fail.

metal mouth. Teenager with braces.

Mickey D's. McDonald's. The company now uses this name in some of its ads, which are obviously aimed at the young consumer. There are other slang fast-food names, including the "B.C. lounge" for Burger Chef and the perennial "D.Q." for Dairy Queen.

mint. Good; great, same as *killer.*

modeiant. Of or pertaining to the rock group Depeche Mode; something worthy of them.

molded. Embarrassed.

money. Friend.

Muffie and Biff. Charactronyms for preppies by high schoolers.

munchie. A cut or scrape gotten from falling off one's skateboard. Inspired by the feeling that the pavement is "munching" on one's skin.

munch on. To treat unfairly; to come down on.

mundo-. Prefix of emphasis along with *mega-.* Something that is very strange, for example, is "mundo-bizarro."

my bad. My mistake.

N

narc. Loser; nerd. Once a term for a narcotics agent or someone giving them information.

neat whistle. Person wearing odd or weird clothing.

nectar. A good-looking girl.

ned. Marijuana.

nice du. Slur aimed at a bad or odd hairstyle.

9.5 fling. As defined by a seventeen-year old female: "When a snobby girl suddenly flings her hair as an act of drawing attention."

nitro. Very good; better than *dope*—a term associated with rap.

no duh. No kidding.

nog. To come into contact with.

nooks. Pain, especially to a high school jock.

not! Interjection used to show disapproval or label as stupid.

nuke. (1) To destroy; "I was nuked by that chemistry exam." (2) To microwave.

O

ollie grab. To kick a skateboard up, catch it, and then jump back on it.

on the strength. Really great, in the rap lexicon.

organ recital. Sex education class.

P

petunia. Man or boy who pays a great deal of attention to his appearance.

pick no squares. Don't fight.

pick up your face. Response to somebody who has just done something stupid or embarrassing.

piece. Junk. Probably from "What a piece of shit!"

player. Person who two-times or flirts, as in, "Look out, she's nothing but a player."

poser. Someone who tries to act and dress like people in another group but is considered a phony by that group.

posse. A group of good friends.

pseudo. (1) Person you think little of, often paired by hyphen with a pseudo type—pseudo-hippie, pseudo-jock, etc. (2) Anything that is suspect.

psych. To exaggerate wildly; to put somebody . on momentarily.

psychotic. Really great; good.

Q

quality. Lousy; bad—the opposite of the real meaning of quality.

queef. Fart.

queer. Stupid or odd; it has nothing to do with sexual orientation.

queeve. To run out of energy, in the parlance of skateboarding.

R

rack. Sleep.

rack monster. A bed.

rack up. To kick somebody in the rear end.

rad / radical. Cool.

radical to the fifth dimension. Terrific.

raggin'. (1) Well-dressed. (2) Beating up on somebody. (3) Beating someone or winning ("He ragged on him in the race"). (4) For a girl to have her period.

raging. A good time; a lot of fun.

rags. Clothes; but most likely concert T-shirts.

ralph. To vomit. It has been pointed out that the name Ralph mimics the sound of regurgitation.

ranker / rank out. One who backs out; to back out.

rat. One who habituates or does—a "gym rat" hangs out in gymnasiums, while a "rink rat" spends spare hours at a skating rink, and a kid who caddies is a "bag rat." Anyone who hangs around shopping centers is a "mall rat." Ancient in terms of this kind of slang, "rats" seem to be a constant.

raw. Great; very good; good-looking.

real slice, a. A bad day.

reeks. To smell.

remo. Same as *Dweeb.*

rents. Parents (from which the word was clipped).

rickety-raw. Good-looking.

ride. A car, as in "My ride is outside."

ride / ridin'. (1) To make fun of; verbal jockeying. (2) To flatter; such as praising a teacher to get a better grade.

rider. Very negative term for someone who tags along when unwanted; a copy cat. It is probably short for "ball rider."

ride the slow train. To not want to party.

rip. (1) n. A rip-off; a bad deal. (2) v. To be cheated or robbed.

road dog. Best friend.

rock and roll. To do something rowdy or noisy.

rocker. Anybody who is into heavy metal.

rock your world. To beat you up.

roll. A fat person.

rouge. To steal.

rude. Out of sight; cool—the same as *rad* or *radical;* totally good.

ruff. Neat, cool.

rush. To confront someone in a hostile or violent mood.

S

sappnin'. What's happening?

scam. To lie, as in "I had to scam my way out of it."

scamming. Flirting.

scarf. To consume quickly; for example, to scarf up a pepperoni pizza.

scoop. To kiss someone.

scope. (1) To hunt for something: "Let's see if we can scope a party." (2) To ogle. "Why you scopin'?" translates into "What are you looking at me for?"

In an article on prep school slang (which is remarkably similar to public school slang), teacher and linguist Richard Lederer suggests that this is a clipping of "telescope."

scrappin'. Fornicating.

scribe. Writing utensil.

scurb. Suburban skateboarder; one who skates on streets and curbs.

seven digits. Telephone number.

sev's. 7-Eleven store.

shagging. Picking somebody up by their underpants.

"She reads *Seventeen*." Said of a trendy teenage girl.

ship to shore. Cordless telephone.

shot who? What? Pardon me.

shout at one's shoes. To throw up.

shun it. To go with it.

sick. Good; awesome.

skanky. Rank or gross. Sometimes uses specifically to describe a teenage girl who is so skinny that she is "gross-looking." One sixteen-year-old definer adds, "Would be pretty if she gained weight."

skater. Skateboarder.

skate rat. Skateboarder. See *rat*.

sketch. To mess up on a skateboard.

skidder. Backwoods teen in New England; after the name of a piece of logging equipment. "A skidder," says a western Maine teen, "has a

mean dog and a broken snowmobile in his yard."

skin it. Slap hands; new way of saying "Gimme five!"

slacking. Not keeping up with one's duties.

slam. To cut down verbally.

slap-down. (1) v. To embarrass. (2) n. An embarrassment.

slaps. Rubber-thonged sandals.

slice up. To criticize or cut down. Sometimes extended to slice up like lunch meat or the like.

slider. An easy course in college—known as a "gut" or a "breeze" to the parents of those who take sliders.

smit. To skip.

smokin'. Looking great.

snake. To steal.

snap. To break a promise. A "snapper" is one who breaks promises.

sounds. Music.

spacin'. Not paying attention; being off in space. Spacin' usually occurs in class.

spazz. To become overly excited.

spent. Cash.

splockenin'. Egging a car or house.

spud. A jerk.

squash that / squash that melon. Forget it.

squid. Nerd, someone with tape

on their glasses. Sometimes used as a joke with friends. By extension, a computer room or center is a "squid tank."

step off. Leave.

stick. Skateboard.

sticks. Needles used to inject steroids.

stoked. Excited; psyched.

stole. To punch out; "I stole him" is to hit him with a knockout punch.

stud. Once a sexy male, increasingly a male who thinks he is *cool/hot/fresh* but is not. Loser; person who is strong and athletic but still a loser.

stud-muffin. An immodest good-looking guy.

stuffies. Stuffed animals.

stupid fresh. Outstanding or spectacular—more than plain *fresh*—in rap terminology.

s'up. Greeting, short for "What's up?"

sure you're right. Said of someone not telling the truth.

sweat. (1) To trash; to break something. (2) To give someone a bad time.

sweet. Good; cool.

swillmobile. Car full of empty beer bottles or cans.

swivel neck. Nerd.

syke. Same as *psych*.

T

take a chill pill. Calm down.

talk out of the side of your neck. To bullshit.

tamale time. Embarrassment.

tard. Someone who is moving or acting slowly.

TBF. A goofy guy. It stands for Top Button Fag because one so described is likely to wear his top shirt button buttoned.

teepee. To cover a house, tree, car, or other large object with toilet paper, from the initials T.P.

that's a plan. Confirmation or agreement of a suggested action.

that's casual. A statement of acceptance.

thrash. (1) To spin a skateboard in midair; to make any good move on a skateboard. (2) To be really good at something.

thrasher. (1) Skateboarder. (2) Skateboarder who doesn't give a damn.

thrashin'. Dancing.

tin grin / tinsel teeth. Braces.

tool. One who studies; a grind.

touron. Annoying tourist; formed, it seems, from blending "tourist" and "moron."

toxic. Astonishing.

trashed. Drunk.

trife. The wrong way. Living trife is living the wrong way; said of a bad person. "This may come from the Yiddish word *treif* [pronounced "trayf"] meaning not kosher," says Robert S. Greenman of Brooklyn, who picked the term up from his students.

trip. An experience on or off of drugs—same as the sixties.

trip-out. One who is out of it; a space cadet.

trippy. Neat; weird; far-out.

'tsup. Catsup, see *'za* for a similar case of clipping.

tubaruba. TV.

tube / tube out. To watch TV.

tweaked / tweaked out. Spaced out.

twink. Loser; nerd.

U

unruly. Gruesome, a term beloved of skateboarders, who talk of unruly falls.

upper story / upstairs. The mind; the brain.

up the ying-yang. A ridiculous amount; for instance, "I have homework up the ying-yang."

V

vamp du. Slur aimed at a bad or odd hairstyle. Also *nice du.*

veg / veg out. To do nothing; to vegetate.

vid. A hassle or a bother.

W

wack. Bad; lousy.

wail. To beat somebody up.

waldo. Out of it.

wanna be / wannabe. An emulator; one on the periphery. The term is sometimes applied to a white who seems to be emulating blacks or a black who is emulating whites.

wassup. What's up?

wasted. Drunk or high on drugs.

wastoid. Person throwing it away on drugs or booze.

waver. New wave teen who goes to clubs, wears black, and "evolutionized" from punk.

way. Plenty; accentuated, as in "way dumb" for very dumb.

weak. Not good; poor.

wedge. Food.

wench. Girlfriend.

wicked. Cool.

wig out. State of agitation.

wiggy man. A cop.

wild. Cool.

wilson. A really bad fall from a skateboard.

winner. Loser; a put-down when you have done something stupid.

wit. What you say when a bad joke has been told; delivered as if it were "nit."

woebetide. Bad news.

woof. To brag.

woofie. Wimp.

word. (1) That which one cannot think of; a word for all words. It comes from rap music, where "word" is used when no rhyming word has been thought of, and can be found in lines like, "That girl is fine. Word." (2) I agree; agreement.

wreck. To fight.

wuss. Wimp or coward.

X

X-ing. Tripping on the drug Ecstasy or X.

Y

yawn in technicolor. Vomit.

yea / yeay. Imprecise unit of measurement, as in "he's yeay tall."

yen. Money of any kind.

Z

'za. Pizza. This is a major clipping in which only the last two letters remain.

zappening. What's happening?

zit. Pimple.

zoiks. An expletive employed when there is nothing else to say. It is without meaning.

zun. Pimple; possible reaction to the co-oping of *zits* by the commercial sellers of skin preparations.

zup. What's up?

SOURCES

Walt Giachini, guidance counselor at Wallenberg High School in San Francisco, obtained contributions from his four daughters—Julia, Brooke, Gina, and Kate—and student Jennifer Massengill (11th grade). Teacher and writer Richard Lederer, writer Geof Huth, and researcher Charles D. Poe helped, as did Willy Risser, 13, and Andrew Dickson, 15.

Robert S. Greenman, teacher and journalist, was kind enough to query students at the Columbia Scholastic Press Association summer workshop in June 1989. Those who responded to the slang questionnaire were, in no special order—Michelle Rowley, 16, Williston Park, N.Y.; Kate Gremmler, 16, Albany, N.Y.; Mary Pflum, 16, Beaver Dam, Wisc.; Sara Walker, 17, Philadelphia; Joy Smith, 16, Manchester, Ky.; Peter Issacs, 17, Farmingdale, N.Y.; Alice Park, 15, Ardsley, N.Y.; Jennifer Marino, 16, Harvard, Mass.; Elizabeth Young, 17, Lima, Ohio; Amy Daily, 17, Westbrook, Conn.; Becky Cowin, 16, Cambridge, Mass.; Angela Barrett, 16, Manchester, Ky.; Sarah Monoky, 17, Toledo, Ohio; Sarah Light, 15, Belmont, Mass.; Michael Carrothers, 16, Albany, N.Y.; Leslie Cregary, 15, Manchester, Ky.; Damon Vagianelis, 14, Colonie, N.Y.; Paula Tusiani, Manhasset, N.Y.; Claudine Cangiano, 17, Plandome, N.Y.; Alexis Martin, 15, Montclair, N.J.; Karen Deutchman, 17, Spring Valley, N.Y.; Ann Goins, 16, Manchester, Ky.; Jennifer Harris, 15, Ardsley, N.Y.; Melanie Rosenberg, 16, Spring Valley, N.Y.; Cheryl Goldman, 17, Farmingdale, N.Y.; Mary Jacobi, 16, Mount Vernon, Va.; Deirdre McEvoy, 16, Fresh Meadows, N.Y.; Susan Kishinchand, 17, Philadelphia; Alessandro Zullo, 16, the Bronx, N.Y.; Christopher Hume, 16, Alexandria, Va.; Katherine Rodi, 17, Hempstead, N.Y.; Liz Barrett, 16, Houston, Texas; Margot Vigeant, 16, Stratford, Conn.; Jill Janson, 17, Rutherford, N.J.; Anne Mogavero, 16, Orchard Park, N.Y.; Carroll Kimion, 14, Montclair, N.J.; Laura and Sarah Scearce, both 15, Manchester, Ky.; Esther Clinton, 17, Brewster, N.Y.; Suyapa Moreira, 17, Brooklyn, N.Y.; Jeannine Morrone, 16, Bellerose Village, N.Y.; Deborah Solomon, 16, Spring Valley, N.Y.; Susan Schneider, 17, Brookfield, Wisc.; Hillary Green, 17, Brooklyn, N.Y.; Jim Stanford, 16, Bethesda, Md.; Sean Gibbons, 17, Alexandria, Va.; Ian Pross, Haddonfield, N.J.; and Christina Martinez, 17, Los Angeles. Robert Greenman also supplied terms from his regular classes.

Also contributing, from Williamsburg, Va., were Scott Callis and Steve Nelson, Becky Day, Lambert Holm, Rick Newton, Nicole Petty, Kayley Harden, Cathy Sanders, Joanne Sanders, Greg Warren, and Lauren Wiseman; and Jason Nicholai from Virginia Beach, Va.

In addition, a number of recent newspaper articles on teenager and college slang were consulted, including those from the *Los Angeles Times, New York Times,* the *Washington Post,* the Detroit *Free Press, Newsday,* the Concord (N.H.) *Monitor, USA Today,* and the San Francisco *Chronicle.*

23 | WAR SLANG

Out of the Jungles of Southeast Asia

"The patois of the Vietnam experience infiltrated the American consciousness slowly, for more than a decade, on a Ho Chi Minh trail of the mind."

—Martin F. Nolan, *Boston Globe*, July 18, 1982

During the war in Vietnam, especially during the early days, it was not unusual for soldiers to use terms the Army had acquired elsewhere at another time. Early in the conflict an Associated Press reporter noted, for instance, that the troops were using such terms as *Ichiban* (Japanese) for "number one" or "very good," *idiwash* (Korean) for "come here," and *bierstube* (German) for "beer hall."

This is how it has always been. Soldiers bring the terminology of one fight or period of occupation to the next and then embellish it with new terms, until it takes on the flavor of that war. "The war in South Vietnam is producing its own vocabulary," wrote Jack Langguth in *The New York Times,* for September 20, 1964. "Among the Americans stationed here, World War II's argot has long since faded away. Even Korea's glossary sounds dated."

231

Generally speaking, it will take a new war to update the slang of combat, and today's war slang is the slang of Vietnam and earlier wars.

————— **A** —————

across the fence. Across a border, as if it were a fence. In Vietnam it referred to missions into North Vietnam, Cambodia, and Laos.

acting jack. Acting noncommissioned officer.

agency. The CIA.

a-gunner. Assistant gunner.

airborne copulation. Euphemism for "I don't give a flying fuck."

AMF. Good-bye; it is short for Adios or Aloha, Mother-Fucker. A popular and long-running television ad for "The Greaseman," a Washington, D.C. radio personality, ends with "The Grease" waving and yelling "AMF."

ammo humper. Artilleryman.

angel. False radar image.

ape. Air Force Air Police, from the A.P. initials.

apple-sauce enema. Mild criticism. Defined in *A Dictionary of Soldier Talk:* "To give a chewing out (the enema) to a subordinate, but to do it so tactfully and gently that he goes away feeling better for the experience."

Army brat. Long-standing name for the son or daughter in a regular Army family.

artie / arty. Artillery.

AWOL. Acronym for Absent Without Official Leave. An "AWOL bag" is a small piece of luggage.

————— **B** —————

baby shit. Mustard.

bad paper. Discharge other than honorable.

banana clip. A curved ammunition clip designed to hold thirty rounds.

Band-Aid. Medical corpsman.

B & B. Booze and broads, used in Korea and Vietnam as a play off *R & R.*

bandit. Hostile aircraft.

BAR. Acronym for Browning automatic rifle. Used in World War II and Korea and still a point of reference for these carrying M-10's.

bare-ass. Barracks.

basic. Basic training; boot camp.

beans and dicks. C-ration hot dogs and beans.

beans and motherfuckers. C-ration featuring lima beans and ham.

Big Red One. Nickname for the 1st Infantry Division.

big twenty. Army career of twenty years.

bird. Aircraft, but usually used for helicopters.

bird colonel. Full colonel, whose insignia is eagles.

birdfarm. Aircraft carrier.

birdland. Quarters for senior officers.

biscuit bitches. USO or Red Cross women, also "donut dollies."

blade time. The time a helicopter is in the air.

blood stripe. Rank achieved at the expense of others.

bloods. Black troops.

blow away. Kill.

blow smoke. To confuse; to cover up.

blue. A body of water, from its color on the map.

blue max. The Medal of Honor, from its blue field.

blues. An airmobile company.

bogey / bogie. Aircraft suspected to be hostile.

bolo. A soldier who flunks his rifle qualifications. A first-person witness, writer Joseph C. Goulden reports, "As punishment at Fort Chaffee, Arkansas, circa May–July 1956, such a cluck was given a 'bolo,' a crude southern scythe, and put to work cutting grass on the entire firing range."

boobies. Boobie traps.

boo-coo. Many. From the French *beaucoup,* which American GI's picked up from the Vietnamese, who picked it up from the French.

boom-boom. Sex. A "boom-boom house" is a whorehouse.

boom-boom girl. Prostitute.

boonie rat. Soldier who has spent a lot of time in the field.

boonies. Backwoods; the jungle.

boot. (1) Soldier just out of boot camp. (2) Adjective for that which is new and untested. At one point in *Rumor of War,* Philip Caputo wrote, "I was alliteratively known as the 'boot brown-bar,' slang for second lieutenant."

bottle-cap colonel. Lieutenant colonel, from the insignia that looks like the tinfoil on a bottle cap.

bouncing betty. A land mine

that, when triggered, pops up waist high and sprays shrapnel.

brace. An exaggeration position of attention which recruits and cadets are sometimes required to adopt. In *The Boo,* a novel about the Citadel, a military school, Pat Conroy describes plebes bracing: "Their chins are tucked in, their shoulders thrown back, and their backs are rigidly straight."

brew. (1) Coffee. (2) Beer.

bring smoke. To attack or punish.

broken down. Disassembled.

brown bar. Second lieutenant, who wears a single gold bar.

brown-shoe army. Anyone or anything that was in the Army prior to September 1, 1956, when the Army went from brown to black shoes. The "existing shoes" had to be dyed, and over that long Labor Day weekend everything was awash in black gook.

buckle. To fight.

Bumfuck, Egypt. Remote site of hardship assignments; East Overshoe.

bunker buster. A satchel charge composed of C-4 explosives and a short-fuse detonation cord, developed in Korea and used extensively in Vietnam.

burp. A Marine, especially to an infantryman.

bush. (1) The field or the boonies. (2) Short for "ambush."

bust. To reduce in rank or grade.

bust caps. To fire rapidly. In *Nam,* Mark Baker says that it is "probably derived from the paper percussion caps used in toy guns." See also *capping.*

butter bar. (1) Second lieutenant, from the brass bar indicating that rank. (2) The bar itself.

buy it / buy the farm. To die.

C

cammies. Camouflage apparel.

canker mechanic. A medic.

cannon cockers. Soldiers whose area of specialty is artillery. A character in Philip Caputo's *Rumor of War* is described as a "cannon-cockin' Texas shitkicker."

capping. Shooting at.

care package. Goodies (candy, cookies, etc.) from home.

Cav. Air cavalry.

chair borne. Describing a military bureaucrat or paper pusher—a play on the term airborne.

Charlie. Short for Victor Charlie; the Viet Cong in the Vietnamese War. Also, variants along the lines of "Mr. Charles," and "Mr. Charlie."

charlie tango. Control tower.

Cheap Charlie. Skinflint.

cherry. New man in unit.

chicken guts. Looped braid on officers' dress uniforms.

chicken plate. Personal armor, such as the kind that helicopter pilots wear across their chest and groin.

chopper. Helicopter.

chow. Food.

chuck. "A term applied by black Marines to identify white individuals," according to James Webb in *Fields of Fire,* who adds that it was often used derogatorily.

Cinderella liberty. Period of freedom that ends at midnight.

civil serpent. Civil servant, especially one who works with the uniformed military.

clerks 'n jerks. Support staff.

click. Kilometer, also *klick.*

cluster fuck. A totally screwed-up situation.

clutch belt. Cartridge belt worn by Marines.

C.O. Commanding officer.

column. A batallion.

COMMFU. Completely Monumental Military Fuck-Up (probably a play on Kung-fu).

commo. Communications, in general, but often specifically used for radio.

connex. Large metal box for shipping and storage.

contact. Firing or being fired upon; engaging in combat.

cots. Apricots. During the Vietnam War a superstition developed among Marine tankers which held that apricots—contained in some rations—brought bad luck. The word was "No cots."

crapper. Latrine.

C-rats / C's. C-rations, which the military began phasing out in 1978. The new rations are called *MRE's,* for Meal, Ready to Eat.

crispy critters. Enemy personnel killed by napalm.

Crotch, The. The U.S. Marine Corps.

crunchies. Ground infantrymen.

cunt cap. Green narrow Army cap.

CYA. Cover your ass.

D

daisy cutter. Very large bomb of the type used in Southeast Asia to clear instant landing zones in the jungle.

day the eagle shits, the. Payday. The eagle is the federal government.

Dear John / Dear John letter. Letter from a girlfriend announcing that she has found another.

deros. Acronym for Date Eligible to Return from OverSeas and/or Date of Expected Return from OverSeas. In his *Everything We Had*, Al Santoli called deros "the sweetest word in the military language."

deuce and a half. A 2½-ton truck; a medium cargo truck.

dich. (Pronounced "dick.") Vietnamese for "dead" and one of the terms used for enemy killed: "We got twenty-nine dead dicks up here and another seventeen hurtin'."

diddy-bopping. Walking carelessly, from black slang meaning to walk ostentatiously, boldly.

di di. To run, from the Vietnamese.

dink. Derogatory term for an Oriental

dirty officer. Duty officer.

DMZ. Initialism for Demilitarized Zone.

dog tags. Identification jewelry.

DOW. Died of wounds.

dream sheet. Official forms on which officers and enlisted members indicate their preference for their next location and job.

dry hole. Any target where you don't find anything and nothing finds you.

DuPont lure. A grenade or C4 plastic explosive used for fishing.

dust-off. (1) Medevac helicopter. (2) To be lifted out by chopper.

E

eight. A master sergeant who is in pay grade E-8.

E-nothing. One at the bottom; an imaginary pay grade below E-1, a recruit.

evak'd. Evacuated.

F

fart sack. Bedroll.

Fast Movers. Jet fighters, usually F-4s.

fat. Describing a unit that is over its authorized strength. In *A Rumor of War*, Philip Caputo talks of a fat battalion.

fatty-gews. Fatigues.

field first. An NCO rank that does not exist in any regulations; the field first is the sergeant who runs the company while the first sergeant is in a rear area.

50-cal. .50-caliber machine gun.

51-cal. Machine gun used by the enemy.

fire base. Remote artillery base.

fire in the hole. Explosives about to be detonated deliberately, such as a satchel charge being dropped into a suspected enemy *hidey-hole*.

flying butterknife. Winged bayonet patch worn by paratroopers.

FNG. Fucking new guy.

four-deuce. A 4.2-inch mortar.

fox. To fire, from the old phonetic alphabet. To report "fox one" is to say that a pilot has fired his first missile.

frag. (1) Fragmentation grenade. (2) To grenade; to wound or kill with a hand grenade.

fragging. Killing one's superiors with a grenade.

freak. Short for radio frequency.

freedom bird. Airplane returning soldiers to the United States.

friendlies. Allies, both military and civilian.

frog hair. Mythical unit of measure denoting a very small distance, such as: "Lay that two frog hairs to the right." Same as *red cunt hair*.

fruit salad. Two or more rows of campaign ribbons.

FTA. Fuck the Army.

full bird. A colonel, from the eagle insignia.

funny money. Military payment script, called this because it looked like Monopoly money. This is traditional military slang as common to World War II as Vietnam.

funny papers. Maps.

---------- **G** ----------

garritrooper. Term invented during World War II by cartoonist and writer Bill Mauldin to describe a soldier who was "too far forward to wear ties and too far back to get shot." The term survived, and Charles D. Poe has noted, "On Barry Sadler's album of Vietnam songs [*Ballads of the Green Berets*] there is one entitled 'Garet Trooper,' and the song's lyrics suggest that Sadler had in mind pretty much the same kind of soldier that Mauldin was describing."

get some. Kill.

getting short. Coming up on the end of one's tour of duty.

ghosting. Special Forces term for hiding out so you wouldn't get put on a shit detail.

G.I. An Army enlisted man, from the World War II initialism for "government issue."

The fact that this term which came into being about 1940 is still used, illustrates the power of slang over officialdom. In 1951 the Pentagon actually issued an edict prohibiting further use of GI within the military, stipulating that the proper term was "soldier."

glad bag. Body bag.

golden BB. Bullet with a soldier or airman's name on it.

gook. Derogatory term for an Oriental, from Korean slang for person.

GOYA. Short for "get off your ass."

grease. To kill. "Brother or not," says a character in Alfred Coppel's *Apocalypse Brigade,* "you come out now or we grease you on the spot."

greased. Killed in action. These gruesome lines appear in John Skipp and Craig Spector's *The Scream:* "The A-gunner's brains blew all over him. His squad was getting greased."

greenbacks. American money.

green bait. Reenlistment bonus.

green beanies. U.S. Army Special Forces (from the Green Berets). To call a member of the Special Forces a green beanie is to risk personal injury.

green machine. The U.S. Army.

grunt. Infantryman.

gun bunny. Artilleryman.

gung ho. Enthusiastic.

gunny / guns. Marine gunnery sergeant.

gunship. Armed helicopter.

gyrene. Marine.

H

hack it. To stand it.

hard rice. Munitions given to friendly tribesmen during the Vietnam conflict.

hash marks. Diagonal uniform bars, each signifying four years of military service.

heart. A Purple Heart, the medal that signifies a combat wound. In *Fields of Fire* James Webb reported on the "Three Heart Rule" which was in effect in Vietnam. It stated that any Marine wounded three times within one combat tour was immediately removed from the combat zone.

hidey-hole. Any hole scratched into the ground or into the brow of a hill where a soldier can take refuge.

Hilton. Name of hotel chain invoked ironically for places totally unlike Hiltons. When Bob Hope returned from Vietnam in 1967, he noted, "Every broken-down hut, hootch, or Quonset hut is called the Chu Lai Hilton, or the Hilton East, or the Hilton something." The most famous Vietnam Hilton was the infamous Hanoi Hilton, a prison in which many American P.O.W.'s were held.

hitch. A period of enlistment or reenlistment.

hog. (1) The A-10 or Thunderbolt II aircraft, sometimes called the "warthog." (2) Helicopter gunship of the UH-Huey series.

Hog-60. The M-60 machine gun.

homesteader. Soldier who manages to stay in one assignment for a long period of time.

honcho. Chief; boss.

hooch. Hut or simple dwelling.

hose down. To shoot with automatic fire.

hot L.Z. Landing zone under fire.

hots. Hot meals.

hot skinny. Information.

Howard Johnson. Fire base built with future occupancy in mind.

HQ. Headquarters.

Huey. Nickname for the UH-1 series of utility helicopters, which one reporter described as a combination of "shuttle bus, supply truck, ambulance, and weapon of war." It comes from the official term Helicopter, Utility or H.U.

hump. (1) March or hike—by extension, to move faster. (2) An infantryman; a grunt.

This is a term that has changed its military meaning. Charles D. Poe reports, "In World War II pilots used the term hump to refer to the terrain between China and India [the high eastern Himalayas], but in the Vietnam War this word was used by infantrymen to describe walking under the heavy weight of their equipment."

hundred and worst. The 101st Airborne.

hurtin'. Injured and dead. A

1964 AP dispatch from Vietnam tells of the use of the word that in one case meant "that a man's head had been blown off by a howitzer shell."

I

I & I. Intercourse and intoxication; a clear play off the initialism R & R.

illum. An illumination flare.

incoming / incoming mail. Hostile artillery fire.

in-country. Country outside the U.S. to which one is assigned. During the Vietnam War it meant being in Vietnam: "After R & R in Bangkok, I was back in-country."

Indian country. Unsecured territory.

ink blot. A fortified enclave for supplies and weapons.

Irish pennant. A loose thread, strap, etc.

J

jacket. One's official service record; the military equivalent of one's permanent record.

jack-off flare. Hand-held flare, tube shaped, about a foot long that is fired by striking the bottom. The projectile comes shooting out trailing a bunch of sparks.

Jesus nut. The bolt that holds the rotor blade to a helicopter.

john. Lieutenant; hence "first john" and "second john" for first and second lieutenant.

John Wayne. (1) To act heroically. (2) Soldier who "acts it up" for the media, especially the camera.

John Wayne High School. The U.S. Army Special Warfare School at Fort Bragg.

Jolly Green Giant. The CH-47 double-rotor helicopter. Also *log.*

junk on the bunk. Inspection in which one's field equipment is laid out and displayed on one's bunk.

K

kaserne. German for "camp," this is now used to describe a military base anywhere in the world.

K-Bar. A military knife.

khaki tit. The Army as provider. A regular Army person is said to suck the khaki tit.

KIA. Killed in action.

kick. Dishonorable discharge.

kill. A downed enemy aircraft.

This term has been in use since World War II, replacing the equivalent "victory" of World War I.

kill-fire. A burst of gunfire that is so effective it leaves nobody to return fire.

klick. Kilometer. Also *click*.

K.P. Initialism for Kitchen Police; mess hall duty.

KYPIYP. Short for Keep Your Pecker In Your Pants, long-established V.D. control motto.

L

Land of the Big PX. The United States. There are a number of "Land of the . . ." variations which mean the same thing. Two which appear in *A Dictionary of Soldier Talk* are "Land of the Round Doorknob" (used in Germany, where most doorknobs are handles) and "Land of the 24-Hour Generator" (used in Vietnam, where power outages were common).

lay chilly. To freeze.

leaflet drop. Spending money on girls and booze with reckless abandon.

legos / legs. Unit that is neither airborne nor mechanized;

ground soldiers to airborne rangers.

lick. A mistake.

lifer. Career military person.

lifer juice. Coffee.

liquid cork. Diarrhea medicine.

log. The CH-47 double-rotor helicopter. Also *Jolly Green Giant*.

long tom. Long-range .155 mm artillery. Essentially a World War II term that lives on in the lore of the infantry.

louie. Lieutenant.

lower than whaleshit. In terms of rank and status, at the bottom of the ocean.

L.P. (1) Listening post. (2) Landing platform.

Lum. Illumination flares.

lurp. Special ration of food packaged for those on long-range patrol.

lurps. Rangers engaging in long-range reconnaissance patrols.

L.Z. Landing zone.

M

Maggie's drawers. (1) Red flag displayed from the target pit on the rifle range when a shot has completely missed the target. (2) A miss.

mechanical. Ambush weaponry

triggered by the enemy; mines, flares, etc.

mess / mess hall. Dining facility.

mess kit repair battalion. Mythical unit to which goofs and *bolos* are sent.

mike-mike. Millimeter.

million-dollar wound / million-dollar zap. A noncrippling wound that is serious enough to warrant return to the U.S.; a ticket home.

missing link. Second lieutenant.

Mr. Zippo. G.I. operating a flame-thrower.

Mr. No-shoulders. A snake, starting in Vietnam, where they were common.

MLR. Initialism for Main Line of Resistance, or front line. Often used in the bravado sense of, "I've got more time on the MLR than the REMF has in-country."

MRE. Meal, Ready-to-Eat; the field ration replacing the C- and E-rations.

mule. Small motorized platform used to carry arms, but sometimes also supplies and troops. Sometimes called a "mechanical mule." In Philip Caputo's *A Rumor of War*, one is described as "a heavy-weapons carrier that looked nothing like a mule, but rather resembled an oversized toy wagon."

mummy sack. Rubber body bag.

mustang. Officer who has come up through noncom ranks; also, one who has been given a battlefield promotion.

mystery meat. Mess hall meat lacking clear identity.

——————— N ———————

Nam. Vietnam.

newby / newfer. Replacement person.

No-clap Medal. Good conduct medal, from the belief that one will be given the medal if one avoids V.D.

no days like that! Not likely to happen.

November Foxtrot Whiskey. Another way of saying "no fuckin' way." From the phonetic alphabet.

number 1. The best.

number 10. The worst.

nylon. Parachute.

——————— O ———————

O-club. Officer's club.

o-dark-thirty. Very early in the morning.

officer material. Not officer material; a goof-off.

O.P. Short for outpost.

ossifer. Officer.

outgoing / outgoing mail. Friendly artillery fire.

outside, the. Civilian life.

outstanding. Term of mock enthusiasm for anything from the terrible to the barely passable.

over-two. More than two thirds of the way through a normal enlistment, which is three years long.

P

palm. Napalm.

PBI. Initialism for Poor Bloody Infantry.

P.I. Political influence or political interest. For instance, a private whose father is a member of Congress would find the initials P.I. on his service jacket.

pick up brass. To leave; to move out. The term comes from the rifle range where soldiers are required to pick up their brass shell casings when they are done.

ping. To criticize.

pocket leave. To take one's leave without leaving the post or base. It is probably called this because the leave papers never leave the leave-taker's pocket.

pogues. Rear-echelon military personnel. Derogatory.

point. Forward man on a combat mission.

police. To clean up.

pop. To shoot or kill.

pop smoke. To ignite a smoke grenade to signal an aircraft.

pos. Position.

prang. To land a helicopter roughly.

Prick-25. The PRC-25, the basic backpack field radio used in Vietnam.

psywar. Psychological warfare.

P.T. Physical training.

ptomaine domain / ptomaine palace. Mess hall.

Puff the Magic Dragon. A C-47 transport plane armed with 7.62mm machine guns, which was used in support of ground troops.

pull rank. To exercise the power of one's position or rank.

pull the pin. To leave, from the rapid exit one makes after pulling the ring on a hand grenade.

purple hurt. Purple Heart.

purple vision. Night vision.

P.X. Short for Post Exchange; military store.

Q

quartermaster property. Dead, because burial is a job of the Quartermaster Corps.

R

rack. Cot or bed.

rack time. Sleep.

rail. First lieutenant, from the single silver-bar insignia signifying that rank.

Rambo. According to a March 20, 1989, *Houston Chronicle* article, this is a term "used derisively by soldiers for someone who is braver than he is intelligent."

Ranch Hand. Allusion to defoliation in Vietnam. A Ranch Hand plane was a C-123 outfitted with gigantic defoliant-filled tanks.

R & R. Rest and relaxation, or rest and recuperation. In Vietnam, R & R was a three- to seven-day vacation from combat zones. "Rape and ruin" is just one of a number of unofficial interpretations of R & R.

rat fuck. Mission or operation that is doomed from the beginning.

ration drawer. Person who collects food, pay, and benefits without working for them.

ration of shit. A hard time.

read. To hear or understand.

reckless rifle. Recoilless rifle.

recon. Reconnaissance.

red cunt hair. Bawdy unit of measure denoting a very small distance, such as: "That is one red cunt hair out of alignment." Same as *frog hair.*

red phone. Emergency telephone reserved for the direst of emergencies.

reefer. Refrigerator or refrigerated vehicle.

REMF. Rear-Echelon Mother Fucker, or base-camp support troop.

repple-depple. Replacement depot, the casual camp where incoming soldiers, replacements, are processed.

re-up. Reenlist.

rifle. An infantryman.

rip cords. Loose threads.

roach wagon. Mobile canteen or snack bar.

rock and roll. (1) To fire an automatic weapon. (2) Automatic weapon fire.

rockers. The lower stripes on a NCO's insignia, which look like the rockers that would be found on a rocking horse.

For instance, a master sergeant (or E-8) wears three stripes and three rockers.

Rocket City. Nickname for any base under constant rocket fire.

roll out. To get up.

Rome plow. Bulldozer with a mammoth blade for jungle clearing.

rotate. To return to the U.S. after a period overseas.

round eyes. American women.

S

sack. Bed; *rack*.

S & D. Search and destroy.

sandpaper. Government-issue toilet paper.

sapper. Infiltrator.

sarge. Sergeant.

scope head. Radarman.

scrambled eggs. Gold embellishment on the hat visors of senior officers.

second balloon. A second lieutenant.

seen the elephant. To have been under fire; to have been in combat is to have "seen the elephant." According to *A Dictionary of Soldier Talk* by Col. John R. Elting, Sgt. Major Dan Cragg, and Sgt. Ernest Deal, this phrase which

cropped up in Vietnam dates back to the Mexican War. A longer original version was, "I've heard the owl and seen the elephant."

sewer trout. Mess hall fish.

shake-and-bake. Describing any sergeant who has earned rank quickly and without much time in the service, such as a graduate of NCO training school.

shavetail. A new lieutenant. This is an old term dating back to a time when the Army used mules. New mules had their tails shaved so that their handlers could distinguish them from the trained mules.

shithook. The CH-47 Chinook helicopter.

shit-on-a-shingle. Creamed beef on toast.

shoot and scoot. Artillery-firing technique in which the unit is moved quickly after firing to avoid return fire.

short-arm inspection. V.D. check.

short-timer. Term for one whose tour of duty or period of enlistment is nearing an end. Such a person is sometimes said to be "short."

short-timer's stick. Defined in

Mark Baker's *Nam,* "[When] a soldier had approximately two months remaining of his tour in Vietnam, he might take a long stick and notch it for each of his remaining days in-country. As each day passed he would cut another notch in the stick until his rotation day when he was left with only a small stub."

shotgun envelope. Manila envelope for interoffice mail, which is punched with holes (so that it is easy to see if anything remains in the envelope).

silk. Parachute.

silo sitters. Those assigned to missile sites around the world.

single-digit figit. Nervous condition of one with less than ten days still at risk in a combat zone.

single-digit midget. One with fewer than ten days remaining in a combat zone.

sitmap. Situation map—that is, one showing the dispositions of friendly and enemy forces.

sitrep. Situation report.

SIW. Self-inflicted wound.

skag. Cigarette.

skate. An easy accomplishment.

sky out. To flee or leave suddenly.

sky pilot. Chaplain.

slant. Derogatory term for Oriental.

slick. Helicopter without rockets or other external armament; one used to carry troops and supplies.

SLJO. Short for Shitty Little Job Officer(s).

slop chute. An on-post beer hall for enlisted men not of NCO rank.

slope. A particularly derogatory term for Oriental, especially Vietnamese.

smadge. Term of address for sergeant major.

smart bomb. One that gains remarkable accuracy because it is guided by a laser beam or TV camera.

smokey bear. Drill sergeant.

snake. AH-1G Cobra attack helicopters.

snake eater. U.S. Army Special Forces soldier; Green Beret.

snatch. A capture or a rescue; an operation in which live subjects are brought back. A squad specializing in such operations goes on "snatch patrol."

snowdrops. White-helmeted Air Force Security Police.

snuffy. Recruit or low-ranking individual.

SOL. Shit Out of Luck.

SOP. Standard (or Standing) Operating (or Operational) Procedure.

"Sorry about that." Ritual response to any bit of ill fortune from the trivial to the tragic.

SOS. Chipped beef on toast, which has been long-known as *shit on a shingle*.

spec. Specialist.

special feces. Special Forces.

spider hole. A camouflaged enemy firing position.

spit and polish. Attention to outward appearance and show; polished.

Spooky / The Spook. A helicopter gunship or Puff the Magic Dragon, which supported beleaguered ground forces with miniguns and rockets or 20mm automatic-fire cannon. It is nocturnal, equipped with lights and loudspeakers, and is said to have been one of the few successful psywar ventures undertaken in Vietnam.

squared away. Prepared; ready for action.

stack pencils. To kill time.

stand down. Rest period for a military unit when all operations, except security, cease.

stand tall. (1) To come to attention. (2) Ready.

stateside. The U.S.

steam and cream. Massage parlors where you could get a steam bath and sex.

steel pot. A helmet.

stewburner. Army cook.

straphanger. A useless person; one who has only come along for the ride.

strike. To barhop.

strings. Ropes tossed out of helicopters that soldiers can lash themselves to for a quick evacuation from an area where helicopters can't land. Strings are usually 120 feet long.

swinging dick. Male soldier.

T

tac air. Tactical air support.

TAD. Temporary active duty.

take fire. To be shot at.

tanker / tankerman / tankmen. Soldier in a tank unit.

TDY. Temporary duty, an initialism that comes out sounding like "teedee-Y."

tent peg. Stupid or worthless soldier.

thirty-year man. Career Army; a lifer.

Thule coolies. Those on duty in Thule, Greenland.

tiger piss. Vietnamese beer.

tiger stripes. Camouflaged tropical uniform.

titi. (Alternative spelling, tee-tee) A little; a small quantity.

toadsticker. Bayonet.

toe popper. Small land mine detonated when stepped on.

top. Top sergeant.

tracer. Round of ammunition treated so that it will glow or smoke, so its flight can be followed.

track / tracks. Armored personnel carrier.

trained killer. Soldier, usually applied facetiously and ironically to boys who seem to be anything but.

treadhead. Soldier whose specialty is armor. A character in Harold Coyle's *Team Yankee* says, "Shit, don't they teach you treadheads anything at Fort Knox?"

trip wire. (1) Booby trap. (2) Soldier with a knack for finding traps.

trip-wire vet. Name given to the handful of Vietnam veterans who dealt with the stress and disapproval of the war by living in the woods in North America.

tube steak. Hot dog.

turret-head. An arguer; one who is always spouting off.

turtles. New replacements—so called because they take so long to arrive.

twink. Second lieutenant.

two hots and a Charlie. Combat fare of two hot meals and a C-ration.

U

ultimate weapon, the. Infantryman.

unass. To get up quickly from a sitting position.

Uncle / Uncle Sucker / Uncle Sugar. Uncle Sam; the U.S. government.

use up. To kill.

V

Victor / Victor Charlie. The Viet Cong; the phonetic alphabet names for V.C.

ville. Village.

W

Wait-a-minute-bush. Any bush that had thorns that you could get hung up on.

warm body. Any soldier.

Warthog. Nickname for the airplane formally known as the A-10 or Thunderbolt II.

waste. To kill.

wax. To kill.

wet read. To study a reconnaissance photo while it is still wet from processing.

WETSU. We Eat This Shit Up, an acronym pronounced "wet-soo."

white mice. Vietnamese police.

white sidewalls / whitewalls. Military haircut clipped close to the sides of the head.

WIA. Wounded in action.

wild geese. Mercenaries.

willy peter / willie pete. White phosphorus.

willy-peter bag. Bag for white phosphorous, alluded to in this sentence from Philip Caputo's *Rumor of War:* "They did not find enough of him to fill a willy-peter bag, a waterproof sack a little larger than a shopping bag."

wire. Perimeter where trip wires set off boobytraps.

wire hangers. Troops who are so far out of the combat zone they can enjoy the luxury of hanging their clothes on hangers at night.

word one. Any word. Someone who cannot get a chance to talk will say that they were unable to say word one.

World, the. The United States.

——————— **X** ———————

X.O. Executive Officer.

——————— **Y** ———————

yobo. Lover, from Korean, it usually is applied to a girlfriend.

——————— **Z** ———————

zap. Kill.

zebra. Noncommissioned officer in the higher grades (E-6 through E-9), because of their insignia stripes.

Z.I. Zone of the Interior, a nickname for the U.S.

zippo raid. Search-and-destroy mission in which villages are set afire.

zippo squad. Those who conduct *zippo raids.*

zulu. Casualty report.

SOURCES

American advisors to this chapter have been Charles D. Poe of Houston, Texas, editor James Thorpe III, military slang expert Frank Hailey, and Henry S. A. Beckett, the distinguished author of *The Dictionary of Espionage*. Mr. Poe has supplied many references from fiction and nonfiction of the Vietnam period to put the terms in context. From Poe's work it is clear that one of the best sources of slang is Philip Caputo's *Rumor of War* (Ballantine, 1977). David A. Maurer of Charlottesville, Virginia, and Gary Grow of Lanexa, Virginia, also contributed.

Books about Vietnam with useful glossaries include Mark Baker's *Nam* (Berkley, 1981), Bernard Edelman's *Dear America: Letters Home from Vietnam* (Pocket Books, 1985), Eric Helm's *The Scorpion Squad #2: The Nhu Sky Sting* (Pinnacle, 1984), Jack Hawkins's *Chopper 1: #2 Tunnel Warriors* (Ivy, 1987), Tom Mangold and John Penycate's *The Tunnels of Cu Chi* (Random House, 1980), Al Santoli's *Everything We Had* (Ballantine, 1981), Wallace Terry's *Bloods* (Ballantine, 1984), Lynda Van Devanter's *Home Before Morning* (Beaufort, 1983), and James Webb's *Fields of Fire* (Bantam, 1978). Two important dictionaries are Frank A. Hailey's *Soldier Talk* (Irving Publishing Co., 1982) and *A Dictionary of Soldier Talk* by Col. John R. Elting, Sgt. Major Dan Cragg, and Sgt. Ernest Deal (Charles Scribner's Sons, 1984).

24

YUPPIES, DINKS, AND OTHER MODERNS

—

A Field Guide to the Last Quarter of the Twentieth Century

There is nothing new about slang nicknames for groups of people who are classified by age or lifestyle. We have had our flappers and beatniks, hippies and junkies, lounge lizards and drugstore cowboys.

During the 1980s, however, there was a whole new wave of these terms. Some of these were the creations of demographers looking for a handle to put on a group, while others were simply clever neologisms that took off. In any event, they collectively serve to show us a new form of slang that has established itself. For lack of a better description, it is the slang of groups and demographics. It is also unusual in that the British seemed as obsessed with these terms as Americans, in fact some are imports from the U.K.

Here, then, is a generous sampling of the crop that came on the scene in recent years, many of which were acronyms or derived from them. The fad of creating new ones seems to have lasted a relatively short time, but most of the terms (save for the most convoluted) seem to have stuck. The day this was written, June 7, 1989, an article about the popularity of tropical fish among young urbans which appeared in the Baltimore *Evening Sun* was titled, Yuppies Find Guppies Are Ideal Low-Maintenance Pets.

A

afterboomers. Those born after the post World War II baby boom was over—from about 1965–74. Contrast with *baby busters* and *post-boomers*.

B

baby boomers. Those 78 million Americans born between 1946 and 1964. In 1986, when the first baby boomer turned forty, they started to be referred to as "aging baby boomers." They have been cited for many social changes, including this one suggested in a 1985 Knight-Ridder News Service headline: Baby Boomers Urge Washington State to Make "Louie Louie" Official Anthem.

baby busters. Consumers born from 1965 to 1974, after the baby boom subsided. This was an era of ecological concern and advocacy of zero population growth, and for the first time in history the population declined for reasons other than war or disaster. Sometimes shortened to "busters."

biddies. (Acronym-derived) Baby boomers in debt.

bimbos. Vacuous, sometimes sexy, females. An old bit of slang given new life in the eighties, with the help of such luminaries as Jessica Hahn (who publicly denied her bimbitude) and Tammy Baker.

boomer babies. Children born between 1965 and 1979, as *baby boomers* had babies of their own.

boomers. (1) Short for *baby boomers*. (2) Those who want to exploit an area's oil, gas, and mineral deposits; who would touch off an economic boom.

buppies. (1) (Acronym-derived) British urban professionals. (2) (Acronym-derived) Black, upwardly mobile professionals.

C

chuppie. (Acronym-derived) Chicano urban professionals.

couch potatoes. Those content to spend great amounts of their free time at home watching television. At first a term of derision, it was quickly embraced by those who took pride in their passive ways.

D

dewks. (Acronym) Dual-Employed With Kids.

diks. (Acronym) Double (or Dual) Income, Kids. Contrast *dinks* and *siks*.

dimps. (Acronym) Couples with Double (or Dual) Income, Money Problems.

dincs. (Acronym) Couples with Double (or Dual) Income, No Children. "Dincs" came first but was superseded by "dinks" about 1987.

dinkies. (Acronym-derived) Variation on *dinks*.

dinks. (Acronym) Couples with Double (or Dual) Income, No Kids. The point of this category is that they have more

disposable income than the average family. In her "Wordwatch" column in *The Atlantic,* June 1987, Anne H. Soukhanov pointed to the distinguishing characteristics of the dink: "The women usually retain their maiden names, the couples are very career-oriented, the husband is likely to cook the meals, and they usually own property in an upscale location." The term seems to have first popped up in late 1986.

(It was noted by researcher Charles D. Poe that in the 1974 sci-fi film *Planet Earth* there is a female-dominated society in which males are turned into cowering slaves called dinks.)

dissident yuppie or **D.Y.** Young urban professional who does not fit the mold; nonconforming yuppie, or as one was quoted as saying, "Yeah, I want a BMW, but I don't necessarily like them."

droppies. (Acronym) Disillusioned Relatively Ordinary Professionals Preferring Independent Employment Situations.

dumpies. (Acronym-derived) Downwardly mobile, middle-aged professionals.

E

echo boomers. Those born after the 1965–74 baby bust who echoed the post-World War II baby boom.

empty nesters. People whose children have left home, whose homes contain empty bedrooms.

F

flyers. (Acronym) Fun-Loving Youth En Route to Success. Identified in 1987 by *USA Today* as a hip group aged thirteen to twenty-five years of age.

folkies. Folk music musicians and their fans.

foodie. Gastronomic faddist.

frumpies. (Acronym-derived) Formerly radical upwardly mobile persons.

fundies. Fundamental Christians. Term is likely to be seen as derogatory by those it is applied to.

G

glams. (Acronym-derived) The graying, leisured, affluent, middle-aged.

golden agers. Old people; senior citizens. The U.S. National Park Service issues passes for discounts in national parks which are called "Golden Ager" cards.

grumpies. (Acronym-derived) Grown-up mature people.

guppies. (1) (Acronym-derived) Gay, upwardly-mobile professionals. (2) *Yuppies* with ecological concerns; a blend of "green" and "yuppie."

H

hackers. Computer zealots who, among other things, have learned to gain entry to other people's computer networks.

hippies. The flower children of the late 1960s and early 1970s who advocated peace, free love, and the use of whatever substance "turned you on." The term is still used in referring to selected groups, such as some of the followers of the Grateful Dead.

hookies. Derived from "Who cares?" Hookies are college students who espouse apathy and noninvolvement. The University of Utah, an apparent hotbed of political apathy, attracted press attention in 1988 because of its large hookie population.

huppie. A blend of "hippie" and "yuppie," for a person who is upwardly mobile but spends his spare time living unconventionally in the manner of a hippie.

J

juppies. (Acronym-derived) Japanese urban professionals.

L

latchkeys / latchkey kids. Children who are left at home alone for at least part of the day—an estimated five to seven million in 1988—while their parents work.

lips. (Acronym) Couples with Low Income, Parents Supporting. Coined in the wake of *dincs/dinks*.

M

maffies. (Acronym-derived) Middle-aged affluent folks.

mallies. Young people who hang around shopping malls.

mensans. Members of Mensa, an organization for people who score in the top two percent of standardized IQ tests. The term is from the Latin word for table and connotes a meeting of minds.

moonies. Followers of the Rev. Sun Myung Moon.

moss. (Acronym-derived) Middle-aged, overstressed, semi-affluent suburbanite.

muppies. (Acronym-derived) Mennonite urban professionals. Presented as evidence of how far people have taken the *yuppie* premise. It was spotted by teacher and writer Robert S. Greenman, who spotted it in Amish country in 1987.

N

new-collar. Term created for the middle class of the *baby boomers* in the context of the workplace. Also called "new-collar workers."

O

oilies. American petroleum workers, but usually used in a foreign context, such as "one of the thousands of American oilies in Indonesia."

P

phonies. People hooked on talking on the telephone.

pink collar. Term for lower-level clerical workers, who are almost always women. The term connotes a level of employment that falls just short of white collar.

pink neck. Sophisticated first cousin of the Red Neck.

post-boomers. People born in 1965 and afterward; after the baby boom.

post-yup. Describing the world of the affluent after the 1987 stock market tumble. It has been described as a less ostentatious world, in which making a living has replaced making a killing.

posy-sniffers. Derogatory term for environmentalists, commonly shortened to *sniffers*.

preboomers. Those born during or just prior to World War II, from about 1935 through 1945.

preppies. People who go to, or went to, private preparatory (or prep) schools.

puppies. (Acronym-derived) Poor urban professionals.

R

rubbies. (Acronym-derived) Rich urban bikers.

Rumpie. (Acronym-derived) Rural, upwardly mobile professional. The Longman Guardian *New Words* defines a rumpie as a "relatively affluent and basically conservative young person living in a rural area and engaged in a professional career."

S

sandwich generation. Those couples who find themselves responsible for elderly parents and young children at the same time.

siks. (Acronym) Single Income, Kids.

skippies. (Acronym-derived) School kids with income and purchasing power. Coined in the summer of 1987 by marketing people targeting this group.

skoteys. (Acronym-derived) Spoiled kids of the eighties.

sniffers. Derogatory label for environmentalists who are often at odds with boomers; it is short for *posy-sniffer.*

snow birds. Northerners who head south in the winter to

escape the ice, cold, and snow.

sofa spuds. Synonym for *couch potatoes.*

spec taters. Synonym for *couch potatoes.*

T

taffy. (Acronym-derived) Technologically advanced family. At a minimum, a taffy owns a computer.

techies / tekky. Technicians, especially those associated with electronics and computers.

ticks. (Acronym) Two Income Couple with Kids in School (and parents in retirement). Columnist Ellen Goodman termed them the "most-wooed voters of the 1988 election."

toolies. Technical folks (architects, engineers, surveyors, programmers, etc.) who are absorbed with numbers, science, and mechanical pencils (which they pull out in restaurants to make calculations). Given a boost in Stephen Clark's 1987 *Toolies: The Official Handbook of Engineers and Applied Scientists.*

truppie. A truck driver whose family travels in living space behind the cab of the truck. The quarters are configured like house trailers and ideally suited to husband-and-wife driving teams.

U

un-yuppies. Term created for those who do not share *yuppie* values, who, for example, are young and professional but don't care much about high status European cars.

Uppie Yuppie. Young urban professional living in Michigan's Upper Peninsula. Anyone from the U.P. is an *Uppie.*

W

wimps. The weak, meek, and the cowardly. Old slang that was propelled into the new in 1987 when it was applied to George Bush. *Newsweek* ran a cover story entitled "George Bush: Fighting the 'Wimp Factor.'" This so-called W-word picked up a quick set of derivatives, including these cited by the Los Angeles *Daily News:* wimpy, wimpish, wimpdom, wimpism, wimplike, wimp out, and wimpismo.

woofies. (Acronym-derived) Those who are well off, over fifty.

woofs. (Acronym) Well-Off Older Folks.

woopies. (Acronym-derived) Well-off older people.

————— **Y** —————

yaps. (Acronym) Young Aspiring Professionals.

yavis. (Acronym) Those who are Young, Attractive, Verbal, Intelligent, and Successful.

yeepies. (Acronym-derived) Youthful, energetic elderly people involved in everything.

yippies. (1) Acronym-derived) Young indictable professional person, a name born of the insider stock-trading scandals. Not to be confused with: (2) (Acronym-derived) Members of the Youth International Party, which became known in the late 1960s for their civil disobedience and antiwar protests. (3) Younger impoverished people.

yorkie. A New York *yuppie*.

Y-people. Same as *Yuppies*.

yucas. (Acronym-derived) Young, upwardly mobile Cuban-Americans.

yuffie. (Acronym-derived) Young urban failure, generally a *baby boomer* making less than $10,000 a year. In her book *Too Smart to Be Rich: On Being a Yuffie,* Patty Friedman says, "The yuffie was born with the trappings of success and infinite potential—his daddy's rich and his mamma's good-looking and his IQ's over 135. He'd be a yuppie if he weren't so smart. But he ran it all into the ground with the aplomb and finesse of a true genius."

yukkies. Young, upwardly mobile communist—term created in the pages of the *National Review* for Gorbachev's supporters.

yummies. (Acronym-derived) Young upwardly mobile mommies.

yumpies. Young upwardly mobile professionals—*yuppies* who earn less than $40,000 a year (or did in 1984, when the term came on the scene).

yuppies. (Acronym-derived) Young urban professionals with a taste for BMW's,

Rolex watches, jogging suits, imported bottled water, and fashionable restaurants.

The term was first put in print and popularized by writer Bob Greene in an article in Esquire (March 1983) on "networking parties" sponsored by former radical leader Jerry Rubin. Writing in the newspaper *Newsday* (April 7, 1985) Erica Jong pointed out that it was a corruption of "Yippie," which was Rubin's own Youth International Party.

The publication of *The Yuppie Handbook* in January 1984 gave the term a monumental boost. The concept and the term were said to have lost their relevance with the stock market crash of October 19, 1987.

Derivates spawned by the term include yuppification, yuppyesque, yupguilt, yuppieback (book aimed at the yuppie reader), yupsters (yuppie gangsters), yuppie tax (such as one put on health-club membership) yuptopia, yuppyish, yuppiegate (for any scandal involving yuppie greed), yuplet (Herb Caen's term for a child yuppie).

SOURCES

The Grackel (Generous Researcher and Contributor of Key ELements) for this chapter was Charles D. Poe of Houston. Ross Reader, Robert Greenman, and Chicquita also helped.

BIBLIOGRAPHY—
SORT OF

One of the ways in which slang differs from conventional English is that one is formal and the other is determinedly informal. It is, therefore, totally consistent to offer these informal working notes on slang sources:

(1) SLANG DICTIONARIES

There are several very good slang dictionaries on the market today. In no special order, the best are:

The New Dictionary of American Slang, which is published by Harper & Row. It is a new book which builds on an earlier work—Wentworth and Flexner's 1960 book—with a lot of new examples (*greenmail, bean counter, glitterati,* etc.) and some purging of old terms (Gypsy and carnival slang get short shrift). A classic with 17,000 terms.

A Dictionary of Slang and Unconventional English, 8th Edition, by Eric Partridge and edited by Paul Beale, published by Routledge. It is a gigantic book that contains more than 100,000 entries and weighs close to five pounds. Collectively, it shows us the stunning richness of slang in the English-speaking world. A word like *damper* has no less than ten slang meanings, ranging from a "wet blanket" or "spoilsport" to a "snack." There are words to be found here that are true rarities, like *degombling.* As used in the Falkland Islands, degombling means to shake the snow off one's clothes. If there is a drawback to this immense work it is that it is much more concerned with Commonwealth and British Isles slang than American slang, especially in areas like baseball and Vietnam-era military slang. One needs an American slang dictionary for terms like *Baltimore chop, frag,* and *tushie.* There are nine meanings of *duffer* but not a single reference to golf, which is its most typical American use.

Slang and Euphemism, by Richard A. Spears, which exists in several versions (hardback, quality paper, and mass market paperback). It is hard to find a bookstore anywhere that does not stock this one; and for good reasons, since it is very good. However, to quote from the dust-jacket cover of the edition at my elbow, it is "a dictionary of oaths, curses, insults, sexual slang and metaphor, racial slurs, drug talk, homosexual lingo, and related matters." It is not a general slang dictionary, but a book of the taboo, with nary a page without, at least, an R-rating.

A fascinating and almost impossible to find work is Joseph A. Weingarten's *An American Dictionary of Slang,* which was privately published in 1954.

(2) SLANG THESAURUSES

First, there is the monumental *American Thesaurus of Slang* by Lester V. Berrey and Melvin Van Bark (Thomas Y. Crowell, N.Y., 1952), which covers everything. A more recent and somewhat more limited effort is the excellent *Thesaurus of Slang* by Esther Lewin and Albert E. Lewin (Facts on File, N.Y., 1988).

(3) JARGON

There are several good jargon dictionaries on the market, including Joel Homer's *Jargon,* Jonathon Green's *Newspeak,* and Don Ethan Miller's *The Book of Jargon.* They are all very good, but one is very British in its orientation and the two U.S. books are topical and very selective—for instance, both have sections on computer jargon, but neither cover educational jargon. The ultimate limitation of these books is that they cover jargon, not slang (after all, medical jargon is a far cry from medical slang).

(4) NEW WORDS BOOKS

By their nature, books featuring new words are great sources of new slang. I found these two to be most useful: The Longman Guardian *New Words,* edited by Simon Mort and published in London (my copy is not dated), and *The Facts on File Dictionary of New Words* (1989) by Harold LeMay, Sid Lerner, and Marian Taylor.

(5) ARCHIVES

The greatest single source of help in preparing this book was the Tamony Collection at the University of Missouri, Columbia. It was recently acquired by the university, which wasted no time in making it public. That collection, put together over the course of a long lifetime by the etymologist Peter Tamony, gives America its own archive of native slang. Tamony was considered to be the leading twentieth century lay expert on American slang, and his collection is the only thing like it anywhere. It has been a major factor in giving this small book its authority and strength, and will fuel other such efforts for many years to come.

(6) NEW EDITIONS OF THIS BOOK

I am planning to keep this book current with contemporary examples. I would like very much to hear from those with suggestions for terms that should be included in future editions. I can be reached at this address:

Paul Dickson
Box 80
Garret Park, MD 20896-0080.

Thank you in advance.

INDEX

A

A.A., 179
ABC, 162
abend, 70
A-bone, 23
above the line, 171
abusak, 212
A.C., 132
Acapulco gold, 112
Acapulco spread, 55
acceptable, 46
account side, 2
ace-high, 212
acid, 87, 212
acid freak, 87
acid head, 87
acid rock, 87
across the fence, 232
across the river, 162
actcom, 171
acting jack, 232
activate, 46
ad, 2
adult, 196
advertorial, 2
advid, 2
affair, 179
Afro, 87
afterboomers, 252
AFTRA, 172
agency, 232
agency copy, 2
aggravation, 9
aggresso, 212
aggro, 212
agitation, 9
agro, 212
a-gunner, 232

airball, 202
airborne copulation,
   232
air breathing, 162
aircraft carrier, 202
airdale, 153
airhead, 212
air mail, 212
air-pocket stock, 56
air support, 162
alarmist, 46
albatross, 143
ALF, 120
algy, 70
alki/alky, 23
all day and night,
   102
alley oop, 202
all for one money, 9
all hands, 153
alligator, 189
alligator spread, 56
all in and all done, 9
all over the house, 9
all the way, 132
also ran, 202
alternative, 87
amateur night, 132
Amerika, 87
AMF, 232
ammo humper, 232
ancestral, 9
anchor, 153, 189
anchors, 23
angel, 232
angel dust, 112
angel lust, 143

ankle, 172
antidote, 70
antipersonnel, 162
A-Okay, 38
APA/-apa, 120
apazine, 121
ape, 232
apologist, 46
apples and oranges,
   46
apple-sauce enema,
   232
apron, 23, 132
arbs, 56
arbuckle, 212
arching/arcing, 23
architecture, 70
arcs, 172
are they in / are they
   out?, 179
Arizona Windsor, 9
ark, 23
ARM, 189
armchair quarter-
   back, 202
armor, 102
Army brat, 232
art, 2
artie/arty, 232
ash can, 153
as is, where is, 9
ass bandit, 196
ass out, 212
A.T., 70
at, 87
Atari Democrats,
   180

at the market, 56
at this point in time, 46
attitude adjustment, 212
auction fever, 9
audible, 202
auntie, 38
awesome, 212
AWOL, 232
Aztec two-step, 143

B

B, 212
B-, 172
babe, 87
Baby Bells, 56
baby bond, 56
baby boomers, 252
baby busters, 252
baby catcher, 143
babylon, 112
baby raper, 102
baby shit, 232
back, 132
back burner, 46
backdoor spending, 46
back end / back-end money, 172
backer, 172
backfield, 10
backgrounder, 46
back in the box, 113
back light / backlite, 23
back off, 23, 56
backout, 38
backpack nuke, 163
bad, 212
badge, 102
bad news, 87
bad paper, 232
bad scene, 87

bag, 87,102, 143, 196, 213
bagbiter, 70
bagel, 23
bag job, 56
bail, 213
bailiwick, 46
bail out, 213
bake, 213
baked, 213
bald, 213
baldhead, 113
baldies, 23
ball, 87
ball of wax, 46
balloon, 189
balloon goes up, the, 163
ballpark figure, 46
banana, 143
banana clip, 232
Band-Aid, 232
B & B, 132, 232
bandit, 232
B & W / black and white, 102
banger, 132
banji, 87
bank, 113, 213
bankable, 172
banzai, 23
BAR, 232
bar, 56
barbecue mode, 38
bare-ass, 232
barefoot, 23
barefoot pilgrim, 23
barf, 70
barfly, 132
barkeep, 132
barnburner, 202
Barnes man, 113
barrel, 23
base, 23
basehead, 113
bases drunk, 202

basic, 232
basically, 46
basis point, 56
bathtub, 202
baton, 102
battlewagon, 153
baud, 70
bazongas, 196
bazooka, 113
bazuco, 38
B-back / beback/ be-back, 23
b-boy/b-girl, 213
b-boy stance, 213
B.C., 196
beach, the, 153
bead, 70
beagle, 102
beanball, 202
beans, 149
beans and dicks, 233
beans and mother-fuckers, 233
beard, 56
bearded clam. 196
bear hug, 56
bear market, 56
bear raid, 56
beast,113
beat, 102, 213
beat bag, 113
beat the bricks, 102
beautiful, 87
beauty bolts, 23
beauty shot, 2
beauty spot, 196
bed and breakfast, 56
bed hop, 196
be down on, 87
bedposts, 202
beef, 213
beefer, 23
beergogles, 133
behind the stick, 133
be-in, 87

belay that, 153
belch, 102
believe he stole it, 10
bellhop, 153
bells and whistles, 70
belly ride, 196
belly up, 56
below the line, 172
belt, 149
Beltway bandit, 46, 163
Belushi cocktail, 113
BEM, 121
bench warmer, 202
bend, 149
bent eight, 23
benz/benzo, 113
beta test, 70
betty, 213
bi/bicycle, 196
bidder's paddle, 10
biddies, 252
biftad, 213
big arm, 23
big banger, 23
Big Blue, 56
big board, 56
big brown eyes, 196
big C, 143
big chow, 153
big crunch, 121
big daddy, 196
big picture, 46
Big Portsmouth, 153
Big Red One, 233
big three, 133
big twenty, 233
biker's speed, 113
bilge, 153
bilge rat, 154
bilge water, 154
billing, 172
bimbos, 252
Bimmer, 23
binder, 133, 189

binders, 24
bindle, 113
biosoft, 121
bird, 38, 233
birdbath, 189
bird cage, 202
bird colonel, 233
bird dog, 46
bird farm, 154
birdfarm, 233
bird hatching, 154
birdland, 233
birdman, 38
biscuit, 213
biscuit bitches, 233
biscuits, 113
bit,70, 102
bite, 24, 113, 133
bizotic, 213
black, 133
Black & Decker, 213
black book, 56
black box, 24
black-box approach, 70
black-flagged, 24
black hole, 56
black knight, 56
Black Monday, 56
Black Panthers, 87
Black Rock, 172
black shoe, 154
black tar, 113
blade, 143
blade time, 233
blast, 113
blaster,102
bleed, 2
blind pig, 133
blitz, 202
bloods, 233
blood stripe, 233
bloom, 172
blotter, 102
blow, 113
blow away, 233

blow back, 57
blower, 24
blow it out, 213
blow lunch, 24
blown engine, 24
blown gasser, 24
blowoff, 38
blow off / blow off his doors, 24
blow smoke, 233
blow your cool, 88
blow your mind, 88
blow your top, 196
blue, 70, 233
blue blower, 143
blue book, 24
blue chip, 57
blue collar, 71
blue flu, 102
bluejacket, 154
blue letter, 38
blue max, 233
blue pipe, 143
blue room, 38
blues, 233
blue shirt, 154
blue sky, 113
blue-sky laws, 57
blue steeler, 196
blue top, 163
blue-water sailor, 154
blunting, 172
boarder, 213
boarding, 213
boards, 202
boat, 113
boat anchor, 10
boat pox, 154
bo dereks, 57
boffo, 172
bofs, 172
bogart, 88
bogey/bogie, 233
bogie, 202
Bogon, 71

bogosity, 71
bogsatt, 163
bogue, 213
bogus, 213
boilerplate, 189
boiler room, 57
Boll Weevils, 180
bolo, 102, 233
bomb, 71, 202
bomb thrower, 180
boner, 196
boneyard, 24
bonzai, 213
boo, 88
boobies, 233
boobs, 196
boo-coo, 233
boogerhead, 213
boogie, 202
book, 2, 102, 202
book / book it, 213
boom, 213
boom-boom, 233
boom-boom girl, 233
boom car, 113
boomer, 154, 163
boomer babies, 252
boomers, 252
boondocks, 24
boonie rat, 233
boonies, 233
boost, 102
boot, 57, 71, 154,
  213, 233
booth, 24
bootie food, 133
bootleg, 202
boots, 24
bootstrap, 71
booze, 133
booze cruise, 133
bopper, 88
boss, 24
Boswash, 121
bottle baby, 102
bottle-cap colonel,
  233

Botts' dots, 24
bounce, 102
bounceback, 143
bouncer, 133
bouncing betty, 233
bouncy-bouncy, 196
boutique, 2
bow, 149, 202
bow-and-arrow
  squad, 102
bowhead, 213
bowl of red, 133
box, 24, 57, 71, 143,
  213
boxie, 213
box tonsils, 196
BPS, 71
brace, 234
brain, 149
brain bucket, 24
brainiac, 213
brains blown out, 24
brainstorm, 47
brandstanding, 23
branwagon, 133
brass hat, 24
brass ring, 57
BRAT diet, 143
bread, 88
break, 172
breakdown, 102
breakup value, 57
breeder, 196
brew, 234
brewpub, 133
brewsky, 133
brick, 88, 213
bricks, 149
Brickyard, 24
bridgeware, 71
brightwork, 154
brig rat, 154
brilliant pebbles, 163
bring smoke, 234
broadbrush, 47
broken arrow, 163
broken down, 234

Brompton cocktail,
  113
bronk, 143
broom, 102
brother, 88
brown bag, 133
brown bar, 234
brownie, 102
brown-shoe army,
  234
bubble, 149
bubs, 102
buck, 172
bucket, 24, 202
bucketing, 57
bucket o'blood, 133
buckets, 196
bucket shop, 57
buckle, 234
Buck Rogers, 57
bud, 88, 113
buff, 24, 213
buff up, 143
bug, 71, 102
buggin', 214
bug juice, 133, 143
bugs in the rug, 143
bug smashers, 38
bule, 113
bulk up, 202
bullet, 57, 113
bulletproof, 71
bull market, 57
bull ring, 24
Bullshot, 133
bumble bee, 25
Bumfuck, Egypt,
  234
bummer, 88, 214
bump and run, 202
bumper tag, 25
bump'n, 214
bum-rush, 214
bundling, 180
bunk, 154, 180, 214
bunker buster, 234
buppies, 252

burger, 133
burger joint, 133
buried, 25
burly, 214
burn, 88, 102, 113, 203, 214
burn bag, 114
burned out, 88
burner, 114, 203
burn in, 71
burn me a copy, 163
burnout, 38, 114
burn-out, 214
burn rubber, 25
burnt, 214
burp, 234
burros, 114
burst, 71
bus, 71
bush, 88, 114, 234
bus head, 214
bush gang, 102
bushing, 25
Business, The, 172
bust, 214, 234
bust/busted, 88
bust caps, 234
busted lung, 25
butter bar, 234
buttonhook, 203
buttons, 149, 214
buy, 47
buydown / buydown mortgage, 184
buyer's premium, 10
buy-in, 10
buy it/
buy the farm, 234
"buy you a suit," 102
buzz, 114
buzza, 214
buzz crusher, 214
buzzmaker, 133
bye-bye, 172
byte, 72

C

CAC, 189
cactus, 88
cafeteria plan, 57
cage, 103
caj/cas, 214
cakes, 196
cali, 114
callable, 57
cam, 25
cameo, 214
cammies, 234
camp, 203
can, 154
cancer, 25
candy, 114
candy-store problem, 58
canker mechanic, 234
canned, 103
cannon cockers, 234
can of worms, 47
C&T ward, 163
can't cut it any closer, 10
cap, 214
capping, 234
captain of the head, 154
car, 58, 149
carcass, 25
card, 203
care package, 234
carryon, 38
carryout, 133
carry-out rape, 103
cartwheels, 114
cascade, 58
casework, 180
caseworker, 180
cash cow, 58
cashed, 214
casual factors, 47
cat, 89, 154
catch a buzz, 114

catcher's mitt, 196
catch one, 214
catered, 10
cath, 143
catnip, 89
CATS, 58
cats and dogs, 58
catslide, 189
caucus, 180
Cav, 234
C.B., 133
CBOE, 58
CC&R's, 189
C-cubed, 163
CE, 121
cellar, 203
cement, 203
cement mixer, 25
CEO, 58
chad, 72
chair borne, 235
chairman, the, 163
chalk talk, 203
change your tune, 10
channel, 25
character, 72, 121
charged, 47
charger, 25
charity stripe, 203
Charlie, 235
Charlie Noble, 154
charlie tango, 235
chaser, 133
chasing the dragon, 114
Cheap Charlie, 235
cheap shot, 203
check, 203
checking, 214
check it out, 89
check you later, 214
cheesehead/
cheese meister, 214
cheesy, 214
cherry, 25, 214, 235
cherry pick, 203

Chevrolet BB, 25
chick, 89
chicken, 25
chicken-fried, 133
chicken guts, 235
chicken hawk, 103
chicken plate, 235
chicken switch, 38
chick with a stick,
    214
chief, 214
chill, 103
chill/chillin', 214
chill out, 214
chill with you later,
    215
chilly, 134, 215
chilly most, 215
Chinese Wall, 58
chip, 72
chiphead, 72
chipper, 114
chippying, 114
chit, 122
chizzler, 25
chocoholic, 134
choice and privilege,
    11
choke point, 189
chomp, 72
chop, 25
chopper, 235
chops, 203
chop shop, 25
chop socky movie,
    173
chow, 235
chow down, 134
Christmas tree, 25
Christmas tree bill,
    180
chuborian, 215
chuck, 235
chugalug, 134
chuppie, 253
church key, 134

churn, 58
chute, 26
Cinderella liberty,
    154, 235
civil serpent, 235
clamshell, 26
clap, 114
clean, 11
clean bill, 180
clean deal, 26
clearance mechan-
    isms, 47
clear title, 189
clerks 'n jerks, 235
click, 215, 235
cloakroom, 180
clockin, 215
clone, 72
closure, 181
cloture, 181
cloud, 189
clueless, 215
cluster fuck, 235
clutch belt, 235
clutter, 3
Clydesdale, 215
C.O., 235
coasties, 154
coast to coast, 203
coattail, 181
cob, 215
cocabucks, 114
cod, 38
Code 3, 163
code azure, 143
code word, 163
coequal, 47
coffee grinder, 154
cognitive skills, 47
coke, 114
coke bugs, 114
cokie, 114
cold call, 58
cold car / cold one,
    26
cold fault, 72

cold gun, 103
cold turkey, 114
collar, 103
collateral damage,
    163
colly weed, 114
column, 235
combo coverage,
    203
comfort letter, 58
COMMFU, 235
commish, 3
commo, 235
commune, 89
community, 47
comp, 3
computer virus, 72
-con, 122
condo, 189
Coney Island white-
    fish, 196
confrontation, 89
conn, 154
connection, 89
connectivity, 72
connex, 235
contact, 235
contact high, 89
contrarian, 58
cooker, 114
cookie monster, 203
cool, 89, 215
cooler, 134
co-op, 3
cooping, 103
cop, 89, 114
copilots, 114
cop killer, 103
cop out, 89
copy, 3, 67
cords, 203
core dump, 72
cork, 196
corn, 114
corner, 26, 58
corset, 103

cosmic, 89
costing, 215
cots, 235
couch potatoes, 253
counter, 203
counterculture, 89
counterfactual, 47
counterintuitive, 47
counterprogram-
  ming, 173
country auction, 11
cousin, 203
cozy, 215
CPU, 73
Crabtown, 154
crack, 73, 114
crackback, 204
cracker, 73
crackhead, 114
crack house, 114
crack of heaven, 196
crank, 26, 114, 189
crankin', 215
cranny, 114
crapper, 235
crash, 73, 89
crash cage, 26
crash pad, 89
crash TV, 173
C-rats / C's, 235
crawl, 173
crawlerway, 38
crawling, 204
cream puff, 26
creative financing,
  190
creative side, 3
creep, 173
creeper, 26
creepers, 215
creeping takeover,
  58
crew, 215
crewby, 215
crib, 103, 215
crib burglar, 103

crispy, 134
crispy critters, 235
critical/crit, 215
crock, 143
Crop, The, 114
crossover artist/
  crossover star,
  173
Crotch, the, 154
Crotch, The, 235
crow, 154
CRT, 73
crudzine, 122
crufty, 73
cruising, 26
crunch, 26, 73
crunchies, 235
crush'n, 215
crystals, 115
cubed out, 163
cubes, 115
cujette, 215
cujine, 215
cum, 196
cumshaw, 155
cunt cap, 235
cup, 204
cursor, 73
cuspy, 73
customer golf, 3
cut, 103, 196
cut a melon, 59
cut down on/
  cut on, 215
CYA, 47, 235
cybercrud, 73
cyberculture, 122
cybermetrician, 122
cyberphobe, 73
cyberpunk, 73, 122
cyberspace, 122
cyborg, 122
cybot, 122

D

d, 215
daddy, 103
daddylac, 215
dag, 215
dagoed, 26
dagwood, 134
daisy chain, 196
daisy cutter, 236
daisy wheel, 73
damages, 134
dance hall, 103
D&D, 123
dark side of the
  moon, 181
Darlington stripe, 26
dash, 26
data, 47
daughterboard, 73
dawn raid, 59
day one, 47
day order, 59
dayside, 38
day the eagle shits,
  the, 236
DDT, 73
dead battery, 149
dead cat bounce, 59
deadhead, 115
Deadhead, 215
deadheading, 38
dead horse, 155
deadlock, 73
dead presidents, 103
dead sled, 26
dead time, 103
deal, 90
"Dear Colleague,"
  181
Dear John / Dear
  John letter, 236
death, 215
death trap, 26
debrief, 47
debugging, 73

decay, 39
decent, 215
deck, 103
deck ape, 155
deck lid, 26
decorate your shoes, 215
deef, 204
deep fry, 144
deep six, 155
deep space, 39
def., 215
default, 73
deffest, 215
Delhi belly, 144
deli, 134
demagogue it, 181
demi-veg, 134
demo, 26
dense pack, 163
derms, 123
deros, 236
destabilize, 47
detailing, 26
detention center, 47
detox, 115
Detroit, 27
deuce, 27
Deuce, The, 103
deuce and a half, 236
deuce-deuce, 103
devastator, 103
developing nation, 47
devil weed, 90
dew, 90
dewks, 253
dexter, 216
dialogue, 47
dice, 149
dicensus, 47
dich, 236
di di, 236
diddle, 73, 196
diddy-bopping, 236
did you want to buy it or rent it?, 11

dig, 90
digger, 90, 103
dig it, 90
digithead, 216
digits, 216
diks, 253
Dilbert dunker, 155
dime bag, 115
dimple, 27
dimps, 253
dincs, 253
DINFO, 3
dinger, 103
dink, 236
dinkies, 253
dinks, 253
dippin', 216
dipstick, 216
dirt tracking, 27
dirty, 103
dirty battlefield, 163
dirty officer, 236
dis/diss, 216
disadvantaged, 47
discipline, 48
disconnected, 149
disequilibrium, 48
dish, 173, 204
disincentive, 48
display, 73
dissident yuppie or D.Y., 253
distortion, 11
district work period, 181
ditz, 216
ditzy, 216
dividend-capture, 59
divorce, 103
divot, 204
D.M., 123
DMZ, 103, 236
do, 90
do-able, 48
do a number, 90
doc, 144
doc-in-the-box, 144

dockominium, 190
docs, 73
doctor shop, 115
docudrama, 173
D.O.E reaction, 164
does windows, 204
dog, 27, 59, 216
dog-and-pony show, 164
doggie bag/ doggy bag, 134
dog house, 103
dog it, 204
dogleg, 204
dogs, 39, 149
dog tags, 236
dolphins, 155
do lunch, 134
D.O.M., 196
domicile, 48
domino transplant, 144
donnez-moi un break, 216
don't dwell, sell, 11
don't shoot, I'll marry your daughter, 11
donuts, 27
doobie, 90
dooky, 216
doolie, 39
doorkeeper, 181
dope, 90, 216
doping, 27
dose, 115
do the do, 216
dot matrix, 73
double bagger, 216
double dipper, 48
double truck, 3
doughnut, 149
dove, 181
DOW, 144, 236
dowager's hump, 144
Dow-Jones, 149

down, 74, 90
down/downstroke,
     27
downer, 90
downers, 115
down size, 59
downsizing, 27
downstroke, 190
downtown, 204
do your own thing,
     90
dozmo, 123
D.P., 27
D.Q., 134
drafting, 27
drag, 90
drain the main vein,
     216
dramedy, 173
dream sheet, 236
Dr. Feelgood, 144
drift, 27
DRIP, 59
drive-by, 103
drive the porcelain
     bus, 216
drive time, 173
drobe, 123
drone, 39
drooling, 173
drop, 90
drop a dime, 103
drop-dead fee, 59
drop out, 90
droppies, 253
drop some iron, 216
drop the hammer, 27
druggie, 115
drum, 103
dry hole, 236
dry run, 39, 196
du, 216
dual, 216
duck, 144,181
duckets, 216
dude, 90, 216
duker, 216

dull tool, 149
dummy, 59, 115
dump, 59, 74, 144
dumpies, 253
DuPont lure, 236
dust bunny, 115
dust-off, 236
dusty, 11
Dutch 200, 204
Dutchman, 155
dweeb, 216
dwindles, the, 144
dyke, 196
dynamite, 90
dysfunctional, 48

E

eagle, 204
ear candy, 173
early, 12
Early bird, 164
early-bird special,
     134
early girl, 115
earnest money, 190
ear sex, 196
earth, 90
earth grazer, 123
easy, 155
easy over, 134
eat chain, 217
eat the ball, 204
echo boomers, 254
edge, 149
edgy car, 27
egg, 217
egoboo, 123
ego pricing, 190
ego trip, 90
eight, 236
eightball, 115
eight-track, 115
85, 104
86, 134
ejecta, 164

elbow, 204
electronics hobbyist,
     74
elegant, 74
elevator, 149
elevator music, 173
eleventh finger, 196
empty, 149
empty calories, 134
empty kitchen, 39
empty nesters, 254
empty-nesters, 190
enchiladas, 149
encounter, 123
ended out, 12
end on, 155
end result, 48
enduro, 204
end user, 74
end-user, 48
enema bandit, 196
E-nothing, 236
equalized, 104
equipment, 39
equity, 3
ERISA, 59
escalate, 164
ESOP, 59
establishment, 91
E.T., 27
etched in sand, 48
etched in stone, 48
ethically disoriented,
     48
ETI, 123
evak'd, 236
event, 164
Everest committee,
     181
evil, 115
ex-dividend, 59
execute, 74
executive, 27
executive session,
     181
exercise, 48
exhaust pipe, 196

exobiota, 123
exosociology, 123
exotic, 39
exotics, 27
expertise, 48
express, 217
eyeball van, 104

F

faaan, 123
face, 3
faced, 217
face paint, 217
facilitate, 48
facility, 48
factory, 28
fade, 204
fade the heat, 104
fair warning, 12
fallback position, 48
family jewels, 196
fanac, 123
fandom, 123
faned, 123
fanger, 144
fan (it), 217
Fannie Mae, 60, 190
fannish, 123
fanzine, 123
farm to arm, 115
far out, 91
fart sack, 236
fascinoma, 144
fast food, 134
Fast Movers, 236
fast track, 60
fat, 217, 236
fat Albert, 39
fat farm, 135
fatidis, 135
fat pill, 135
fatty-gews, 236
favorite, 204
feasless, 164

Fed, 91
Fed, The, 60
Fed time, 60
feed, 12
feedback, 48
feeder, 12
feep, 74
feero, 104
fen, 123
fender belly, 155
fender-bender, 28
fern, 196
fern bar, 135
fetus, 217
FIAWOL, 123
field day, 155
field first, 237
fierce, 217
FIFO, 60
50–cal, 237
51–cal, 237
56, 104
FIJAGH, 124
file, 217
filibuster, 182
fill or kill, 60
finalize, 48
finding story, 12
fine tune, 48
finger, 104
finger roll, 204
finger wave, 144
fire base, 237
fired up, 217
fire in the hole, 237
fire on (someone),
   217
fireworks, 104
firmware, 74
first, 190
first strike, 164
fish, 104, 155
fishing, 149
fish skin, 196
five B's, 135
fix, 104, 115

fixed pie, 124
fizzbo, 190
flack/flak, 3
flagging, 173
flail, 217
flake, 12, 104, 217
flamin' 217
flanker, 204
flash and trash, 173
flatline, 124, 144
flat-out, 28
flats, 204
flat top, 155
flavor, 74
flea, 28
flea-market kit, 12
flesh session, 196
flight, 135
flip, 104
flip / flip out, 91
floater, 104
floor, 60, 182
floppy disk,74, 217
flop sweat, 173
flow, 205
flow blue, 12
flower child, 91
flower power, 91
flu, 217
fluff and fold, 135
fluids and electro-
   lytes, 144
fly, 104
flyback, 74
fly-boy/fly-girl, 217
fly by wire, 39
flyers, 254
flying butterknife,
   237
flyover people, 173
FNG, 237
folkies, 254
folky, 13
food, 115
foodie, 135, 254
fooled out, 104

footer, 74, 205
footprint, 39, 74, 164
forked-eight, 28
for real even?, 217
Fort Fumble, 164
fouled, 155
four-banger, 28
four-deuce, 237
455 air-conditioning, 28
four-five, 104
four-oh / four-point-oh, 155
four-oh sailor, 155
four striper, 155
fourth medium, 164
four-to-four, 104
four-walling, 174
fox, 237
frag, 237
fragging, 237
fratricide, 164
freak, 91, 237
freak / freak out, 92
freaky, 92
freebase, 115
freedom bird, 237
free-range, 135
free trip, 205
freeware, 74
freeway dancer, 104
freeze, 48
French letter, 196
French tickler, 196
fresh, 217
freshman, 182
Freshwater Navy, 155
frickles, 135
friendlies, 237
friendly takeover, 60
frobnitz, 74
frog hair, 237
front, 217
front end, 174
front-end bra, 28

front foot, 190
frontloading, 135
front money, 190
front run, 60
frozen, 28
FRP, 124
fruit salad, 237
frumpies, 254
fry, 74
FTA, 237
FTL, 124
FUD/FUD factor, 74
fueler, 28
full bird, 237
full deck, 149
full hank, 217
full house, 28, 135
full of acid, 217
fully-on/fully, 217
fun bags, 196
functional, 48
functional utiliza-
tion, 48
fund, 48
fundies, 254
funding, 48
fungible, 49
funk, 217
funny money, 237
funny papers, 237
furniture, 205
fuzz, 49, 92
F.Y., 49

G

gaffer, 174
GAFIA, 124
gag, 217
gag rule, 182
gallery, 13
galley yarn, 155
gamer, 124
gangsta, 217

ganja, 92, 115
gank, 217
garbage, 74, 135
garbage fees, 190
garbitrageur, 60
Garden of Eden, 197
garritrooper, 237
gas, it's a, 92
gas guzzler, 28
gasser / gas passer, 144
gat, 104
gate, 115
-gate, 182
gauge, 104
gavel-to-gavel, 182
gay, 92, 217
gazump, 190
GCD, 164
gearhead, 75
gee, 104
geed, 217
geedunk, 155
geek, 115, 217
gel, 218
generic, 218
Georgia credit card, 28
geronimos, 115
gerrymander, 182
Gertrude, 155
get busy, 104
get down, 92
get horizontal, 218
get into, 92
get it on, 92
get it together, 92
get naked, 218
get paid, 104
get small, 104
get some, 237
getting off with your bad self, 218
getting short, 238
getting stiffed, 135

getting your plumb-
  ing snaked, 197
get up!, 218
get yours, 218
ghosting, 238
ghost senator, 182
ghost speech, 182
G.I., 238
gig, 92
gigaton, 164
GIGO, 75
gilt edge, 60
gimmie what?, 13
gimp, 218
Ginnie Mae, 190
girly-mon, 218
Gitmo, 155
give 'em away for
  Christmas, 13
G.J., 135
G-joint, 104
glad bag, 238
gladiator school, 104
glams, 254
glass, 28
glass beat/glass post,
  104
glitch, 75
glitterbag, 218
global, 75
glory hole, 155
glove, 197
G.M., 124
gnarly, 218
goat, 182
goat food, 182
gobble, 28
god box, 218
godly, 218
go-go, 164
Golden Age, 124
golden agers, 254
golden BB, 238
golden gater, 174
golden handcuffs, 60
golden parachutes,
  60

gold tin, 104
gomer, 144
go naked, 61
gone, 13
gone camping, 144
gone to ——, 144
gong, 115
go-no-go, 39
goob/gooker, 218
good, 13, 49
good answer!, 218
good, early ware, 13
good hands, 205
good trade, 13
gooey, 218
goof on, 92
goo-goos, 182
gook, 238
go on the box, 105
go over the moun-
  tain, 197
go public, 61
gorilla, 174
gorked, 144
gorp, 135
gorpoblorcho, 218
go straight, 92
gouge, 156
gourd guard, 28
gowser, 13
GOYA, 238
G.Q., 128
grandfather, 190
granny glasses, 92
granola, 218
grapes, 144
grass, 92
grassroots, 183
graunch, 75
graveyard, 205
grav field, 39
gray ghost, 183
gray knight, 61
gray market, 61, 75
grazing, 136
grease, 61, 238
greased, 238

greasy spoon, 136
greek, 3
greenbacks, 238
green bait, 238
green beanies, 238
greenhouse look,
  136
greenies, 183
green machine, 238
greenmail, 61
greenmailer, 61
Green Room, 174
grenade, 28
grid, 28
gridiron, 205
gridlock, 28
grill, 218
grind, 28
grinder, 136, 156
grip, 174
gritch, 75
grok, 75, 124
gronk, 75
gronked, 75
gronk out, 75
groove, 28, 92
groovy, 92, 218
gross player, 174
ground, 218
grounder, 105
ground hog, 136
ground zero, 165
group grope, 197
groupies, 92
growzy, 75
grumpies, 254
grunt, 238
G spot, 197
GTC order, 61
gubbish, 75
guest, 149
GUI, 75
guidette, 218
guido, 219
gulp, 75
gumby, 219
gummer's mate, 156

gun bunny, 238
gung ho, 238
gunny/guns, 238
guns, 219
gunship, 238
gun shy, 205
guppies, 254
guru, 92
gut, 29
guts, 29
gutter wear, 219
guzzler, 29
gweep, 75
Gypsy Moth, 183
gyrene, 238

H

H, 115
hack, 75, 219
hack attack, 75
hacker, 75
hackers, 254
hack it, 238
Hail Mary, 205
hair, 76
hair bag, 105
haircut, 61
hairlines, 13
hairy, 29, 92
ham, 219
hammer, 174
hammock, 174
hand-holding, 3
handshake, 76
hands off, 49
hands on, 49
handyman special,
    190
hang, 29, 76, 219
hang me up, 92
hangtime, 205
hang up/hang-up, 92
happening, 93
happy camper, 136,
    219

happy hour, 136
happy man, 29
hard, 165, 219
hard copy, 76
hardcores, 219
hard disk, 76
hard money, 191
hard rice, 238
hard science/
    hard s.f., 124
hard time, 105
hardware, 76
hard way to go, 219
harsh, 219
hash, 76, 93, 115
hash bash, 115
hash mark, 156
hash marks, 238
hassle, 93
hat, 29, 149
hat trick, 205
hauler, 29
haver, 191
hawg, 205
hawk, 39, 183
hay, 93
head, 93, 156
headbanger, 219
head count, 183
header, 29, 76, 238
head shop/
    head store, 93
he ain't too drunk,
    let him bid
    against himself,
    13
heart, 238
heat, 93, 105, 174
heavy, 93
heavy bead, 165
hedgehog, 76
heeled, 105
he/him, 165
heifer, 219
hein, 219
hella-, 219
he'll be back, 14

hellified, 219
hellish, 219
hello, 219
hemp, 93
herb, 93, 116
heretofore, 49
hernia special, 14
hero, 136
Heroic Fantasy/
    Heroic Fiction,
    or H.F., 124
he/she, 105
he/she came early,
    14
hibernaculum, 125
hickey, 61
hides, 29
hide the salami, 197
hidey-hole, 239
high ball, 29
high beams on, 116
High Frontier, 125
high jack, 219
Hill, the, 183
Hilton, 239
hinges, 149
HINT, 174
hip, 93
hip-hop, 219
hippie/hippy, 93
hippies, 254
hippy witch, 219
his, 116
hit, 105, 116
hitch, 105, 239
hit list, 183
hittin'/hit'n, 219
hit up, 219
ho!, 219
ho/hoe, 219
hoagie, 136
hobble, 197
hobbler, 197
hockey, 149
hog, 239
Hog–60, 239
hokey, 61

hold, 93, 136
hold your mud, 105
hole, the, 105
hole in one, 144
holiday, 156
holler at / hollerat,
    219
Hollywood shower,
    156
holmes / homes /
    homie, 219
home, 76
homeboy/homegirl,
    220
homebrew, 205
home run, 61
homesteader, 239
honcho, 239
honest, 14
honking, 29
honky/honkie, 93
hooch, 93, 239
hoofer, 174
hook, 156, 220
hooked, 93
hookies, 254
hook-up, 220
hooligan, 156
hooter, 116, 136
hooters, 197
hoovering, 61
hopper, 183
hopping, 136
horizontal bop, 197
horn, 220
horror stories, 165
horse, 105, 116, 197
horsemen, 105
hosebag, 220
hose down, 239
hospitalitis, 144
host, 76, 205
hot, 105, 220
hot bunk, 156
hot car, 29
hot dog/hotdog, 205

hotdogger, 3
hot L.Z., 239
hot new issue, 61
hots, 239
hot shot, 116
hot skinny, 239
house, 29, 105, 149,
    220
house ape, 220
housekeeping, 76
house nut, 174
housewife time, 174
HOV, 29
Howard Johnson,
    239
HQ, 239
hubba, 220
Hudson River
    whitefish, 197
Huey, 239
huff duff, 156
huffer, 116
huffers and puffers,
    29
hugger-mugger, 105
Hugo, 125
human resources, 49
humint, 165
hump, 197, 239
hundred and worst,
    239
hung, 197
hung up, 61
hungus, 76
huppie, 255
hurtin', 239
hushmail, 61
hush puppy, 136
hustings, 183
hustle, 93
hustler, 116
hygiene, 76
hymns, 3
hype, 61, 220
hyped, 220
hyperspace, 125

I

I&I, 240
IBM, 105
I can live with, 49
I can't buy 'em for
    that, 14
ice, 116
ice cream habit, 116
iceman, 205
icing, 39
icon, 76
idiot buttons, 29
idiot cards, 175
idiot lights, 29
if you was that old
    you'd have a lot
    more than chips,
    14
igniter, 29
I heard that, 220
illin', 220
illum, 240
ily, 116
impact, 49
implement, 49
implementation, 49
important, 14
in, 93
-in, 94
in a crack, 105
incoming / incoming
    mail, 240
in-country, 240
Indian country,
    240
Indians, 39, 165
indicated, 49
Industry, The, 175
indy, 175
Indy, 29
indyprod, 175
I never would have
    thought of it, 14
influence peddler,
    183

information process-
ing center, 49
infraction, 14
infrastructure, 49
inhale, 137
in-house lawyer, 105
ink, 3
ink blot, 240
inner space, 94
inoperative, 49
inside, 205
inside lot, 191
inside/outside, 105
insiders, 62
insufficiency, 49
interconnect, 49
interdependent, 49
interdisciplinary, 49
interpersonal, 49
intervention, 49
in the can, 175
in the free, 106
in the loop, 49
in the ozone, 173
in the trees / in the
weeds, 137
into, 94
in view of, 49
in-your-face, 205
Irish pennant, 156,
240
Irish sweetener, 137
iron, 30
iron man/woman,
205
iron pimp, 220
irrespective, 49
ish, 125
is of the opinion
that, 49
it ain't all that, 220
Italian, 137
it rules, 220
it's got some age on
it, 14
it's no, 14

ivy pole, 145
Izod, 220

J

jab, 116
jack, 30
jacked, 220
jacket, 106, 240
jackknife, 30
jack-off flare, 240
jack shit, 220
jack up, 220
Jade Squad, 106
jakes, 106
jam, 165, 205, 220
james bond, 62
jammin', 220
jank, 220
January effect, 62
jarhead, 156
jar wars, 116
Jesus freak, 94
Jesus nut, 240
jigger, 137
Jim Jones, 116
jingle, 3
jingus, 220
jitter, 76
jive, 94
joanin', 220
jo-bag/jolly bag,
197
jock, 205
jocker, 106
jockin', 220
joe, 156
john, 240
John Law, 106
Johnnie, 197
johnny, 220
John Wayne, 240
John Wayne High
School, 240
joint, 94, 106

Jolly Green Giant,
240
jolt, 116
joy hole, 197
joy popper, 116
joystick, 76
juco, 220
jug, 30, 106
juice, 106, 116
juicehead, 94
juicer, 220
juke, 116, 220
jump, 156
jump his/her bones,
220
jumpouts, 106
jump-seat sniffer, 40
June bug, 30
jungle rot, 145
junior / junior lien,
191
junk bonds, 62
junker, 30
junket, 183
junkie, 116
junk on the bunk,
240
junks, 221
junque food, 137
juppies, 255
jury rig, 156

K

K / kilobyte, 77
kaserne, 240
kazoonie, 106
K-Bar, 240
keel haul, 157
keep, 106
keeper, 206
keeping six, 106
kennel, 191
key, 206
key grip, 175

keystone, 206, 221
K.G., 106
khaki tit, 240
KIA, 240
kibbles and bits, 116
kick, 240
kickapoo, 4
kick back, 221
kicker, 191
kickin' it, 221
kiddy condo, 191
kidvid, 175
kill, 221, 240
killer, 221
killer bees, 62
killer technology, 62
killer weed, 94
kill-fire, 241
kill-jamming, 165
kill shot, 206
kilo, 94
kippers, 14
KISS, 77
kissed by the Santa
    Fe, 30
kite, 106
klepto, 106
klick, 241
kludge/kluge, 77
kneecap, 165
knife-happy, 145
knitting, 150
knob, 197
knock back, 137
knockdown, 191
knockdown auction,
    14
knocked, 106
knock-off, 30
knockout, 62
knot, 150
Kojak light, 106
KOPS, 40
kosher, 197
kotex, 4
K.P., 241

K-12, 49
KYPIYP, 241

L

L.A., 184
labonza, 197
LAHA, 30
lajaras, 106
lamb, 62
lame, 221
lame duck, 184
lame time, 221
lampin', 221
Land of the Big PX,
    241
Langley, 166
lardo, 221
latchkeys/
    latchkey kids,
    255
later, 221
laughter, 206
launch, 77
launder, 106
lavaliere, 175
law, law, 221
lawyer's bill, 184
LAX, 40
lay, 30
lay chickie, 106
lay chilly, 241
lay day, 157
layover, 40
lay your cane in a
    dusty corner, 197
leader board, 206
Leadership, The,
    184
leadfoot, 30
leads, 62
leaflet drop, 241
leak, 150
leaning, 184
leatherman, 206

leather or feather, 40
lech, 197
left bid, 14
left hanging, 221
leg counsel, 184
legos/legs, 241
legs, 175
Le Mans start, 30
lemon, 30
Leprosy Effect, 166
les, 197
let's cruise, 221
let's discuss, 50
let's show a little
    respect for this
    one, 14
lettered stock, 62
letter-quality, 77
LGM, 125
liberty, 157
liberty hound, 157
LIBOR / LIBID, 62
lick, 241
lid, 94, 116
lifeboat ethic, 125
lifer, 241
lifer juice, 241
lifestyle, 94
LIFO, 62
light sailing, 125
light the rug/
    light the tires, 30
like, 221
limousine liberal,
    184
lips, 255
lipstick, 30
liquid cork, 241
lit / lit up, 116
lite, 137
liver rounds, 145
live tag, 4
liveware, 77
living large, 221
load, 221
loaded, 30

loaf, 221
lobby locust, 40
lo-cal, 137
lock, 206
lock down, 106
loco weed, 94
loft, 221
log, 241
logic board, 77
logic bomb, 77
logrolling, 184
loid, 106
London fix, 62
long, 62
long list, 137
long neck, 137
long tom, 241
lookers, 14
looks like somebody
    missed the road
    to the dump, 15
loop, 30
loose, 221
lop, 221
lost between the
    bells, 221
lost in the sauce, 221
lot, 15
lots per hour, 15
louie, 241
love boat / lovely,
    116
love fest, 184
love juice, 197
low ball, 30
lower than whale-
    shit, 241
low profile, 50
low-rider, 31
low-watt bulb, 150
LOX, 40
loxie, 221
loxing, 40
L.P., 241
lubie, 197
luded out, 116

'ludes, 116
LULU, 191
Lum, 241
lump, 31
lunch, 31
lunchin', 221
lunger, 145
lurp, 241
lurps, 241
L-word, 184
LYON's, 63
L.Z., 241

M

Ma Bell, 63
MAD, 166
maffies, 255
mag, 31
magalog, 4
Maggie Mae, 191
Maggie's drawers,
    241
magic, 77
magnet, 221
Magnum, 197
main, 31
mainframe, 77
majolica, 15
major, 175, 221
make, 31
mall, 191
mall crawler, 221
mallies, 255
man, the, 106
Manhattan eel, 197
Manny Hanny, 63
maracas, 197
marahoochie, 117
marbles, 31, 150
marital aid, 197
mark, 106
mark one eyeball, 40
Mark1 Mod 1, 166
married, 15

marsdoggle, 40
Martian Statue of
    Liberty, 125
Mary Jane, 94
mashed potato
    drive, 31
mast, 157
mat, 157
match box, 94
mating dance of the
    lead-bottomed
    money-gobblers,
    157
Maui Wowie, 117
maxi, 94
maximize, 50
maxin', 106
mayo, 137
Maypole, 198
maytag, 107
McGovern Demo-
    crat, 184
McQ, 198
meat market/
    meat rack, 137
meat puppet, 125
meatware, 77
mechanical, 241
Med, the, 157
media, 4
media center, 50
medley, 137
Medusa, 117
meeting of the
    minds, 191
mega-, 221
megacharacters, 126
megadeath, 166
megadiner, 137
MEGO, 184
melba, 221
mellow up, 221
Melody Hill anemia,
    145
melon, 63
meltdown, 63

mensans, 255
mental, 221
mention, 4
mentor, 63
menu, 77
menuese, 137
mess / mess hall, 242
mess 'em up, 221
mess kit repair
    battalion, 242
mess up, 221
metal mouth, 222
methodology, 50
metsat, 40
Mexican overdrive,
    31
MFR, 166
M.I., 145
Mickey D's, 222
Mickey Mouse
    rules, 157
micro, 77
mike, 94
mike-mike, 242
mike sock, 175
milicrat, 166
mill, 31
million-dollar
    wound / million-
    dollar zap, 242
mindfucking, 94
mindshare, 78
mingling, 191
mini, 78
mint, 222
MIPS, 78
Mirandize, 107
missing link, 242
MLR, 242
mobile response
    unit, 50
moby, 78
mode, 78
modeiant, 222
modem, 78
moguls, 206

molar masher, 145
molded, 222
mole, 107
mommy track, 63
Monday morning
    quarterback, 206
money, 222
money bus, 107
monkey, 191
monkey fist, 157
monster fodder, 126
Montezuma's
    revenge, 145
monty haul, 126
mooch, 107
mooner, 107
moonies, 255
moontel, 126
MOR, 175
morf, 117
mortgage-backed, 63
MOS, 175
mosquito boat, 157
moss, 255
mothballs, 157
moth-eaten, 31
motherboard, 78
mother's helper, 117
mother ship, 126
motivationally
    deficient, 50
motor, 150
motors, 63
Mount Joy, 198
Mount Saint Else-
    where, 145
mouse, 78
mouse house, 31
mouse-milking, 63
mousing, 157
Movement, The, 95
MRE, 242
Mr. Happy, 198
Mr. No-shoulders,
    242
Mr. Zippo, 242

Ms., 95
mud doggin', 31
mud pie, 138
Muffie and Biff, 222
mug, 107
muggle, 117
mug shot, 107
mule, 107, 157, 242
mullets, 63
mulligan, 206
multidisciplinary,
    50
mummy sack, 242
munchie, 222
munchies, 138
munchkin, 126
munch on, 222
mundane, 126
mundo-, 222
mung, 78
muppies, 255
muscle, 31
mushfake, 107
mush mind, 117
mushrooms, 117
mustache ride, 198
mustang, 242
mustard, 150
mustard chucker,
    107
must list, 184
Mutt and Jeff act,
    107
my bad, 222
mystery meat, 138,
    242

N

n, 78
nail, 117
Nam, 242
narc, 95, 222
navy shower, 157
near space, 41

neat, 138
neat whistle, 222
Nebula, 126
nectar, 222
ned, 222
needless to say, 50
nemmies/nimbies, 117
neofan, 126
neonatal unit, 50
nerdling, 78
nerd pack, 78
nerf, 31
nerf bars, 31
new blood, 15
newby / newfer, 242
new-collar, 255
new issue whore, 63
New Jersey, 15
New Jersey tourist birds, 15
New Wave, 126
nextish, 126
nibble, 78
nibbling, 138
nice du, 222
nickel, 117
nickel defense, 206
nightcap, 138
NIMBY, 191
9.5 fling, 222
nitro, 222
nitty gritty, 95
nix, 175
No-clap Medal, 242
no days like that!, 242
no duh, 222
no excuses to be made on this one, 15
NOFUN, 166
nog, 222
noise, 63
no-load, 63

no more partying, let's get with it, 16
noncon, 126
nonpaper, 184
nonpro, 175
nookie, 198
nooks, 222
nooner, 198
no-op, 41
No refund. No return. This isn't J. C. Penney, 16
normals, 126
no's, 16
nose bleeder, 206
nose candy/ nose powder, 117
nose guard/tackle, 206
nosh, 138
noshery, 138
no-show, 41
nostril shot, 175
not!, 222
not even in the ball game, 145
nothing to hide, 16
nothing wrong with it, it just needs a new home, 16
"Not that well-known in these parts", 16
no way, 95
November Foxtrot Whiskey, 242
NPC, 126
nuc, 158
nuke, 222,
number crunching, 78
number 1, 242
number 10, 242
numbers, 175
nutmeg, 206

NUTS, 166
nuttier, 150
nutty, 150
nylon, 242

O

O, 198
O & O, 176
oar, 150
oater, 176
ocean fenders, 31
O-club, 242
O.D., 138, 158
o-dark thirty, 242
odd lot, 63
off, 95, 107
officer material, 242
offline, 141
offload, 166
off-load, 50
off-the-shelf, 78
of the period, 16
oids/roids, 145
oilies, 185, 255
O.J., 138
old, 16
Old Guard, 185
old lady / old man, 95
Old Lady of Thread-needle Street, 63
old man, the, 158
old-timer's disease, 145
ollie grab, 222
omnibus bill, 185
once over easy, 138
one-eyed wonder, 198
one hundred per-cent, 16
110 percent, 207
one-minute, 185
one-night stand, 198

one-percenters, 107
one would think, 50
onload, 166
on the arm, 107
on the floor, 31
on the grain and
    drain train, 107
on the hook, 32
on the pipe, 117
on the rocks, 138
on the strength, 223
on wheels, 138
O.P., 243
open architecture,
    79
open dating, 138
open house, 191
open the tap, 32
orange pouch, 185
oregano, 95
organ recital, 145,
    223
orphan, 79
O sign, 145
ossifer, 243
OTE, 50
other end of Penn-
    sylvania Avenue,
    the, 185
OTR, 198
outgoing/outgoing
    mail, 243
outlaw, 32
out of it, 95
out of sight, 95
out of the chute/
    gate/hole, 32
outreach, 50
outside, the, 243
outstanding, 243
overcrowded, 50
overdrawn, 150
overexposure, 4
overkill, 95, 166
overnights, 176
over on the floor,
    185

oversight, 50
over the shoulder
    boulder holder,
    198
over-two, 243

P

P.A., 4
PAC, 185
pacer, 32
packing, 32
Pac-Man defense, 63
pad, 95
padre, 158
paint, 207
painter, 158
palm, 207, 243
pan, 145
panic, 117
paper, 108, 117
paper dolls, 150
paper hanger, 108
paper profit, 64
paper pusher, 50
paper trail, 50
parallel parking, 198
parallel world, 126
paraphernalia, 95
parsec, 127
parsley patch, 198
pass, 16
paste, 207
past history, 50
patch, 108
pavement princess,
    108
PAX, 41
payola, 176
PBI, 243
PC, 79
Peacekeeper, 166
peg, 4
penalty box, 41
pencil in, 50
penny stock, 64

Pentagoose Noose,
    166
people meter,176
People, The, 95
peripherals, 79
perks, 117
perp, 108
personality, 176
pessimal, 79
Peter, Paul, and
    Mary, 198
petunia, 223
P-funk, 117
phantoms, 16
phase in, 50
phase out, 50
phase zero, 50
phoner, 176
phonies, 256
phony collar, 108
phreaking, 79
physical, 207
physics package, 166
P.I., 108, 243
picker, 16
pickets, 150
pick no squares, 223
pick-up, 4
pick up brass, 243
pick up your face,
    223
pickin' bids, 16
piddling, 108
piece, 32, 108, 223
pig, 95
pigeonhole, 185
pig out, 138
pigskin, 207
pilot light, 150
ping, 243
pink collar, 256
pink house syn-
    drome, 192
pink neck, 256
pink puffer, 145
pink sheets, 64
pip, 64

pipes, 32, 158
pit, 32, 41, 64, 207
PITI, 192
pitman, 158
pit stop, 138
pit, the, 146
pixels, 79
place, 4
place, the, 108
planar / planar
    board, 79
Planet, The, 96
Planet X, 127
plant, 108
plant your seed, 96
plastic, 64, 96
platform, 185
player, 146, 223
plug, 4, 150, 198
pluggers, 207
pluggery, 5
pluke, 198
plum, 50
plumber, 146
plunge, 64
PMSB, 146
pocket leave, 243
pocket man, 108
pod, 41
podmall, 192
pogues, 243
point, 64, 243
points, 176, 192
poison pill, 64
police, 243
policy, 51
pood, 198
poodle, 207
pool, 17
pop, 243
pop caps, 108
popcorn machine,
    108
pop it right out of
    here, 17
pop one's cookies,
    198

pop smoke, 243
pop the clutch, 32
porcupine provi-
    sions, 64
pork, 185
pork barrel, 185
porking, 198
pork out, 138
ports, 79
Port Said garter, 198
POS, 17
pos, 243
poser, 223
posse, 117, 223
post, 32
post-boomers, 256
postcard pressure,
    185
posteds, 17
posture, 185
post-yup, 256
posy-sniffers, 256
pot, 32, 96
pothead, 96, 117
pot luck, 138
pounds, shillings,
    and pence, 96
power, 32
power breakfast/
    power lunch, 138
P.P., 108
PPPP, 146
PR, 5
praisery, 5
prang, 243
preacher's car, 32
preboomers, 256
prebrief, 51
preemie, 146
preplanning, 51
preppies, 256
Prick–25, 243
prime time, 17
prioritize, 51
private sector, the,
    51
privatize, 64

proactive, 51
probably, 17
procedural safe-
    guards, 51
process, 51
procurement/procur-
    ing, 51
product, 64
product PR, 5
program, 51, 166
project, 51
prompt, 79
promulgate, 51
propars, 127
propeller-heads, 79
propho, 198
prudent man rule, 64
prune, 51
prunes, 198
pseudo, 223
psych, 223
psychedelic, 96
psychoceramic, 146
psychotic, 223
psywar, 243
P.T., 243
ptomaine domain/
    ptomaine palace,
    243
public sector, 51
public trough, 185
pud, 198
pudding, 96
puddle, 64
puds, 64
puffer, 17
puffery, 5
puffing, 192
puff piece, 5
Puff the Magic
    Dragon, 243
puke, 32
pull, 5, 32
pulling teeth time,
    18
pull rank, 243
pull the pin, 243

pull yourself
    together, 96
pumping, 117
pump priming, 186
punchboard, 198
punch job, 108
punch on, 207
punk, 108
puppies, 256
puppy, 117
pups, 64
purple hearts, 117
purple hurt, 243
purple shirt, 158
purple vision, 243
putdown/put down,
    96
put his papers in,
    108
put-on/put on, 96
put on the map, 5
Puzzle Palace, 166
P.X., 243

Q

Q, 176
QBE, 79
Q sign, 146
quacks, 117
quad, 146
qualifying, 192
qualitative, 51
quality, 223
quantification, 51
quantitative, 51
quants, 64
quarter, 117
quartermaster
    property, 244
quarters, 158
quarts, 150
queef, 223
queer, 223
queeve, 223

quick fix, 51
quickie, 198
quick knockdown,
    18
quiet sun, 41

R

R and R, 32
R&D / R and D, 51
R & R, 244
rabbit food, 138
rack, 223, 244
rack monster, 223
racks, 198
rack time, 244
rack up, 223
radical to the fifth
    dimension, 223
rad/radical, 223
rad weed, 117
ragged edge, 32
raggin', 223
raging, 223
rags, 223
ragtop, 32
ragweed, 117
raider, 65
rail, 244
rail job, 32
railroad, 186
railroad flat, 192
rails, 32
railway thinking, 127
raincoat, 198
raked, 32
ralph, 223
RAM, 79
Rambo, 244
ramscoop, 127
Ranch Hand, 244
ranker / rank out,
    224
rap, 32, 96, 108
rap sheet, 108

rat, 32, 224
ratboy, 117
rates, 158
rat fuck, 244
ration drawer, 244
ration of shit, 244
raw, 224
razor blades, 158
razor boy/girl, 127
read, 244
real slice, a, 224
rear admiral, 146
reckless rifle, 244
recon, 244
red cunt hair, 244
red devil, 117
red dog, 207
red-eye, 41
red flag, 118
red herring, 65
red lead, 158
redlining, 192
red phone, 244
red pipe, 146
redshirt, 207
red shirt, 158
redundancy of
    human
    resources, 51
reefer, 96, 108, 244
reefer ship, 158
reeker, 146
reeks, 224
ref, 207
rehab, 192
reinventing the
    wheel, 51
release, 5
REMF, 244
remnant space, 5
remo, 224
rents, 224
repeaters, 138
repo, 65
repple-depple, 244
reserve, 18

resident, 80
resistance level, 65
reskilling, 51
rest cure, 32
retool, 166
retros, 41
re-up, 244
revenue enhance-
    ment, 186
revenue shortfall, 52
reverse, 150
revise to reflect, 52
revolving door, the,
    166
revolving the door,
    52
RFP, 52
rice burner, 32
Rice Krispies, 150
rickety-raw, 224
ride, 32, 224
ride on, 108
ride-out, 108
rider, 224
ride/ridin', 224
ride the rails, 32
ride the slow train,
    224
rifle, 244
RIF / riff, 52
rig, 65
riggers and juicers,
    176
right, 18
right on!, 96
"right where we
    should've
    started", 18
rim shot, 176
ringer, 207
ring his bell, 207
rings, 118
ring the register, 65
rinse, 138
rip, 224
rip cords, 244

rip off, 97
rip-off artist, 97
RIPP, 65
ripped, 97
roach, 33, 97
roach clip, 97
roach coach, 41, 138
roach wagon, 244
road dog, 224
road tar, 33
robo, 186
rock, 118
rock and roll, 224,
    244
rocker, 150, 224
rockers, 244
Rocket City, 245
rocket fuel, 118
rock glass, 139
Rocky Mountain
    oysters, 139
rock your world, 224
roll, 108, 224
roll call, 150
roller, 33, 118
roller skate, 33
roll out, 245
ROM, 80
Roman, 198
Rome plow, 245
rookie, 207
room, 150
roostertail, 207
root cause, 52
roots and berries,
    139
rope, 118
roscoe, 108
rotate, 245
roto rooter, 198
rouge, 224
rough off, 109
rough rider, 198
rounder, 109
round eyes, 245
round lot, 65

RPG, 127
R's and T's, 118
rubber, 33
rubber duckie, 158
rubberneck, 33
rubbies, 256
rude, 224
ruff, 224
rug rank, 166
ruined, 97
rules lawyer, 127
Rumpie, 256
run-and-gun, 207
rush, 224
rust bucket, 33
R.V., 167
RYFM, 80

S

S & D, 245
S&J, 109
S&S, 128
S&W, 109
sack, 207, 245
safe, 198
safe seat, 186
safety net, 186
Sagebrush Rebels,
    186
salami attack /
    salami technique,
    80
Sallie Mae, 65
sameway, 18
sandpaper, 245
sandwich, 208
sandwiches, 150
sandwich genera-
    tion, 256
sandwich man, 5
sandwich /
    sandwich lease,
    192
sanitize, 167

sapper, 245
sappnin', 224
sarge, 245
satch, 109
Saturday night
    special, 109
saving roll / saving
    throw, 128
say hello, 33
scam, 224
scamming, 224
scare book, the, 167
scarf, 139, 224
scenario, 52
scenario-dependent,
    167
scene, 97
scenery, 65
sci-fi, 128
scoop, 224
scope, 146, 224
scope head, 245
scorched earth, 65
scramble, 41
scrambled eggs, 245
scrambler, 176
scrappin', 225
screw, 109, 150, 158
scribe, 225
scrim, 176
scrimmages, 150
scroll, 80
scrub, 41, 80
SCSI, 80
scuff, 33
SCUM, 109
scurb, 225
scuttlebutt, 158
scuz/scuzz, 97
sea gull, 158
sea-gull model, 65
search and destroy,
    167
seat, 65
seatwarmer, 186
seaweed, 158

Secdef, 167
second, 192
second balloon, 245
second effort, 208
second-story man,
    109
second wind, 208
second strike, 167
secure, 158
securitization, 65
seed money, 52
seen the elephant,
    245
segue, 176
selected out, 52, 167
sell ya' one in a
    minute, 18
sensetapes, 128
sercon, 128
SETI, 128
set it in at, 18
seven digits, 225
sev's, 225
sewerman, 158
sewer trout, 245
s.f., 128
shades, 97
shadow gazer, 146
shagging, 225
shake, 118
shake-and-bake, 245
shakedown, 109
shake out, 65
shallow river run-
    ning fast, 65
shank, 109
shareware, 80
shark, 66
shark repellent, 66
shaved, 33
shavetail, 245
shellback, 158
"She reads Seven-
    teen", 225
Sherwood Forest,
    158

shill, 18
shillelagh, 33
shine on, 109
ship over, 159
ship to shore, 225
shirts vs. skins/
    shirts 'n' skins,
    208
shit, 97, 150
shithook, 245
shit-on-a-shingle,
    245
shiv, 109
shock jock, 177
shoe, 109
shoestring, 208
shoot and scoot, 245
shooter, 139
shoot your wad, 199
shop, 5
shopping list menu,
    139
short, 66, 109
short-arm inspec-
    tion, 245
short dog, 139
shortfall, 52
short-timer, 245
short-timer's stick,
    245
shot, 5, 139
shot glass, 139
shotgun envelope,
    246
shot who?, 225
shout at one's shoes,
    225
shovel / shovel pass,
    208
shower cap, 199
showstopper, 66
shrink, 146
shtup, 199
shuck, 97
shun it, 225
sick, 18, 225

sick bay, 159
SICU, 146
sigint, 167
signage, 52
signed, 18
significant contribu-
    tion, 52
sign off on, 167
siks, 256
Silicon Valley, 80
silk, 246
silo sitters, 246
single-digit figit, 246
single-digit midget,
    246
sinker, 139
sinsemilla, 118
SIOP, 167
sitcom, 177
sitmap, 246
sitrep, 246
SIW, 246
six-banger/six-holer,
    33
six-pack license, 159
six-pack Republican,
    186
size the vic, 109
sizzle, 5
skag, 246
skanky, 225
skate, 246
skater, 225
skate rat, 225
skeeching, 33
skell, 109
sketch, 225
skidder, 225
skid-drop, 118
skiffy, 128
skin, 199
skin it, 225
skins, 33, 159
skippies, 256
skitcom, 177
skoteys, 256

skunk, 159
skunk works, 66
skyhook, 208
skylarking, 159
sky out, 246
sky pilot, 246
slacking, 225
slam, 199, 225
slam dunk, 41, 66
slammer, 109
slant, 5, 246
slap-down, 225
slaps, 225
slash and hack, 128
slasher movie, 177
slave, 80
sleaze factor, 186
sleaze TV, 177
sled, 33
slice up, 225
slick, 246
slicks, 33
slider, 225
slim jim, 109
slingshot, 33
slippery, 33
slipstreaming, 33
SLJO, 246
SLOB, 66
slop chute, 159, 246
slope, 246
slot, 177
slow motion, 33
slug, 33
slush / slush box, 33
smadge, 246
smalls, 19
smart bomb, 246
smashed, 97
smidge, 66
smit, 225
smof, 128
smokables, 97
smoke, 97, 118
smoke test, 80
smokey bear, 246

smokin', 225
smoking gun, 186
smoking materials,
    41
smothered, 139
smurfing, 109
snake, 225, 246
snakebit, 208
snake eater, 246
snap, 225
snarf, 81
snatch, 199, 246
sneakers, 33
sniffers, 256
snipe, 159
snitch, 109
snow, 118
snowballs, 33
snow birds, 256
snowdrops, 246
snuffy, 247
sofa spuds, 257
soft, 167
soft money, 192
software, 81
SOL, 247
solo, 128
so much for one,
    take 'em all, 19
so much for one;
    take one, take
    all, 19
songbird, 109
SOP, 247
"Sorry about that",
    247
SOS, 247
soufflé, 146
soul, 97
soul brother, 97
soul sister, 97
sound of the city, 52
sounds, 225
soup, 42, 159
souped up, 33
southpaw, 208

southside basing,
    167
space, 5
spaced / spaced out /
    spacey, 97
space junk, 42
space opera, 128
spaceship ethic, 129
spacetug, 42
spacin', 225
spaghetti, 34
spaghetti suit, 42
spazz, 81, 225
spearing, 208
spec, 247
spec taters, 257
special, 34, 177
special feces, 247
speedball, 118
spent, 225
spider hole, 247
spike, 81, 208
spin doctor/
    spin master, 6
spin / spin control, 5
spit and polish, 247
spit on the sidewalk,
    109
spitter, 109
splash, 81, 139
splashdown, 42
splatter movie, 177
splatterpunk, 129
splice the main-
    brace, 159
spliff, 97, 118
splinters, 150
split, 97
splockenin', 225
spoiler, 34
Spooky / The
    Spook, 247
spread, the, 208
spritzer, 139
sproutsy, 139
spud, 140, 225

SQL, 81
squared away, 247
square grouper, 118
squash that / squash
    that melon, 225
squat, 109
squeal, 110
squeeze, 66
squid, 225
squint, 34
squirrelly, 34
squirt, 34
Squish, 187
stack, 140
stack pencils, 247
Stalingrad, 66
stall, 110
stalled vehicle, 150
stamps, 159
stand down, 247
stand tall, 247
stardust, 118
starship, 42
starter home, 192
stash, 97
state of the art, 52
stateside, 247
staties, 110
steal of the evening,
    19
steam and cream,
    247
steel collar, 81
steel pot, 247
steenth, 66
steerer, 118
stem, 118
step back, 110
step off, 226
step on, 118
stern-wheeler, 199
stew, 42
stewburner, 247
stew zoo, 42
stick, 34, 118, 226
sticker, 34

sticks, 34, 140, 226
stick shaker, 42
stick-um, 208
stick-up boys, 118
stinking rose, 140
stir, 110
stirrups, 146
stock, 34
stoked, 226
stole, 226
stoned / stoned out,
    97
stooge, 110
stove bolt, 34
straight, 97
straight eight, 110
straight up, 140
strange, 199
straphanger, 247
strapped, 110
strawberry, 118
straw hat, 34
street name, 66
stretch, 177
strike, 247
striker, 159
strings, 247
strip, 192
stripes, 159
stripped, 66
stroked, 34
stroker, 34
strung out, 97
stud, 226
stud-muffin, 226
stuffies, 226
stump, 187
stunt, 6
stunting, 177
stupid fresh, 226
stutter step, 208
subject matter, 52
submarine, 34, 140
substandard hous-
    ing, 52
suburbs, the, 209

sudden death, 209
suds, 140
sugar scoop, 34
suicide squad, 209
suitcase war, 129
suit up, 209
Summer of Love, 97
sunny side up, 140
sunset law, 52
sunshine rule, 52
s'up, 226
superstation, 177
sure you're right,
  226
surf-n-turf, 140
surviving spouse, 52
swab / swabbie /
  swab jockey, 159
swacked, 97
sweat, 226
sweep, 209
sweeps, 6
sweet, 226
swill, 140
swillmobile, 226
swinging dick, 247
switch hitter, 199
swivel hips, 209
swivel neck, 226
swooner, 66
syke, 226
system hacker, 129
system, the, 110
System, The, 66

T

T&A, 199
T&T, 140
tab, 118
table from hell, 140
tabletops, 19
tac air, 247
tachyon, 129

TAD, 247
tadpole, 159
taffy, 257
take a chill pill, 226
take fire, 247
take a fix / take a
  reading, 52
talent, 177
talk out of the side
  of your neck, 226
tamale time, 226
tank, 34
tanker/tankerman/
  tankmen, 247
Tank, the, 167
tape watcher, 66
tard, 226
target, 52, 66
task, 52
tasker, 52
task force, 53
tatas, 199
tater, 140
taxi squad, 209
TBF, 226
T-bone, 34
TDY, 247
tea, 98
tea / tea 13, 118
team, 150
teaser, 6
teaser rate, 193
techie, 81
techies/tekky, 257
tech-mech, 81
technoslut/
  technotrash/
  technoweenie, 81
teeny, 66
teepee, 226
teeth, 119
tell it like it is, 98
ten-and-ten, 19
10/13, 110
tenant, 209
tent peg, 247

termites, 150
tern, 146
terraforming, 129
Texas disease, 66
Texas rat, 35
Tex-Mex, 140
thanks for your help,
  19
that's a plan, 226
that's casual, 226
The Man, 98
the old (insert name
  of color) paint,
  19
there's still plenty of
  money to be
  made on this
  one. There's still
  money in this
  one, 19
thermal radiation,
  167
thin, 209
thing, 98
Third Industrial
  Revolution, 129
30 Rock, 177
thirty, 6
thirty-year man, 248
Thorazine shuffle,
  146
thrash, 226
thrasher, 226
thrashin', 226
threat tube, 168
three-humped
  camel, 168
three I's, 187
three-martini lunch,
  140
three P's, 146
three pointer, 42
threesome, 199
three-toed sloth, 146
throwaway, 6, 110
throw bricks, 110

throw it in the
  swamp, 19
thrust, 53
Thule coolies, 248
thunder jug/
  thunder mug, 20
ticket puncher, 168
ticks, 257
tie the President's
  hands, 187
tiger piss, 248
tiger stripes, 248
TIGR's, 66
tiled, 81
time bomb, 81
time frame, 53
time to open your
  eyes, 20
tin, 110
tin can, 159
tin fish, 159
tin grin/
  tinsel teeth, 226
tinman, 42
tin parachute, 67
tired iron / tired rat,
  35
Titanic analogy, 129
titi, 248
titty shake, 199
T-man, 119
toadsticker, 248
toe popper, 248
together, 98
to go, 140
toilet, 177
toke, 98
tolly, 119
tongue wrestle, 199
tonsil hockey, 199
tool, 35, 119, 226
toolies, 257
tools of ignorance,
  209
tootsie roll, 119
top, 248

top eliminator, 35
top fueler, 35
topline, 177
topspin, 177
top tick, 67
torpedo, 140
tossing a rod, 35
touch, 209
touchdown, 42
touron, 226
towered, 187
toxic, 226
toys, 199
tracer, 248
track/tracks, 248
tracks, 119
trade out, 6
trades, the, 177
trained killer, 248
train wreck, 146
trannys, 35
transparent, 81
transphotic, 129
trap door, 81
trash, 98
trashed, 226
trash fish, 140
trash TV, 178
traveling , 209
treadhead, 248
tree, 150
tree huggers, 187
treewood, 20
Trekker, 129
Trekkie, 129
trey, 119
trey-eight, 110
Triad, 168
tribes, 98
trickle-down, 53
trife, 227
trip, 98, 227
triple-double, 209
triple witching hour,
  67
trip-out, 227

trippy, 227
trip wire, 248
trip-wire vet, 248
Trojan horse, 81
trouser trout, 199
trucking, 98
truppie, 257
TSR, 81
'tsup, 227
tub-thump, 6
tubaruba, 227
tube, 168
tubed, 146
tube steak, 140, 199,
  248
tube/tube out, 227
tune in, 98
turbo lag, 35
turkey, 119, 209
turn, 35
turnaround, 178
turn around / turn
  around flight, 42
turn his/her head
  around, 98
turn off, 98
turn on, 98
turnover, 209
turnpike cruiser, 20
turret-head, 248
turtle shell, 35
turtles, 248
T.V., 199
tweak, 35, 82
tweaked/
  tweaked out, 227
24/24, 110
24/24 rule, 110
twenty-percenter,
  20
twig, 199
twiggy bond, 67
twink, 227, 248
twist, 140
twitcher, 129
two-foot-itis, 159

two hots and a
    Charlie, 248
typewriter, 150

U

udders, 199
ufology, 129
uforia/ufomania, 129
ultimate weapon,
    the, 248
ultra, 67
Umbrella Room,
    The, 140
ump, 209
unass, 248
unblown, 35
Uncle / Uncle
    Sucker /Uncle
    Sugar, 248
underground, 98
under the gun, 159
underutilized, 53
unfortunately, he
    isn't here, 20
unglued, 35
unhorsing, 35
unk-unks, 168
unloading, 35
unobtanium, 42
unruly, 227
unsubstantiated
    rumor, 53
un-yuppies, 257
up, 82, 98
up-cut, 6
up front, 98
up-front exposure,
    178
upgrade, 42
upgrades, 193
upper story, 151
upper story / up-
    stairs, 227
uppers, 119

Uppie Yuppie, 257
upside down, 35
up the ying-yang,
    227
up tick, 67
uptight, 98
up to speed, 53
use it for packing, 20
use up, 248
user, 82
user-friendly, 82
USP, 6
utilization, 53
utilize, 53

V

vamp du, 227
vanilla, 82
vanity plate, 35
vaporware, 82
VAR, 82
vegetable garden,
    147
veggies, 141
veggy, 141
vegucation, 141
veg / veg out, 227
velvet, 67
ventilate the block,
    35
Venus mound, 199
verbalize, 53
vette, 35
viable, 53
vibes, 99
vic, 110
Victor/
    Victor Charlie,
    248
vid, 227
Videocart, 6
ville, 248
viper, 119
virtual, 82

virus, 82
visualize, 53
vitals, 147
vitamin A, 119
VO or voice-over, 6
voice-over or VO,
    178
vulture, 42
vulture's row, 159

W

wack, 227
wacky t'backy, 99
wacky weed, 99
wagger, 110
waggle, 209
wagon, 35
wail, 35, 227
Wait-a-minute-bush,
    248
waldo, 130, 227
Waldorf Astoria, 110
walk-on, 209
wall job, 199
wallpaper, 82
walls, 111
wallyball, 210
wanna be/
    wannabe, 227
war babies, 67
war chest, 187
ward X, 147
warm body, 248
Warthog, 249
wash tub, 67
wassup, 227
waste, 111, 249
wasted, 99, 227
wastoid, 227
watchdog, 53
water, 119
water bug, 35
watering hole, 141
waver, 227

wave, the, 210
wax, 249
way, 227
wayback, 35
WBFP, 193
W/E, 199
weak, 227
weapons system, 168
wedge, 141, 227
wedged, 82
weed, 99, 119
weeper, 178
wench, 227
went toes, 67
we're goin' the other way, 20
western, 141
W.E.T., 159
wet dog, 141
wet read, 249
WETSU, 249
wetware, 82
whale, 147
what's happening?, 99
what's wrong with it?, 20
wheel, 151
wheels, 35
when deemed appropriate, 53
where it's at, 99
where's the pleasure?, 20
whimsy, 20
whip, 187
whisper stock, 67
whistleblower, 53
white-blue-white, 160
white Christmas, 119
white coat rule, 6
white goods, 21
white hole, 130
white knight, 67

white knuckler, 210
white mice, 249
white sidewalls/ whitewalls, 249
white snow, 119
white squire, 67
whiz kid, 168
whore, 67
WIA, 249
wicked, 227
wide on, 199
wide / wide break, 178
widget, 67
wiff, 210
wig out, 227
wig picker, 147
wig-wag, 210
wiggle room, 53
wiggy man, 227
wild, 227
wildcard, 210
wild card, 130
wild geese, 249
willy peter/ willie pete, 249
willy-peter bag, 249
wilson, 228
Wimby, 210
wimps, 257
wind sprint, 210
windmill, 35
window, 42, 53, 83, 168
window dressing, 67
winger, 187
winner, 228
wipe, 178
wiped, 35
wire, 249
wired, 53, 111
wire hangers, 249
wirehead, 83
wires, 35
wiring diagram, 168
wisdom weed, 119

wit, 228
witch doctor, 147
with ice, 67
within the frame-work of, 53
woebetide, 228
wolf down, 141
Women's Lib, 99
wooden ticket, 67
woof, 228
woofie, 228
woofies, 258
woofs, 258
woopies, 258
word, 228
word one, 249
word wrap, 83
works, 119
work station/ workstation, 83
World, the, 249
worm, 83
wrangler, 178
wrapped, 151
wreck, 228
wrecked, 99
wrecker, 35
wuss, 228
WYSIWYG, 83

X

xd, 68
X-ing, 228
X.O., 160, 249
X.T., 83
XTAL, 42
XXX, 199

Y

yankee bond, 68
yaps, 258
yard, 68

yard hack, 111
yavis, 258
yawner, 178
yawn in technicolor, 228
yea/yeay, 228
yeepies, 258
yellow sheet, 111, 160
yellow stuff, 168
yellowjackets, 119
yellowtail, 36
yen, 228
Ye Olde Peruvian Marching Powder, 119
yeoman, 160
yield, 193
Yippie, 99
yippies, 258
yips, 210
yobo, 249
yoking, 111
yorkie, 258
you battin' a fly or are you bidding?, 21
you folks on this side are allowed to bid, 21

you just can't seem to win, 21
you wanna stand up so everyone can see you?, 21
you'll never see another one like this, 21
you're the expert, 21
your court, 53
yo-yo mode, 83
yo-yos / yo-yo stocks, 68
Y-people, 258
Y, the, 199
yucas, 258
yuffie, 258
yukkies, 258
yummies, 258
yumpies, 258
yuppies, 258

Z

z, 36, 99
'za, 228
zap, 83, 99, 147, 249
zappening, 228
zapper, 141

zebra, 210, 249
zenology, 130
zero, 68
zero fund, 54
zero-g, 43
zero lot line, 193
zero out, 68
zero-sum game, 54
Z-gram, 160
Z.I., 249
zip, 210
zip-code wine, 141
zip fuel, 43
zippo raid, 249
zippo squad, 249
zit, 228
zoiks, 228
zombie, 119
zombie food, 141
Zoning, 210
zonked, 99
ZOO, 7
zorch, 83
zulu, 249
zun, 228
zup, 228

ABOUT THE AUTHOR

PAUL DICKSON is a free-lance writer and author of 22 books who lives in Garrett Park, Maryland, with his wife and two sons. He has written for a number of newspapers and magazines, including *Esquire, Smithsonian,* and *Playboy. Slang!* is his fifth book on the fascinating American English language. Others include: *Words; Names;* and *The Dickson Baseball Dictionary.* He currently holds the record in the *Guinness Book of World Records* for most synonyms for one word. Dickson was able to find 2,231 synonyms for the word *drunk.*